B53 083 805 7

D1337099

2

DINN

MA

THE THREE DEGREES

Also by Paul Rees

Robert Plant: A Life

The Three Degrees

Paul Rees

Constable • London

Constable & Robinson Ltd
55–56 Russell Square
London WC1B 4HP
www.constablerobinson.com

First published in the UK by Constable,
an imprint of Constable & Robinson Ltd, 2014

A copy of the British Library Cataloguing in
Publication data is available from the British Library

ISBN 978-1-47210-690-2 (hardback)
ISBN 978-1-47210-691-9 (ebook)

1 3 5 7 9 10 8 6 4 2

Printed and bound by CPI Group (UK) Ltd, Croydon, CR0 4YY

This one's for Mom, Dad and 'G' – for bringing me up to be a Baggie and with much love.

Contents

Prologue: The Final Whistle

The last full day of Laurie Cunningham's life began like most others had done in the red hot Madrid summer of 1989. He spent the morning of 14 July in the city negotiating the terms of a new contract with Pedro Garcia Jimenez, the incoming president of Rayo Vallecano, the most recent and tenth football club he'd played for during his career. The previous season Cunningham scored the goal that got Madrid's third-biggest club promoted to Spain's top division, La Liga. However, his one-year deal with them had run down on 30 June, and discussions about an extension had become complicated and drawn out.

Cunningham was made an overnight millionaire ten years earlier when he signed for Real Madrid as a prodigiously talented 23-year-old. Fresh from the English First Division, he was bought by Spain's royal club to be their new star player and they had acceded to all his demands. He'd revelled in Madrid for a time. Standing out not just as a young black man in Real's pure white strip, but because he was capable of outrageous feats of skill – regularly making fools of the toughest full-backs in Spanish football and swinging the ball in from corners with the outside of his foot. He did such things with apparent insouciance, as if it all came too easily to him. Real's followers christened him the Black Pearl – the jewel in their crown.

This was before it all began to go wrong for him. A succession of injuries took their toll physically, and disciplinary issues soured his relationship with the club. Most damaging of all, a broken toe took away from him his greatest asset, an uncanny ability to glide past opponents and across the pitch with the grace of a dancer. Without that, he was a busted flush.

For as long as he could remember, Cunningham had clung to the belief that being exceptional at football would be his passport to making his mark on the world. After all, it had taken him from the grim backstreets of north London to great riches and celebrity in Spain. He believed that his fame would allow him to progress to becoming something more substantial than a successful sportsman. Through it, he hoped to evolve into all that he wanted to be: an artist, poet, designer, architect, philanthropist, or any of the other many things that occupied his thinking outside of the game he happened to excel at. But not now, not robbed of his powers and in this reduced state. He knew now that he would only ever be recalled – if at all – as the one thing he'd least desired to be: as just another footballer.

The tragic irony is that Laurie Cunningham had already by then made a greater impact on the world around him than he could have ever imagined, and as a footballer. This hadn't been as a result of his feats in Madrid, but rather during the time he spent at a much less glamorous provincial football club in the heart of England's industrial Midlands – West Bromwich Albion. It was while he was in Albion's first team and alongside two other black players, Cyrille Regis and Brendon Batson, that he'd used his manifest talents as a weapon against the terrible racist abuse that had poured off the streets and down from the terraces in the Britain of the 1970s. This was a time when black footballers were scarce in the British game and the presence of three in one team was enough to inflame and incite prejudices amongst overwhelmingly white crowds. Together with Regis and Batson, Cunningham made up the front line in a war against ignorance within the sport and also the gathering forces of an extreme right-wing menace that was taking root in the country.

The three of them were focal points of an especially exciting West Bromwich Albion team, and the spearhead of a wider battle for the nation's soul. They empowered a generation of disenfranchised black youths, bringing to it a sense of hope and inspiration. They were agents of change as well, and helped set in motion a domino effect that would allow a new order to assert itself in the British game and across the country as a whole. Yet the full scope of this was not yet apparent to Cunningham or to anyone else.

Soon enough, Real Madrid cut him loose and since then he'd led a peripatetic existence, drifting from one club to another in search of a place to settle and to be. Belatedly, Rayo Vallecano had appeared to offer him that, albeit in much more mundane circumstances. Based on the south-eastern fringes of the Spanish capital, Vallecano played their home games at the compact Campo de Futbol de Vallecas, which held 14,000 spectators on a good day. This was a far cry from the grandly magnificent Estadio Santiago Bernabeu where 85,000 baying Real Madrid fans had once been Cunningham's adoring gallery. But then, he was not the player that he had been then. The longer Vallecano prevaricated over the offer of a new contract, the more starkly he was forced to confront this fact and the greater then his hurt.

Cunningham and his Spanish wife, Sylvia, had just recently celebrated the birth of a son, Sergio. Yet he seemed to be in the grip of a deep, dark psychological pain, so much so that his close family and friends feared for his state of mind and well-being. He'd been home to London on a visit the previous weekend and something then appeared to have died in his eyes. It was as if the fire that had once danced behind them had been extinguished. His mother, Mavis, had confided to friends her worries that her son had fallen in with a bad crowd in the Spanish capital. For all his reported wealth, she was concerned that he'd also apparently run into financial troubles.

Cunningham's mother and others close to him back in England often told each other that he'd not been the same since he'd split with his childhood sweetheart, Nicky Brown. This was six years ago and around that time things had first started to unravel for him in Spain. Whenever she was fretting about her youngest son, which was most of the time these days, Mavis felt a cold dread creeping upon her.

Much of what happened that fateful day in July remains a mystery to Mavis and to most everyone else. Cunningham left his meeting with Jiminez with his contract situation still unresolved and appears to have gone on to a horse-racing meet that evening at the picturesque La Zarzuela hippodrome, located five miles from the city centre and bordered by the verdant Monte El Pardo forest. He met up there with a young American named Mark Cafwell Latty, who was studying at the city university and with whom he'd recently become acquainted. To this day, no one from Cunningham's immediate family or any of his closest friends has found out anything but the barest of details about Cafwell Latty. There is speculation that he was about to enter into a business deal with Cunningham to buy a restaurant, though how he was going to fund this as a student remains a mystery.

Cunningham lived in a gated community in Las Matas, a wealthy suburb of Madrid ten minutes' drive from the racecourse. Yet rather than return home after the meet, he and Cafwell Latty went on to a nightclub. They remained there until the early hours of the next morning, a Saturday, moving on next to a pizza joint. It was past 6 a.m. when the two of them finished eating and set off again in Cunningham's car, a silver-coloured Seat Ibiza. Cunningham had always been fastidious about wearing a seatbelt, insisting upon doing so even when backing his car out of the garage. However, for some reason he didn't put one on for this, his final drive.

He headed into the city centre that morning on the main A6 road. A 370-mile highway running north-west from Madrid to the coastal town of Arteixo, the A6 was a notorious accident black spot that was characterised by sharp, fast bends. One of the most extreme of these was just outside of the city at Pozuelo de Alarcon and Cunningham sped into this at 6.45 a.m. As he came out of the bend, he was forced to swerve to avoid a car parked on the side of the road. Cunningham's Seat crashed into the central reservation, overturning and buckling like a crushed tin can. He was flung ten metres from the vehicle, his head taking the brunt of the impact on the road. A passing municipal police patrol stopped at the scene and rushed Cunningham to hospital along with Cafwell Latty, who had remained in the car and suffered no more than minor injuries.

Laurie Cunningham never regained consciousness and was pronounced dead on arrival at hospital, having sustained severe head trauma. Brain matter was visible through an open wound to his head. He was thirty-three years old. Mark Cafwell Latty checked himself out of hospital that same day and seems to have then vanished without trace.

Later that Saturday morning, Cunningham's elder brother, Keith, was walking to work in north London. He was stopped by his girlfriend pulling up behind him in their car and frantically beeping the horn. She told him Paul was dead, Paul being Laurie's middle name and the one by which his family called him.

'At first I thought she was talking about her brother, because his name's also Paul and he's a roofer,' Keith recalls. 'I thought he must have fallen off a roof. Then she said, "Your brother's dead." We went round to my mom and dad's. I'd never seen my mom and dad cry until then. We all sat and cried. As we did it came on the TV – pictures of his car being lifted off the road by a crane.'

The phone didn't stop ringing at the Cunningham household that terrible morning. One of the first to call was Bobby Fisher, who'd played with Cunningham at Leyton Orient in the mid-seventies. He remembers Mavis Cunningham being hysterical with grief.

Chapter One: Roots

Laurence Paul Cunningham was born in the north London district of Holloway on 8 March 1956. His parents, Elias and Mavis, had come to England from Jamaica the previous year. They brought with them Cunningham's elder brother, Keith, who was just one year old at the time. Elias had been a racehorse jockey in Jamaica, but he and Mavis both took factory jobs in their adopted city, he moulding ashtrays and she as a machinist.

Holloway still bore the scars of the intensive bombing it had suffered from the German Luftwaffe during the Blitz and was among the capital's most densely populated and multicultural areas. Its bustling streets buzzed with voices from the Caribbean, Cyprus and Ireland, and were rich with the smells of North African and Asian spices.

When the boys were still infants, the family moved a couple of miles down the road to settle in Finsbury Park. The brothers attended the same primary school, St Paul's, until Keith was expelled for kicking a teacher. The two of them were otherwise inseparable. Together with a gang of friends, the young

Cunninghams went off looking for adventure in the warren of streets around the area; they would steal apples from their neighbours' gardens, pick blackberries from railway sidings and forage in the shells of houses that had been left to ruin after the war. Elias, although a genial man, was a distant father and not given to outward displays of affection. However, Laurie was the apple of his mother's eye, and Mavis doted on him.

'If anything happened to him I got the blame for it – and he was very accident prone,' remembers Keith Cunningham. 'We were always playing cricket back then, not football, and Laurie would be wicketkeeper. One time, someone swung the bat right round and hit him in the face, mashing his nose. I had to take him home and Mom had a right go at me for it. He'd fling his clothes all over the bedroom we shared and yet I'd be the one who'd have to tidy it up. I was definitely the black sheep, but we stuck together and it was me who taught him to do things like swim.'

Entering their teens, the two brothers joined the 22nd London Company Boys' Brigade and it was through this that they first started to play football. The company was run by a Mr Cottingham, who worked in the probation service. A significant influence in the Cunningham brothers' early lives, he would take the boys into Regent's Park with a ball and coach them in the basics of the game. Both Cunninghams soon graduated to the Boys' Brigade football team.

'Mr Cottingham was like a father figure to us,' says Keith. 'He always had time for us and would give us advice. He was a white guy, but he and his wife had an adopted black daughter, Phillipa. She pretty much became our half-sister.'

Aside from such selfless individuals as Mr Cottingham, there was not much else to encourage or inspire young black kids in the Britain of the early 1970s. The world that was projected back at them through the media was almost exclusively white-looking and most often hostile-seeming. Two of the most popular programmes on TV at that time were sitcoms – *Till Death Us Do Part* and *Love Thy Neighbour*. The lead character in the former, Alf Garnett, was a ranting working-class bigot given to spouting such supposedly hilarious rhetoric as, 'He understood yer coon did Shakespeare.' The latter show derived comic conflict from a white couple in leafy Twickenham coming to terms with having a black couple as their next-door neighbours. Eddie Booth, the white male character, habitually referred to his black counterpart, Bill Reynolds, as 'nig-nog' or 'Sambo'.

The Reynolds' were nonetheless among the very few black faces to be seen on British television at the time. More commonly, white actors would 'black up' to play ethnic characters in sitcoms such as *It Ain't Half Hot Mum*, which was set in India during the Second World War, or the Saturday night variety staple, *The Black and White Minstrel Show*. Both of these programmes were screened by the national broadcaster, the BBC. The BBC's commercial rival ITV was marginally more inclusive. In 1973, it employed the first black news reporter, Trevor McDonald, and the next year introduced a black family to the cast of one of its signature soaps, *Crossroads*.

The economic tide was also then turning in the country as the era of post-war boom reached an end and both inflation and unemployment began an inexorable rise. Once the soaring cost of living began to bite, those at the sharpest end looked for someone to blame. The growing immigrant communities drawn from the Commonwealth became a target for their anger and frustrations. This influx from the Caribbean and the Indian subcontinent had begun in the immediate post-war years and at the invitation of the British government. Britain's manufacturing industries had seen their workers decimated by the war, and also due to the fact that the indigenous population had begun to aspire to more skilled and better-paid professions. The new immigrants had filled the nation's factories and foundries, but now were seen as having stolen 'our' jobs.

In their corner of north London, Keith and Laurie Cunningham grew up accustomed to having insults hurled at them by white neighbours. On the streets around their home, a pressure-cooker atmosphere was pervasive. One of the brothers' closest friends, Eustace 'Huggy' Isaie, recalls there always being 'a feeling of tension. I can remember being out on the street with white kids and their mothers opening up the front window and shouting at them, "How many times have I told you not to play with those black boys?"

'Skinheads used to chase our big brothers and we'd get beaten up all the time. You'd call up the Old Bill for assistance and eight times out of ten they'd turn up and be more interested in nicking you for something.'

The louder and more rebellious of the brothers, Keith was at first thought to be the most promising footballer of the pair. He had trials for the district team and encouraged his brother to follow in his footsteps, but Keith was hot-headed and lacked discipline. It was rare indeed during a game that Keith didn't get involved in an argument with the referee or an opponent. By the time he was sixteen, he was invariably spending each night drinking and clubbing with his mates. Much the quieter and more reserved, Laurie enjoyed drawing and was learning to play the organ. He also spent hours kicking a ball against a wall, and while his brother was running wild Laurie was beginning to get noticed playing for both the Boys' Brigade and his school team.

In 1973, he was picked up by a scout from London's top First

Division team, Arsenal, and signed apprentice forms with the club. Arsenal's Highbury Stadium was a stone's throw from the Cunningham family home in north London, but Laurie had a relaxed attitude to timekeeping and often as not arrived late to training sessions. The Arsenal manager of the time, Bertie Mee, had served in the army and ran the club to the same strict disciplinary code he'd encountered in the forces. Erratic free spirits like Cunningham weren't tolerated at Arsenal for long, and the club released him less than a year after he'd joined them. Nevertheless, his unrefined talent had impressed the Arsenal coaching staff enough for them to recommend him to the manager of another London club, George Petchey at Second Division Orient.

Based in London's East End, Leyton Orient was the capital's second-oldest football club, having been founded in 1881. In their long history, 'the O's' had spent just a solitary season in the top division of English football. Orient played their home games at the ramshackle Brisbane Road, which during night matches was often shrouded in the mist that drifted over from nearby Hackney Marshes. The club had almost gone bankrupt in the mid-sixties, but was enjoying a relative golden period in the seventies under Petchey and his head coach, Peter Angell. Like Mee, Angell had come from an army background and was known to punish wayward players by having them cut the Brisbane Road pitch with a pair of scissors.

Under the stewardship of Petchey and Angell, Orient had been promoted to the Second Division at the start of the decade. The pair had begun to build an attractive team based around a group of youthful players. Among these was a young Londoner named Bobby Fisher, a sixteen-year-old of mixed race who had been adopted into a Jewish family. Fisher had just then broken into the Orient first team. At training one morning, Petchey pulled him aside and told him a young lad would be joining them from Arsenal the next morning. The manager asked his teenage full-back to look out for the new recruit, suggesting he might be a bit on the wild side.

Fisher arrived early the following morning to welcome Laurie Cunningham to Orient, but there was no still sign of him at 10 a.m. and no sign still when training started. Fisher and the rest of the players went out onto the Brisbane Road pitch to do their warm-up and then gathered around Petchey for his morning briefing.

'Ten, fifteen minutes into this chat, I saw a figure emerge from the dressing rooms and start walking over to us – not running, but walking,' recalls Fisher. 'By the time he got to the group everyone was looking at him and yet he didn't say a word. George eventually asked him why he was late and Laurie said he'd missed his bus. That was it. He didn't plead or apologise. I thought there was either something wrong with him, that he was completely mad, or that he must be super-confident in his own ability.'

By the end of that morning, Fisher had his answer. Training sessions at Orient were rounded off with the first team playing a game against the reserves and apprentices. Fisher found himself up against Cunningham and resolved to kick some sense into this upstart the first chance he got.

'Two minutes into the game, the ball was moved out to Laurie on the halfway line,' says Fisher. 'I went in to smash his ankle, and the next thing I knew I was on my backside and he was running away from me with the ball. The rest of the game continued like that. He actually took the piss out of me and kept knocking the ball through my legs. The other players could see it as well – they knew that I wasn't a bad player, so to have someone come along and do that to me, it was obvious he must be pretty special.'

Petchey and Angell were also fast convinced that they had a unique player on their hands in Cunningham. So much so that that they made allowances for him. He didn't get drummed out of the club on account of his habitual lateness, or even on the occasions when he went missing altogether and would claim to have overslept. The steadfast Angell would always be there to put a paternal arm around his shoulders and to smooth things over with the other players whenever they complained about the preferential treatment Cunningham was getting.

'Peter would stick up for Laurie and stand in his corner,' says Fisher. 'There was a special sort of love there which most guys, and most clubs, didn't have. But George also looked into things a little deeper. I'm sure he'd have researched Laurie's background and spoken to people about the challenges he'd had growing up. He's a very decent, caring man and he had a real hatred of racism, so he was going to go out of his way to make an exception of Laurie.'

In his first few months at Orient, Cunningham turned out for the reserve team, being as raw as he was precocious. He was a self-contained lad, something of a loner and sat apart from the raucous dressing room banter. But he grew close to Fisher. The two of them would take off together after training and go to Kensington Market to shop for clothes. The introverted Cunningham came out of his shell whenever he dressed up. He had a particular fondness for forties-style double-breasted suits and wide-brimmed hats, a look he'd picked up from his favourite film stars, the song-and-dance men Gene Kelly and Fred Astaire.

'With Laurie, it wasn't like having a conversation with the archetypal footballer,' says Fisher. 'There were other things going on with him, different levels, and he was buzzing with ideas. He was very much into his poetry, for instance. You could sense that he wanted to do something different and also that there was this thing that was holding him back. I think he was scared to vocalise all these thoughts he had, inside and outside of football, because he feared he'd be laughed at or not taken seriously.

'We'd go out together and after a few glasses of wine he'd loosen up and different things would come out. He would say that he'd had it pretty tough growing up, with racism and prejudice, and also that he hadn't had much contact with his dad.'

The other great passion that lit a fire in Cunningham was dancing. He was as flamboyant and expressive on the dance floor as he was on the football pitch. It was as if this, too, unlocked something deep within him that he had to get out. No one ever saw him chat up girls, he was too shy for that, but they flocked around him whenever he danced. Sundays he'd go to a club in Tottenham called the Royal for the weekly funk night, and it was here that he was first drawn to a red-headed girl who also dressed in vintage clothes and appeared just as lost to the music as he did.

In most other respects, fifteen-year-old Jacqueline 'Nicky' Brown had come from a different world to Laurie Cunningham. She was white, well educated and had been born into a comfortably middle-class family in Camden, north London. Her father, Mike, was something of a showbiz entrepreneur and worked variously as a booking agent, stand-up comic and bit-part actor. He'd appeared as an extra in the popular ITV soap *Coronation Street* and was a well-known face on the London club and theatre circuit.

Nicky Brown was the kind of girl that stood out in a crowd. She was pretty, vivacious and self-assured. Her striking hair seemed to explode from her head in a wild shock. She was in her last year at school when she first met Cunningham and was already doing bits and pieces of part-time modelling and acting work. She'd come to the Royal that night with her then boyfriend, but found herself facing off with Cunningham on the dance floor.

'He was suddenly there in front of me, and what a dancer he was,' she recalls. 'He was unbelievable, like he'd been born with rhythm. It was a stand-off – you did what the other person did and then added a move of your own. I joined in with him and we just connected straight away.'

Cunningham introduced himself to Brown as 'Paul' and since he was wearing a fifties work shirt with the Esso logo emblazoned across it, she assumed he was employed as a mechanic. The pair of them began to meet up at the Royal both on Sunday and Thursday nights, when they would jive to jazz records until the early hours of the next morning.

'One night, we missed the night bus and he walked me and my friend home to Camden,' says Brown. 'We swapped phone numbers that night, but it was pure innocence. We'd go ice-skating or into Finsbury Park on a Friday afternoon where we'd take a portable stereo with us and practise dance moves together. It was all just good fun back then; we'd have a picnic and a peck on the cheek.'

The eighteen-year-old Laurie Cunningham was now on the verge of playing in Orient's first team. As a young black man, he would be a rare, almost alien sight in the English Football League of the time. Ever since the formative years of the game during the Victorian era, only a handful of black players had represented British football clubs.

Arthur Wharton, a goalkeeper, became the first black professional footballer in England when he joined Rotherham from Preston in 1889. The first black outfield player was Walter Tull, who was born in Folkestone in 1888 to a Barbadian father and English mother. Tull made ten appearances for Tottenham Hotspur from 1909 and later enlisted in the army for the Great War, rising to the rank of Second Lieutenant in the 23rd Battalion. He survived the Battle of the Somme, but was killed in action during the spring offensive against the Germans in March 1918.

More recently, Albert Johanneson, a black South African, had signed for Don Revie's Leeds United in 1961. Johanneson had completed a three-month trial at the club, having been told he'd have to pay his own fare home if unsuccessful. He became the first black player to appear in an FA Cup final when he turned out in Leeds' 2-1 defeat to Liverpool in 1965. Yet his rewards from the game were scant and he was to die destitute in 1995. West Ham United, located just up the road from Orient in London's East End, had groomed three black players during the sixties and early seventies. These were defender John Charles and two strikers, Clyde Best and Ade Coker. Best was the most prominent of the three and went on the make 186 appearances for the club up to 1976.

Laurie Cunningham joined this select group on 12 October 1974 when he made his debut for Orient against Oldham Athletic, coming on as a substitute in a 3-1 win at Brisbane Road. He made an instant impression, gliding past defenders as if they were static. It was one that was picked up by the London Weekend Television cameras, filming the game for the following afternoon's *The Big Match* highlights show. Nicky Brown's father, a keen football fan, was watching it the next day when she happened to walk into the room.

'I looked at the TV and there was Paul taking a tracksuit off and running onto the pitch,' she says. 'I told my dad that they must have his name wrong. I said that I knew him and that he wasn't called Laurie Cunningham. When he phoned later to arrange to go out, I wouldn't talk to him. I told my mom to tell him he was a liar.

'He came and sat on the wall outside our house for hours until Mom made me go out to him. He said his family called him Paul and that he'd told me that was his name because he saw me as a friend and that he hadn't wanted me to think he was boasting about his football. He took me home with him that night and I met his family for the first time. I don't think we were ever apart after that. I had to have a room at his house and he had one at mine.'

In his first full season at the club, Cunningham went on to make a further sixteen appearances for Orient, scoring one goal as the team finished the campaign in a secure mid-table position. Even then, people in the game had begun to speak of him as a shining prospect. On one of those Saturday afternoons, another black youngster who was then on Arsenal's books came down to Brisbane Road to see what all the fuss was about. Brendon Batson remembers sitting next to Clyde Best in the main stand that day, the two of them looking on admiringly at Cunningham.

'He was graceful, almost balletic, and so confident,' says Batson. 'He could go from a standing start to flat out like a Formula One car. He'd walk with the ball, almost inviting a challenge, and then he was gone. I thought he was quite extraordinary.'

In the tight circle of friends that Cunningham cultivated were Brown, Bobby Fisher and another of the other young Orient players, Tony Grealish, an Irishman who was known to one and all as 'Paddy'. The four of them went everywhere together, heading into the West End to see Bruce Lee films or to support Brown when she did fashion shows at stores such as Selfridges.

On afternoons after training, they'd go dancing at a club in Soho called Crackers. Another of their favourite haunts was a champagne bar on Oxford Street.

'We used to enjoy making a scene there,' says Bobby Fisher. 'There was a big spiral staircase leading down to the bar and Paddy would go down first of all. He had long ginger hair and a big Viking beard, not the sort of person you'd normally see in that kind of place. Then I'd come down with my afro, a satin shirt and platform shoes. And after that Nicky would emerge in tight white trousers and knee-high boots.

'The people who drank there were very middle class, very pukka, and they'd be staring at us. But Laurie was another thing altogether. A black guy in a champagne bar – that just didn't happen. He'd make his entrance last of all, wearing a suit, a cravat, a fedora hat and carrying a cane. Once we'd all arrived, the manager would get up from his seat and salute us. You could see all the other customers thinking, "Who *are* these people?"'

Cunningham was also a man apart among his team-mates. He'd begun to take yoga and ballet lessons to help make him suppler, and before each game he'd take himself off to the kit room and warm up dancing to James Brown records. At home, he'd go out into the garden and practise with a ball until it got too dark for him to see what he was doing.

'What he could do with a football was amazing,' says Brown. 'He'd keep it off the ground for nine, ten minutes at a time, and under total control. Or he'd kick it way up in the air and catch it under his chin. The first few times he tried that the ball would whack him in the face, but he'd stick at it for days on end.'

'After a game on a Saturday, the typical footballer of the time would take his wife or girlfriend out to a steakhouse, sink a few pints of lager and be home in time to watch *Match of the Day* on the telly,' says Fisher. 'Laurie and Nicky would go off to a bar, have a glass of wine and then go home at 6.30 p.m. to get something to eat and have a nap. Then they'd get up again at midnight and go out dancing till five o'clock in the morning. He mixed with a completely different set of people.

'On a Friday night, he'd go to a club in north London where they had these dance-offs for money. It was like a scene from Studio 54 in New York. This big group of girls and guys would form a circle around the dance floor and there would be Laurie in the middle of it all, dancing off against some other guy.'

The money Cunningham regularly received for winning such dancing competitions came in useful. He used it to pay off the fines Orient gave him just as frequently for reporting late to training or team meetings. On one occasion, he and Brown found themselves marooned after a night out, having spent all their money. Cunningham was due at training in a couple of hours, so Brown rang George Petchey and asked him to come and pick them up. The Orient manager – as he would always do – obliged his star player.

During the 1975–76 season, there would be no doubting Laurie Cunningham's exalted status within the Orient team. The club once again finished in mid-table, but Cunningham brought to them the look of something exotic and an edge of excitement. He looked slight, frail even, as if a gust of wind might blow him over. But he was quick as a flash and would skip past opponents. He was a showman too, teasing defenders by beating them once and then turning back to bamboozle them all over again. He didn't score many goals, just eight that season, but they were invariably of a kind to take supporters' breath away.

'Brisbane Road had one of the worst pitches in the division,' says Orient fan Steve Jenkins. 'The ground was brown, not green, so to see Laurie Cunningham come out and give some of the performances he did was amazing.

'At that time, there were also some very uncompromising defenders in football, and he was getting hacked to pieces. However, I never saw him get involved in a fight. He used to get up, brush himself down and get on with it. I remember he scored one goal at Chelsea that was so good, both sets of fans applauded it – and also the Chelsea players and the referee.'

Cunningham's eye-catching performances soon enough brought him wider recognition. Writing in the *Sun* newspaper, football reporter John Sadler suggested that Orient's flying young winger was the best thing to happen to the British game since George Best. Mavis Cunningham had begun to keep a scrapbook that bulged with such pieces. On a clipping of the Orient team line-up for that season she highlighted her youngest son with an arrow and underneath it wrote a single word: 'Star.'

Yet there was another, uglier kind of attention that was being focused on Cunningham and also Bobby Fisher that season. At almost every ground Orient visited away from Brisbane Road, the two players would be subjected to continuous racist abuse. This became so prevalent that it got to the point where the two of them would express surprise if they weren't greeted with a chorus of monkey noises.

'Laurie had got it when he was growing up and so had I, so it wasn't a shock going into professional football, but it was barbaric,' says Fisher. 'As soon as we came out of the tunnel there'd be shouts of "black bastards" and "niggers". And then, of course, there'd be bananas getting thrown onto the pitch. At some places we couldn't go and take throw-ins, because you'd be too close to the crowd and people would try to grab you or spit at you.

'You would also get racial slurs on the pitch from opposition players and the referees would often say things too. If Laurie was called a black bastard by a full-back, he'd fight back by putting the ball through his legs and making him look a fool. That would hurt them even more.'

'Laurie and I had death threats – on the street, in clubs, every-where,' says Nicky Brown. 'It could be very intimidating and frightening, but we dealt with it back to back. On the whole we tried to talk to people, so they'd think twice the next time they came across a mixed-race couple. The next option was to see if it was possible to walk away and if not, you'd have to stand your ground.'

These dark, savage undercurrents were ebbing and flowing through the country as a whole at a time when more than a million people found themselves out of work. The first Race Relations Act that passed through Parliament in 1976 was established to prevent discrimination on the grounds of race, colour or ethnicity. It appeared a significant step forward, but Britain was still very much a divided nation.

As a rule, ethnic workers – who were invariably doing blue-collar manual jobs – got paid less than their white counterparts and were often as not being denied union recognition. Parliament itself was then exclusively white, and of the Metropolitan Police's 22,000-strong force, there were just seventy officers from an ethnic background. An extreme far-right political party, the National Front, had also emerged as an electoral power and advocated the forced repatriation of immigrants. In May 1976, the NF fielded 176 candidates in local elections across the UK.

The summer of '76 brought a stifling heatwave to Britain; also, the touring West Indian cricket team came to play a five-match Test series against England. Prior to the series starting, the English cricket captain, Tony Greig, a South African by birth, had said his team intended to make their opponents 'grovel'. Greig was made to eat his words. The dazzling West Indies side, which included a fearsome four-man fast-bowling attack and a dashing batsman, Viv Richards, crushed England 3-0.

There was no escaping the symbolic nature of this victory. Next to the thrilling and colourful West Indians, the English team appeared dull and staid, the stuffed-shirt remnants of an era turning to dust. The touring cricketers had struck a resounding blow for black pride in Britain. And at a time when black faces were barely seen on the country's football terraces, thousands of jubilant West Indian supporters had turned out to see each of the test matches.

That summer also witnessed the founding of a new youth-led movement in the UK, Rock Against Racism. This was established in opposition to the National Front in the battle for hearts and minds on Britain's streets. It was the brainchild of two men – Roger Huddle, a designer at the *Socialist Worker* newspaper, and a photographer and activist, Red Saunders. The pair of them had begun promoting a series of pub gigs in London under the *RAR* banner. These shows had British reggae groups such as Aswad and Misty in Roots playing alongside some of the emerging punk rock bands such as the Buzzcocks, the Ruts and Generation X.

'Both Red and I thought you could fight the cultural battle through music,' says Huddle. 'Right from the start, we were going to have black and white united on the stage, no matter what. In our minds, there was hard racism and soft racism. The National Front discussed racism and used tactics. They were political thinkers and hard core. The people on the estates that voted for them did so because they felt completely powerless and blamed their neighbours.'

Rock Against Racism was given added impetus by a drunken speech the rock guitarist Eric Clapton had given at a concert in Birmingham on 5 August, during which he'd suggested that all of Britain's 'foreigners' should be sent home. Like England's cricketers when contrasted with the West Indians, next to the upcoming punk and reggae acts, Clapton appeared representative of British rock's old guard. He was made to seem embarrassing, out of touch and time.

Later that month, Laurie Cunningham began a new football season with Orient, though he was destined not to finish it with them. He had started to enjoy his success at the club. He was now getting clothes made for him by a Jewish tailor in the East End and had bought his first car, a vintage Volvo that he'd picked up for £250 and customised with leopard-print seats.

On the pitch, he continued to be the team's heartbeat and he was attracting scouts and coaches from First Division clubs. Orient's near neighbours, West Ham United, were first to consider buying him, but they didn't have the money. In the end, it was a team that he'd starred against the previous season that took the plunge: newly promoted West Bromwich Albion.

Cunningham made the last of his seventy-five appearances for Orient in a 2-0 defeat to the club he'd debuted against, Oldham, at Brisbane Road on 5 March 1977. Two days later, Orient accepted an offer of £110,000 for him from West Brom, and on the eve of his twenty-first birthday, Laurie Cunningham left home.

Chapter Two: Black Country

West Bromwich Albion's home ground, the Hawthorns, is sited at a point equidistant between the town of Smethwick in the West Midlands and Handsworth in Birmingham. Smethwick and the clutch of other towns that lie within a two-mile radius to the north-west of the Birmingham conurbation were transformed into one of the centres of coal, iron and steel production in Britain during the Industrial Revolution of the 1800s. At that time of sweeping change the region was christened the Black Country on account of the thick, acrid smoke that poured out from its thousands of factory chimneys.

By the 1950s the Black Country's coal deposits were almost exhausted, but it continued to be a base for heavy industry and manufacture. During the post-war boom years, the prospect of work brought more migrants to Birmingham and the West Midlands than to any other area of the UK outside of London. A substantial Asian population developed in Smethwick. In Handsworth and another of Birmingham's inner-city districts, Balsall Heath, large Afro-Caribbean communities grew up. This influx soon stirred resentments and hostilities in a region that was predominantly working class and suffering from a general shortage of council housing, and later of jobs.

As early as 1962, race riots were reported in the Black Country town of Dudley. That summer, crowds of white men and youths rampaged along North Street in the town centre, which was largely populated by Afro-Caribbean and Asian families. One of the bitterest battles in the General Election of 1964 was fought in Smethwick. The Conservative candidate, Peter Griffiths, bucked the national trend in unseating the incumbent Labour MP and Foreign Secretary-designate, Patrick Gordon Walker. Griffiths ran an anti-immigration campaign, claiming his rival was soft on the issue. In the lead-up to the poll, posters began to appear around the town stating, 'If you want a nigger for a neighbour – vote Labour.' Griffiths later maintained that these were not of his doing. The incoming Labour Prime Minister, Harold Wilson, nevertheless suggested in a speech to the House of Commons that Griffiths should 'serve his time here as a parliamentary leper'.

Among Griffiths's first acts was an incitement to the white residents of Marshall Street, one the town's most populous addresses, to urge the local council to buy up its remaining houses to stop immigrants from moving into them. Such was the furore this created that Malcolm X, the black American civil rights leader, was prompted to visit to Smethwick. He arrived in the town on 12 February 1965, just nine days before he was assassinated in New York City.

Griffiths declined an invitation to meet and debate the issue with the visiting American. When asked why he had come to the town by an accompanying BBC news reporter, Malcolm X said: 'Because I am disturbed by reports that coloured people in

Smethwick are being treated badly. I have heard that they are being treated as the Jews under Hitler.'

Perhaps most notorious of all was the infamous 'rivers of blood' speech given by another West Midlands MP, the Conservative firebrand Enoch Powell, to a group of party members in Birmingham on 20 April 1968. Powell told an approving audience of his fear that 'in this country in fifteen or twenty years' time the black man will have the whip hand over the white man.' He went on to paint an apocalyptic vision of the future, quoting from the ancient Roman poet Virgil's epic, the *Aeneid*: 'As I look ahead I am filled with foreboding. Like the Roman, I seem to see the "River Tiber foaming with much blood".'

A poll in the local *Birmingham Post* newspaper the next day suggested that 80 per cent of local people agreed with Powell's sentiments. However, these were not tolerable in the mainstream political arena and Powell was sacked from his post as Shadow Defence Secretary by the Tory leader, Edward Heath. He would conduct the rest of his career from the margins.

The month after Powell gave his speech, West Bromwich Albion defeated Everton 1–0 in the FA Cup final at Wembley. It was the fifth time the club had won the trophy in its history and was its last major honour to date. Founded as West Bromwich Strollers in 1878 by a group of local factory workers, ten years later the club became one of the dozen founding members of the English Football League. The Albion, as they were known from 1880, finished in sixth place in that first fledgling season and since then have been crowned champions of the League on just the one occasion – for the 1919–20 campaign that immediately followed the Great War.

Albion moved to the Hawthorns in 1900. The club's official

nickname, the Throstles, also originated at this time. It was a local term for the Song Thrush, a bird that was commonly found nesting in the Hawthorn bushes that gave the ground its name. Yet among their supporters the Albion would most often be referred to as the Baggies. This dates from 1905 and is attributed to the fact that on match days at that time, a pair of gatekeepers would gather up the takings in large cloth bags and be escorted with them to an office under the main stand. Their appearance gave rise to a chant from the terraces, 'Here come the bag men!', and this evolved into, 'Here come the baggies!'

The afterglow from the club's '68 triumph was soon dimmed and they were relegated to the Second Division in 1973 under the dour management of Don Howe, a former Albion player who'd been coach when Arsenal won a League and FA Cup double just two years before. Howe was dismissed in 1975 and replaced by a player-manager, Johnny Giles. An Irishman, Giles had joined Matt Busby's Manchester United straight from school in Dublin. He made his first-team debut as an eighteen-year-old in the aftermath of the Munich air crash of 1958 that had decimated the club's playing staff. Yet Giles was best known as the midfield fulcrum of Don Revie's fiercely competitive Leeds United side of the late sixties and early seventies. His last game for Leeds before joining Albion had been their 2-0 European Cup final defeat to the German champions, Bayern Munich.

Giles's Albion tenure had started slowly, with just a single win coming from his first ten games in charge. However, he'd gradually imposed himself on the club, introducing a methodical style of possession football and securing promotion back to the First Division on the final day of the 1975–76 season. His promotion-winning side was made up of a core group of seasoned professionals that had been brought to the club by his immediate predecessor and also by the man Don Howe had succeeded, Alan Ashman. To this, Giles had added a sprinkling of promising youngsters from Albion's youth team.

Of the younger team members, the most notable were an eighteen-year-old local lad, full-back Derek Statham, and twenty-year-old Bryan Robson. An all-action midfielder, Robson would go on to captain England. The more experienced group included a couple of dogged centre-halves, John Wile and Alistair Robertson, and the midfield pairing of Len Cantello and Tony Brown. The latter of these had been at the club since 1963 and was nicknamed 'Bomber' on account of his charging runs into opposition penalty areas. Then there was a fleet-footed Glaswegian named Willie Johnston. A skilful winger, Johnston was also a genuine maverick. He put his shocking disciplinary record down to the fact that he believed in getting his retaliation in first against opposition defenders. Johnston had also been cautioned for such infractions as kicking a referee up the backside and taking a swig from a can of beer during a game. In one particularly memorable exchange with a supporter, Johnston negotiated the sale of a greenhouse.

'I'd let it be known that I was looking to buy one and a young lad sitting in a corner of the ground, right on the track-side, began shouting out to me that he had one to sell,' recalls Johnston. 'I started talking to him about a price while the game was going on and in between taking corner kicks. It took me a couple of weeks, but I eventually bargained him down from £80 to £45.'

Back in the First Division that season, the team had more than held its own under Giles and were looking at a top-ten finish. At the point of signing Laurie Cunningham, West Brom were in the middle of a five-match winning run, having seen off local rivals Birmingham City and Derby County, and won at Arsenal in their three most recent games. A stickler for discipline, Giles had developed an excellent team spirit and was universally adored by his players.

'He was a hard man, but fair too,' says Alistair Robertson. 'He used to say, "I'll tell you once, I'll tell you twice, but don't let me have to tell you a third time." If there was a third occasion, you wouldn't be in the team, simple as that. We were all given a specific job to do. He'd say to John Wile and me, "If you two were good passers of the ball, you'd be midfielders. But you're not, are you? You win tackles and headers, and when you've got the ball, give it to me because I'm able to do something with it."'

'John knew the game inside out and his man-management skills were second to none,' adds Len Cantello. 'Earlier that season we'd got beaten 7-0 at Ipswich and he'd stopped the bus on the way home and got the beers in.'

Laurie Cunningham had been recommended to Giles by Ronnie Allen, Albion's chief scout. Allen had been a striker for club in the 1950s and was still then West Brom's record goal scorer. The week of his arrival, Giles pitched Cunningham straight into the first team. He made his debut in a 2-0 win at Tottenham on 12 March 1977 and in doing so became the first black player to represent the club. In its report on the match, the *Birmingham Post* declared: 'Cunningham played the sort of dream game that suggests Johnny Giles has got himself a bargain.'

Four days later, Cunningham made his first appearance at the Hawthorns in a midweek fixture against Ipswich Town. Albion won the return match against their early season conquerors that night 4-0, with Bryan Robson scoring a hat-trick and Cunningham netting his first goal for the club. By the end of the game, Albion's supporters had begun to chant his name, instantly won over by his dancing feet.

However, there were few other bright sparks to savour at that time for people in the Black Country. The economic woes afflicting Britain as a whole were hitting the area hard, and the outlook for its blue collar workforce – then the foundation of any football club's fan base – seemed especially bleak and unforgiving. Soaring inflation led to a series of bitter industrial disputes, as management attempted to keep down wage rises and unions called mass walk-outs in protest. It was a vicious circle that accounted for ten-million working days being lost to strike action that year. A significant number of these came at the British Leyland car plant in Longbridge, Birmingham, where union leaders had adopted an especially militant stance.

The state of English football was no less grim. The national team, World Cup winners in 1966, had failed to even qualify for the finals of the tournament in 1974, an inglorious feat that was to be repeated four years later. This decline had permeated all levels of the game. The country's archaic pre-war stadia had fallen into disrepair, and pitches that were arid and bone-hard in the summer months became quagmires through the winter. A new social disease, football hooliganism, had begun to manifest itself on the terraces, with violent clashes between opposing fans becoming a regular aspect of the match-day experience. Things were no more edifying on the pitch, with the introduction into the game of the offside trap prompting a shift towards a joyless brand of defensive football.

Against this kind of backdrop, a player such as Cunningham, whose talents seemed as untamed as they were unpredictable, was bound to be conspicuous. Yet the ease with which he appeared to slip into the West Brom team and begin to bend it to his will also kept hidden the fact that Cunningham was struggling to settle into his new surroundings. Just as he'd done at Orient, he often seemed to his team-mates in the dressing room like an outsider looking in, and his introverted nature was initially taken for aloofness or arrogance.

'Laurie was a funny character,' says Tony Brown. 'I found him hard to get to know and I think other people in the team felt the same. He was very quiet. Even in the dressing room, where lads are always cracking jokes and pulling your leg, he'd keep out of things. On some mornings, he'd come into training and wouldn't say a word all day. But then, out on the pitch he'd be completely different, expressing himself with the ball and doing tricks.'

Cultural differences between Cunningham and the others were also soon evident. One morning after training, his colleagues watched agog as he stood before them in the dressing room, applying a moisturising cream to his face and body. His white team-mates had not witnessed another man doing anything of the kind before. Their own post-training regimen extended to nothing more outlandish than going off to a local café for a pot of tea and a fry-up, the smokers in the side all huddled together around one table, non-smokers at another. It further marked Cunningham out as being someone different among them.

'He had to moisturise otherwise his skin would dry and blister,' says Nicky Brown, who had moved from London to the Midlands with Cunningham. 'But at that time, if you did some-thing like that and looked after your hair, then you must be gay. I think the other players were very much afraid of that kind of thing, although Laurie couldn't have cared less what they said about him.

'There was a bit of passive racism towards him at first. It was nothing nasty, but there'd be comments made about him not forgetting to have his bananas before a game or his having 'nappy hair'. Laurie was a very evenly distributed man, shall we say, but once they'd seen him in the bath, there were remarks like, "Well, you don't live up to that rumour, do you?" People at the club would also ask Laurie and me if we had lots of sex, as if that were the only reason a white woman could possibly be with a black man.'

Cunningham shared these initial feelings of isolation and alienation not just with the handful of other black footballers then playing for British clubs, but in general with black people across the country. At the Hawthorns, the West Brom players ran out for home games to an instrumental track titled 'The Liquidator', which had been a Top 10 hit in the UK for the Jamaican reggae producer Harry Zephaniah Johnson and his All-Stars band back in 1969. Yet this was in no way reflective of there being a multicultural mix among supporters on the terraces. Albion's gates that season averaged around 25,000, of which the vast majority were white, and such statistics were repeated at football grounds throughout the League.

'There were a couple of Asian lads and two or three West Indians who'd just then started to come to games,' says John Homer, chairman of West Brom's supporters' club. 'I can recall one Jamaican lad called Bowie. He and a couple of his mates used to come on the coach with us to away games. They took a hell of a lot of stick wherever they went, but they were big blokes and could look after themselves.'

The increased presence of the National Front at English football grounds hardly encouraged ethnic supporters to games, the far-right organisation having targeted the sport's white working-class fan base as a potentially fertile recruiting ground. NF activists became a common sight outside stadia on a Saturday afternoon, particularly in London and the northern cities, handing out their poisonous pamphlets and literature.

In May 1973, one of the National Front's most senior figures, Martin Webster, had contested a by-election in West Bromwich. He polled 16 per cent of the vote, then a record for the party. Three years later, the NF fared even better in local elections in the area, on average picking up a 17 per cent share of the vote, a markedly higher figure than it achieved in most other areas of the country.

For young blacks growing up in places such as Birmingham and the West Midlands as a whole, there was an acute sense of having been cut off both from the rest of society and from their own culture. Their parents, who'd emigrated from the Caribbean in the fifties and sixties, had been brought up to regard Britain as the mother country and a land of milk and honey. The reality they experienced upon arriving on these new shores proved to be very different.

'My parents came to Birmingham from Jamaica in 1959 expecting to be welcomed with open arms and instead walked into a country that hated them,' says Derrick Campbell, a civil rights activist who spent his childhood in Handsworth. 'My mother can remember being stood at the bus stop and white women coming up to her and touching her face, asking her if she was the same colour all over.

'Because our parents suffered such oppression and discrimination, we were taught at home to believe that white people were to be feared and not to trust them. As a youngster, I can recall being chased through the streets by police vans, which we used to call Black Marias. The police would regularly beat black kids with truncheons, or turn their dogs on us.'

'More than anything, my memories of growing up are of the

isolation we felt,' says David Hinds, who was also born in Handsworth and later formed the British reggae band, Steel Pulse. 'We saw it through the state of our housing and in our schools. Every now and then, the National Front would march through the community and put bricks through the windows. It was extremely hard to get a job in the area, because of the racial divide.'

The first signs of protest were seen in Birmingham in the late sixties and early seventies with the emergence of a group of young black men calling themselves the Natty Bongos. The Bongos based their dreadlocked hair and idealism on the Rastafarian movement, which had developed among working-class blacks in Jamaica in the 1930s in response to oppression from the island's white landowners. The Rastafarians took the Bible as their sacred text and advocated a return to their ancestral homelands in Africa, believing that the slave trade had robbed them of their heritage. In the minds of the Bongos, their fight was with white Britain.

'There was a reggae club called the Santa Rosa, which was on the main Soho Road that ran from Handsworth to West Bromwich, and that was on the front line,' says Hinds. 'A lot of Rasta-looking guys used to hang out there. These guys had wild-looking hair and they wore their pants halfway up their ankles. They began burning Bibles because they didn't believe the King James translation could be trusted, since it was written by a white man. And they went to the extreme in their beliefs, refusing to eat white flour or sugar. But they could also be intimidating. Even for a black kid like me, it was a scary experience having to walk past them on the street.'

★

On 19 March 1977, West Bromwich Albion travelled to the North East to play high-flying Newcastle United at St James' Park. For the first time in an Albion shirt, Laurie Cunningham was subjected to a diatribe from the Newcastle supporters on each occasion he touched the ball. One particularly ugly chant rose up and followed him along the touchline: 'Pull the trigger, shoot the nigger.' It was repeated over and again in a menacing monotone.

Cunningham appeared unruffled and was outstanding that afternoon, as if driven to greater heights by the continual abuse he was being subjected to. He scored Albion's equalising goal, a header, in a 1-1 draw, further enraging his would-be tormentors. It was through performances such as these, facing down the mob and putting one over on them, that Cunningham became a figurehead for the nascent black pride that was fermenting in the country, especially in the West Midlands.

'Laurie Cunningham was part of the process of black kids starting to find themselves,' says Brian Travers, who grew up in Balsall Heath and is a founding member of the reggae band UB40. 'He came through just as black culture was starting to emerge, and as a white guy, I could see how much he meant to my black pals. He gave them a sense of recognition and I'd guess that it helped them to stop feeling as if they were second-class citizens.'

Muhammad Ali's triumph in retaining his world heavyweight boxing title in the epic 'Rumble in the Jungle' contest of 1974 with George Foreman was instrumental in awakening this new black consciousness in Britain. Before it, tremors were also set off by the emergence of such black-centric American record labels as Motown and Stax. Just three weeks after Cunningham's ordeal in Newcastle, the BBC screened the smash-hit American TV series

Roots, a pivotal moment for black Britons. Telling the true-life story of an African-born slave, Kunta Kinte, *Roots* was the first instance in which a drama told from a black perspective, and with a black man in the leading role, had been seen on British television.

Such things doubtless resonated, but what they didn't or couldn't do was articulate the experience of black kids growing up in Britain at the time, or suggest anything that might be attainable to them. For that, they would have to look to role models such as Cunningham and also to emerging British reggae bands such as Aswad from London and Handsworth's Steel Pulse.

Reggae had been born in Jamaica, its bass-heavy sound evolving from the 'bluebeat' and ska scenes that had risen up on the Caribbean island in the fifties and sixties. These had generated such international hits as Millie Small's 1964 single 'My Boy Lollipop' and Desmond Dekker's 'Israelites' from 1968, and also heralded the emergence of a group called the Wailers that was fronted by a young Bob Marley. It was another band, Toots and the Maytals, that gave reggae its name with their 1968 song, 'Do the Reggay'. But it was Marley who popularised the music through such defining anthems as 1973's 'I Shot the Sheriff' and 'No Woman, No Cry' from the following year.

In the spring of 1977, reggae was still very much an underground music in Britain. It was barely heard on local radio stations, let alone the national broadcaster, the BBC's Radio 1. Its impact was being felt instead on the streets of places such as Brixton in south London, and Birmingham's Handsworth and Balsall Heath, among strong and growing black communities and where specialist reggae clubs and record shops had been founded. Following Marley's lead, the new young British reggae bands used their music as a platform from which to sing about their own lives and experiences.

'Reggae music was of the utmost importance to us, because it was like the tale that was never being told,' says David Hinds. 'As kids, we didn't know the historical events that took place to bring us here, and the music started to connect the dots for us. Reggae was what we used to learn the history of ourselves as a people.'

'Every second kid in my class at school was West Indian or Asian, and reggae was all that was played in the youth clubs or at the church-hall discos on a Friday night,' recalls Brian Travers. 'You could dance with girls to it and it was sexier [than white pop music]. When all the black kids began finding their own identity and started to become Rasta, I can remember feeling distinctly left out as a white kid, but reggae in general worked wonders.'

Soon, Cunningham and Nicky Brown found their way to the heaving reggae clubs in Handsworth and elsewhere in Birmingham. There they resumed their London lifestyle, dancing through the night and into the next morning. As at Orient, Cunningham began to turn up late to training. This brought him into conflict with not just his disciplinarian manager, but also with the club's captain, John Wile, a domineering figure in the dressing room.

'Johnny Giles had instilled in us the ethos that the team was the most important thing and there's no doubt about it, Laurie lacked discipline,' says Wile. 'You couldn't have a player behaving as he did, although later on he was given a fair bit of latitude. But if someone came into the club at that time and felt they could take liberties, a little bit of glory seeking, it was stamped on straight away. And this didn't always go down well.'

'Laurie didn't hit it off with some of the older players,' admits Derek Statham. 'He was forever parading in front of the dressing room mirror, combing his hair and wouldn't accept friends too easily. You had to win his trust and then he'd take you in a little bit. I went out with him socially a couple of times and got to see the other side of him. He loved showing off with his dancing and he knew how to have a right good laugh. He was a lovely guy really, but unfortunately not everybody was able to see that.'

Cunningham found an unlikely ally in one of the West Brom directors, John Gordon. A flamboyant character, Gordon was a self-made millionaire who'd grown up friends with the media impresario Lew Grade in the thriving London East End Jewish community of the 1920s. He owned the Adelphi Ballroom in West Bromwich and had brought the Beatles to the Black Country to perform at the venue in November 1962.

Perhaps empathising with the prejudice Cunningham was encountering on the football pitch, having himself been subjected to anti-Semitism, Gordon took the young player under his wing. He offered Cunningham financial advice and entertained him and Brown at his penthouse apartment in Birmingham, whisking them off there in his Jaguar car. The football club had lodged the couple at the Europa Hotel, just down the road from the Hawthorns. When they were asked to leave following complaints about noise, Gordon found them a place to live.

'John Gordon liked our naughtiness and daring, but he felt protective towards us as well,' says Nicky Brown. 'From his own youth, he understood what Laurie was dealing with, and doing so with dignity, and he treated him as if he were his own grandson.

'There was one time when we went to Scotland with him on a private plane. Laurie and I did one of our things that day. We got all dressed up and pretended to be Fred Astaire and Ginger Rodgers. We made out that we didn't know each other and sat on opposite sides of the aisle on the plane. When we took off, Laurie came over and started talking to me as if we'd just met. I don't know if John had ever had children, but I think he liked that kind of innocent life in us.'

At the end of that April, Cunningham's rise through the game was further accelerated when he was selected for the England Under-21 team. He wouldn't quite be the first black footballer to represent his country, as the *Birmingham Post* claimed when announcing the news, since that honour had gone to another Londoner, Benjamin Odeje, who'd turned out for the England Schoolboys side six years earlier. Cunningham's ascension was nonetheless a hugely significant milestone for both the game in England and for the burgeoning ideal of an empowered black Britain.

He re-enforced this when making his international debut against Scotland at Sheffield United's Bramall Lane ground on 27 April. In a tightly contested match, he scored the only goal of the game, a diving header just after half-time. After the match, the U21s boss, Les Cocker, told waiting reporters: 'This boy can certainly play and I was very pleased for him, because he was under a lot of pressure before the match and had something to prove.'

'Laurie was very much aware of the significance of his playing in that game,' says Brown. 'He was a British boy. He loved his bacon sandwiches and his roast dinner on a Sunday.'

A week previous to the international fixture, Johnny Giles announced his intention to quit as West Bromwich Albion manager at the end of the season, having taken issue with the club's failure to offer him an improved contract. His shell-shocked team won their next two games, beating Leicester City 5-0 and Stoke City 3-1, results that secured them a seventh-place finish in the First Division. Giles' final game was a local derby at Aston Villa, a couple of miles up the road in Birmingham. Yet there would be no glorious send-off for him, with Albion losing 4-0 and doing so without Laurie Cunningham. On the evening of the game, he'd had the last of his run-ins with the manager.

'We'd come in to have a warm-up that morning and Laurie hadn't turned up,' says Tony Brown. 'He didn't actually show up till teatime, when we were all on the coach and ready to go to the game. John asked him where he'd been all day and I forget his excuse, but his usual one was that he'd not heard his alarm clock. John ordered him off the coach and sent him home.'

'I doubt very much whether that attitude of Laurie's would've continued had John stayed on,' says Wile. 'He'd have been told to toe the line regardless of how good a player he might have been. But after John left, people tended to put their arm around Laurie, pamper to him if you like, and other players perhaps didn't get the same sort of attention.'

One of Giles' other last acts as manager of West Brom would have a deeper meaning for not just the football club, but on a much greater scale, though he couldn't possibly have known it at the time. In the first week of May 1977, Giles sanctioned the signing of another young black player scouted by Ronnie Allen, this time from non-league football in London. He was a strapping centre-forward named Cyrille Regis.

Chapter Three: Smokin' Joe

The mass migration to Britain from its Caribbean colonies was instigated by the 1948 British Nationality Act, which permitted islanders holding a British passport to legally reside in the UK. On 22 June that year, the SS *Empire Windrush* sailed into Tilbury Docks in Essex, delivering the first 492 of the 80,000 migrants that would arrive from the Caribbean by 1957.

There was the general sense among the islanders that Britain was a land of boundless opportunity. However, harsher realities also drove them to leave their homelands. The British West Indies had long suffered from the neglect of its colonial master, and as a result poor wages, poverty and squalor were facts of life on the islands. The British government had also not shied from using an iron fist to keep its colonial subjects in check. During the 1930s, a series of workers' revolts had occurred across the region. These protested pay and conditions at various subsidiary companies of the British sugar giant, Tate & Lyle. The British army was sent in to crush one such uprising in Kingston, Jamaica, in 1938, with forty-six protestors being killed.

Decamping to Britain's urban areas, the new arrivals were grouped together in run-down inner-city housing and ushered into low-skilled manual work. Most often they were paid less than their white counterparts, despite a mere 9 per cent of them being classed as unskilled. A common sight at this time were hand-made signs displayed in the windows of lodging houses that read 'No blacks, no Irish, no dogs'. The Irish had made up the greater number of migrants to Britain in the pre-war era. The frigidity of this welcome took on a hostile edge in 1958 when white gangs spilled onto the streets of London's Notting Hill and the East Midlands city of Nottingham in the country's first race riots for a generation.

In 1963, Cyrille Regis left the Caribbean island of St Lucia for Britain with his mother and two siblings, a sister and brother. Regis was born four years earlier in French Guiana, a protectorate of France on the north Atlantic coast of South America. His father, Robert, was a fisherman by trade but had come to the mountain town of Maripasoula from the Caribbean to prospect for gold. He'd had little success and in 1962 had gone on to England ahead of his family to look for work. His wife, Mathilde, took the children to stay with relatives on St Lucia. From there they were able to pick up British passports.

The remaining Regis family members sailed into Southampton as the British winter was biting. They took a train from the coast to London, where Robert had got a job working as a labourer. He was renting a room on Portobello Road and to begin with the four of them crammed into it. The family subsequently moved to a two-bedroom lodging house in Kensal Rise to the north-west of the city, where the three children attended the local primary school.

'I can remember that it always seemed to be cold,' says Regis.

'But I was a kid, so England was new and fun to me. For my parents, it was tough and there was a constant struggle with housing. The house in Kensal Rise was two-up, two-down with an outside toilet and no bathroom. We used to have to go to a place in Paddington once a week to get a bath.

'Later on, my parents made us aware of the prejudice they'd encountered. They told us about things like the "No Irish, no blacks . . ." signs. That's when I came to understand why there were only ever Irish and black people living where we lived. But I personally never experienced anything of the sort growing up, or at least nothing that affected me too much or stayed with me.'

In 1969, the family was broken up again, driven out of Kensal Rise by a steep increase in rent. Robert, Mathilde and their daughter moved into a nearby hostel, while Cyrille and his brother were sent off to board at a convent school in the Hampshire town of Aldershot for nine months. The five of them were reunited the following year and settled down in north London. They found a council house on a new housing estate in Stonebridge, near Wembley, a neat maisonette over which loomed six concrete tower blocks.

Brought up a Roman Catholic, Regis was sent to the Cardinal Hinsley secondary school in Harlesden. A big lad even then, he soon proved to be an adept sportsman. He was naturally broad and muscular, but quick-footed too, and he regularly picked up certificates for winning the 100-metre and 200-metre sprint races on the school's sports days. However, cricket was his first love, and he was selected to represent both the school and the borough of Brent at the game.

'Even as a kid, I'd got a really strong work ethic from my dad,' he says. 'I had a paper round and a milk round. On a Saturday, I used to stack shelves in a shop on Church Road in Harlesden. I also gave up an entire summer holiday from school to go and work with my mom for £10 a week. She was a seamstress, but she'd got a job in a lace-making factory. For the six weeks I was there, it was my responsibility to load up the bobbins on the machines.'

At school, Regis used to join in with the other boys kicking a ball about in the playground. Yet he didn't take an active interest in football until he was thirteen. His games teacher, a Mr Ward, encouraged him into the school team. At first, he played on the right wing, but with his pace and power was soon converted into a striker. Regis also gravitated to his local youth club team in Kilburn. He turned out for them alongside the future Arsenal player Steve Gatting and his elder brother Mike, who would later captain England at cricket.

'Quite a few of the lads at school then started to play for a team called Ryder Brent Valley on a Sunday morning, so I joined them,' says Regis. 'This was in 1973 and the side was run by a wonderful man named Tom Dolan. People like Mr Dolan kept a lot of kids like me out of trouble, ferrying us around all over the place and encouraging us. He worked for a van rental company, so each week he used to get us a big yellow van and drive us out to Regent's Park or wherever else we were playing. We'd get changed in the back of the van on the way and be falling about all over each other.'

Nonetheless, the young Regis did step out of line on occasion. In 1974, during his final year at school, he received a police caution. He was caught breaking into a house in Harlesden intending to steal money from the gas meter. By then he was running with a group of older lads that was led by a pair of brothers, the Crawfords, who frequented the local reggae clubs. They turned Regis on to the music of Bob Marley, Dennis

Brown and Augustus Pablo, as well as to the pleasures of drinking beer and smoking.

'The Crawford brothers were twenty, twenty-one at the time and they had their own sound system,' Regis recalls. 'We'd go off in their car to all these different nightclubs that they were playing at. I fell in love with that heavy bass sound and became a reggae man. I was going out each night, listening to and learning from these guys, drinking Special Brew. They were great times.'

In the summer of 1974, aged sixteen, Regis left school. His father had drummed into him the need to get a trade and he signed up for a three-year apprenticeship with a firm of electrical contractors, Higgins & Castle, who were based in Cricklewood, north-west London. His starting wage was 32p an hour. Working towards qualifying as an electrician, he laboured on building sites by day and took classes at the local technical college in the evenings.

Each Sunday morning he continued to turn out for Ryder Brent Valley. At the time, he had no concept that it might lead him on to anything more permanent or grander. As much as anything else, he enjoyed football for the social side of the game and the chance to be with his mates. In any event, in one game, Ryder Brent Valley had been pitted against a junior side from Queen's Park Rangers and he'd scored a hat-trick. Yet no one from the professional club had whisked him off for a trial.

'I didn't even get into the Middlesex county side, like a few of the other Brent Valley lads did,' he says. 'But then, I loved the camaraderie and the banter, winning and losing together, supporting each other. For me, it was all about the whole experience. I learned so many lessons about discipline, sacrifice and commitment. I also felt as though I was living the life, going out to work and playing football at the weekend.'

★

A typical suburb of London, the small Surrey town of Molesey sits on the banks of the River Thames to the west of the city. By the 1970s it had become a haven for middle-class commuters. The town boasted a successful rowing club and also a non-league football team, Molesey FC. Formed in 1892 by a local doctor, by 1975 the club was playing in Division Two of the Athenian League, and also the Premier Midweek Floodlit League.

Molesey's chairman and manager, John Sullivan, was a brash figure who worked as an agent in the music business and drove a gold-painted Pontiac Firebird. Sullivan enlisted a friend of his to go out talent-spotting young players for the club at park pitches across London. One Sunday morning, Sullivan's scout happened across Cyrille Regis playing in Regent's Park for Ryder Brent Valley. Regis was invited down to Molesey for a trial, impressing Sullivan, who took him on at the club. He was given £5 a match, the first money he'd made from the game. His Molesey debut was against Tooting & Mitcham United on a Tuesday night in the Floodlit League.

The level Molesey competed at was significantly higher than anything Regis had been used to, but he took to it with apparent ease and became a regular in their first team. Sullivan would pick him up from home in Stonebridge on a Saturday morning, or meet him from work on a Tuesday evening, and speed them off across London to a game or to training.

'John was always going on about what was happening in the music business and who he was looking after, but I didn't listen too much as I was half-asleep most of the time,' Regis recalls. 'It was a long way from north-west London to Molesey and it was tough for me. During the week, I'd be getting home at one or two o'clock in the morning and having to be at work for 6 a.m. to do an eight-hour shift. I'd be battered and bruised too, because playing as a striker you'd have these big defenders whacking into the back of you all the time.'

Regis spent just a single season at Molesey, scoring twenty-seven goals. The club won their section of the Floodlit League that year with a record points haul and also reached the Fifth Round of the FA Vase for the first time. By then, the performances of Molesey's centre-forward had attracted the attention of another club based to the west of London, but a further step up the non-league ladder.

Hayes FC played in the Isthmian League, the strongest in the south of England. They had just signed a goalkeeper from Molesey named Ian Bath. It was Bath who recommended Regis to the Hayes manager, Bobby Ross. A no-nonsense Scot, Ross was a former professional footballer who'd played for Heart of Midlothian in Edinburgh, Brentford and also Cambridge United, where he'd briefly been a team-mate of Brendon Batson's.

'Ian and I went to see Cyrille playing for Molesey the next Saturday,' says Ross. 'He was easy to spot when the teams came out because he had his socks rolled down around his ankles and wasn't wearing shin-pads. With my professional eye, having played five hundred or six hundred games by that time, I could tell straight off that he had outstanding ability. He was quick, won balls in the air and was obviously capable of hurting teams.

'We waited around for him after the game and I told him I was interested in signing him for Hayes. We were in a better league than Molesey and I believed I could get him to go on and do what I'd done. Right away, I let him know I thought he could be good enough to get into the pro game.'

Hayes' chairman, Derek Goodhall, was a wealthy builder and the club paid decent wages for a non-league side at that level of the game. Ross clinched the deal by offering to more than double the money Regis was getting at Molesey. Together with his apprenticeship wages, he would now be pocketing the princely sum of £38 a week.

Once he began working with Regis, the Hayes manager determined that he'd got a unique footballer on his hands. After training, Ross would keep Regis out on the pitch and give him one-to-one coaching. He hammered cross after cross at him to power into an empty goal until his head ached, cajoling and urging him on as if he might will him to greatness. Ross insisted to his reluctant new recruit that he wore shin-pads. He told him that if he didn't, he'd get his legs broken, since defenders in the professional game would set out to hurt him. It was the only issue Ross had to force, since he found Regis to be an otherwise exemplary member of the team. He was reliable, attentive, always on time and blessed with an easy manner that charmed everyone at the club.

Regis made his first appearance for his new club against Wycombe Wanderers before a 300-strong crowd. Just as he'd done at Molesey, he seemed to grow in stature among better players. That 1975–76 season, he charged through opposition defences like a battering ram and plundered goals. He was fast and strong, near impossible to knock off the ball and just as hard to ruffle. However much centre-halves kicked at him and whatever insults were tossed at him from on or off the pitch, Regis carried on regardless. He seemed unbending and unbreakable. His team-mates nicknamed him Smokin' Joe, after the heavyweight boxing champion Joe Frazier, since it was well known that Frazier would never go down during a fight.

'Cyrille wasn't one of those guys that worried about colour, he didn't take it at all personally,' says Ross. 'But you couldn't do so, because it's a fact that you get lunatics near football pitches.

The lads could have a laugh with him too. One night we were having a darts competition to raise money for the club and the boys asked Cyrille if he was bringing along his blowpipe. He took it the way it was intended, as a joke.'

'I've been in that situation myself and we're expected to laugh off things like that blowpipe joke,' counters civil rights activist Derrick Campbell. 'If you don't, you're seen as having a chip on your shoulder. I'm sure that if Cyrille had reacted, the response would've been, "What's his problem?"'

In a short time, Ross grew used to seeing Football League scouts peppering the small main stand at Hayes. Representatives from Chelsea, Millwall and Watford each enquired about taking his statuesque number 9 on trial. But Ross rebuffed them, telling his chairman to wait until a club came along that was prepared to pay good money for Regis and then they would all benefit. 'I told Derek that we should all watch and enjoy Cyrille in the meantime,' he says, 'because I knew that he wouldn't be with us for long.'

By the end of that season, Regis had helped himself to twenty-five goals for Hayes and won the club's Player of the Year award. The last month of the campaign, Ronnie Allen, a scout from from West Bromwich Albion, came to see him playing against Dagenham. Allen had a particular affinity for strikers, having scored 234 goals in 458 appearances for West Brom between 1950 and 1961. He had gone into management after retiring as a player, becoming one of the first British managers to coach overseas during stints with Athletic Bilbao in Spain and Sporting Lisbon in Portugal.

Allen was a quiet, aloof-seeming man, but he was stirred by Regis. He came back to watch him on three further occasions. He then told his employers at West Brom that if they wouldn't commit to buying him, he'd pay for Regis out of his own money.

Allen was given the go-ahead to make an offer to Hayes for their prize asset: a down-payment of £5,000 with a further £5,000 due when and if Regis made twenty appearances for the Albion first team. It was enough to buy Hayes a new set of floodlights.

'I had told Cyrille that he was being watched, because if you're good enough, then you've got to be able to do it when the pressure is on,' says Ross. 'When we got the bid from West Brom, I drove him up there to speak to them. We met with the chairman, Bert Millichip, Ronnie Allen and also Johnny Giles.

'Their offer to Cyrille was £60 a week, plus travelling expenses. As we were sat there in the chairman's office negotiating the deal, a ceiling light started to flicker. I said, "Mr Chairman, one thing I know for a fact that Cyrille is able to do for you is fix that light."'

Returning to London with Ross, Regis said he needed time to think the offer over. He'd just recently passed his final exams to qualify as an electrician and had the promise of a steady wage. To take this great leap into the unknown, he'd have to leave his home and all that was familiar to him, and he was barely being offered more money to do so.

'Being from London, I didn't even know anything about West Bromwich Albion,' he says. 'So I went and asked my dad what he thought I should do. He told me that I'd got something to fall back on now and that if it didn't work out, I could always go back to being an electrician.'

Taking his father's advice, Regis signed his first contract as a professional footballer with the Baggies in May 1977. Local newspapers in the West Midlands didn't deem the club's latest acquisition significant enough to be reported on and focused instead on the imminent departure of Giles. Regis had three more months at home before he was due to move to the Midlands. He spent this time doing the same thing he'd done for the previous three years: getting up at the crack of dawn and going to work on a building site.

Arriving at Birmingham's New Street station that July, Regis was met off the train by Ron Jukes, a part-time coach at West Bromwich Albion. Jukes drove him to Smethwick, where the club had arranged digs for him with a Jamaican family, the Groces. The household was presided over by Murtella Groce, a warm-hearted matriarch who became a surrogate mother to Regis during the two years he lodged at her home in Maple Court.

'I paid her £15 a week rent and that was the first time I'd had my own room,' he says. 'Up until then, I'd always had to share with my brother. It was a real home from home for me. Mrs Groce made great food and she loved me. She also had a grandson living with her named John, who was two years younger than me, and we buddied up.

'The West Brom training ground was just around the corner from the Groce house on Spring Road and I used to walk there each morning. But to begin with I was bored. We finished training by 12.30 p.m. and I'd been used to getting up at six in the morning and working a full day.'

West Brom initially viewed Regis as a low-cost gamble. The club had only given him a one-year contract. It was intended that he'd be groomed in the reserves, before a decision was taken on whether to retain him or not. It was Regis' good fortune that Ronnie Allen, who'd been so instrumental in signing him, was appointed the club's new manager that summer. Allen wasn't popular with the club's fraternities of defenders and midfield players, who felt neglected by him, but he devoted himself to developing Albion's strikers and the young Regis especially.

The week after his arrival from London, the new manager threw Regis into a training game between the reserves and West Brom's first team. To the senior players, this was an opportunity to check out the competition in the 'stiffs', as the reserves were derided, and assert their authority over them. The first team captain, John Wile, lined up against Regis. A towering and singularly uncompromising defender, Wile prided himself on the fact that he and his fellow centre-half, Alistair Robertson, could be bullied by nobody.

'Cyrille was raw as raw could be and the ball was bouncing off his knees and shins,' Robertson recalls. 'Then they got a corner. Now, nobody beat John Wile to the ball in the air, ever. You just used to say, "Your ball, John," and that was that. But all you heard on this occasion was a thud and the ball was in the back of the net. And John was laid flat out on the floor.

'Next time they got a corner, Cyrille did the same thing again and he must have got up a good foot above John. I said to Wiley, "I think we need to slow this one down a bit, don't you?" So then I went in and whacked Cyrille. And he just turned and stared at me, never said a word.'

'We were all of us watching this, mouths agape,' says Derek Statham. 'After the game the lads were going to each other, "What the fuck was that? Who the hell is this guy?"'

By the end of the match, Regis had scored a hat-trick of headers. The next day, the first team departed for their annual pre-season tour, but he remained behind in Smethwick. For now at least, he was still a stiff.

Chapter Four: The Deadly Duo

When Cyrille Regis announced himself at West Bromwich Albion, Laurie Cunningham was the one player absent from pre-season training. He was off on international duty. It was in the course of this that Cunningham became unwittingly embroiled in an incident that signified how far it was that he'd then travelled, and also all that he hadn't been able to leave behind. If one were to scratch further at this surface, it would expose as well the conflicts and complexities that ran like fissures throughout his short life.

Following his successful debut, Cunningham had been selected to join up with the England U21 squad for a tour of Scandinavia. It was anticipated to be a low-key trip, but it was marred by an altercation that centred on him. After the final game in the Finnish capital of Oslo, a number of the young England players went out to enjoy a night on the town, Cunningham among them. The party ended up at a nightclub, where a bouncer refused Cunningham entry at the door. He was told that the club operated a colour bar. The next morning, the story was picked up by several British newspapers, each of which reported the basic details but without additional comment.

'I was so happy when I read that story,' claims Eustace 'Huggy' Isaie. 'It made me think, "Yeah, that brought you back down to earth, you prat." You're living in that high society world and on good wages, flying here and there, and all of a sudden someone's telling you that you can't come in because you're the wrong colour. To me, that was a reminder to Laurie that he was black.'

'I actually think Laurie had got a little bit lost by then,' says Bobby Fisher. 'I didn't have the same bond with him that we'd had together at Orient. In fact, since he'd left the club, I'd kept more in contact with Nicky. Laurie was great at being able to cut off certain ties, to go from having been quite close to someone to separating from them. Perhaps it was a defence mechanism he used so that he was able to move on, but in my opinion he'd also started to buy in to all the other nonsense that was going on around him at the time.

'To us, all that stuff had always been a joke. Going out to champagne bars and things like that, it'd be very easy to adopt that whole middle-class attitude of thinking you had to sit there looking and acting like everyone else and speaking properly. We'd always fought against that, not wanting to be the norm. We'd rebelled a little bit by going so over the top with it. It felt to me as though Laurie and I had lost that connection between us and he wasn't the same grounded guy that I'd known previously.

'But then, I don't think Laurie was ever really happy as a person. There was always something missing from his life. He was kind of like a lost soul and there may have been an inner frustration at not knowing what to look for, or what it was that was going to make him feel satisfied.'

That summer, the country as a whole appeared to be engaged in a battle with itself. The surging optimism of the post-war era turned to dread and despair as the self-image Britain had of itself as a global power vanished to the past. With it, the nation's moral compass began to shift.

The new Labour Prime Minister, Jim Callaghan, encapsulated a general air of resigned desperation when dolefully announcing a marked decline in British living standards. Real take-home pay had fallen by up to 5 per cent. A more vociferous response was still then brewing among Britain's white working classes, and this rising tide of bitterness and resentment continued to benefit the National Front. In council elections around the UK, the NF polled over a quarter of a million votes. In more than a third of the ninety-two seats it contested in Greater London, it usurped the Liberals as the third-most popular mainstream political party. That August, there were violent clashes between NF supporters and bands of protestors on the streets of Lewisham in south London and the Birmingham district of Ladywood.

The preceding June, Queen Elizabeth II had celebrated her Silver Jubilee. To mark the occasion, millions joined in street parties the length and breadth of the land. These festivities had a sepia-tinted afterglow to them, as if refracting a fading idyll – the dying idea of the nation as both united and glorious. The opposing view, one of a younger and more cynical generation, was articulated by the spitting guitars and sneered vocals of the Sex Pistols. Their venomous 'God Save the Queen' single was the most-bought pop song of those long, hot months in spite – or because – of it being banned by the BBC. A gentler, but just as emphatic tilt at the country's prim and proper traditions was taken by an otherwise unremarkable sitcom, *Robin's Nest*. This was the first programme of its kind to show an unmarried couple living together on British television.

Looking at football, one could see the state of the nation in microcosm. At the end of the previous season an English club, Liverpool, had defeated the German champions Borussia Monchengladbach in the European Cup final in Rome. This was a flickering monument to English supremacy, a panacea for the failures of the national team and the turgid fare that was being served up in the Football League. It also brought some respite from the ugly spectres of hooliganism and racism that were stalking the game's terraces.

Euphoria at Liverpool's triumph passed like a shadow, with deeper and more lingering truths to be derived from the item that replaced it on the national newspapers' back pages. This was the story of the resignation of the England team manager, Don Revie. A grubby saga, it was shaped three summers earlier when Revie, who'd built a successful Leeds United side in his own stern image, took over the national team from Sir Alf Ramsey. The buttoned-up Ramsey had won England the World Cup in 1966, but failed to guide them to the finals of the tournament in 1974.

Revie's reign was ill-fated from the start. England crashed out of the next major international tournament, the 1976 European Championships, again at the qualifying stage. They were making a faltering start to their campaign to reach the 1978 World Cup finals in Argentina when Revie walked out of his job, having negotiated a £340,000 contract to coach the United Arab Emirates. In the press and the corridors of power at the Football Association, Revie was portrayed as having the morals of a snake, a gutless captain abandoning his sinking ship. The FA banned him from working in England for ten years.

Media and public alike lobbied for the brazen, outspoken manager of Nottingham Forest, Brian Clough, to be Revie's replacement. Clough's Forest side played exciting attacking football, almost an anomaly at the time, and he'd led them from the depths of the Second Division to promotion the previous season. However, he was no diplomat and his barbed outpourings had frequently ruffled feathers among the game's top brass. Clough ultimately was too much for the people running the English game to stomach and the FA ignored the clamour for him, opting instead for West Ham's Ron Greenwood, the very image of the dutiful company man.

Laurie Cunningham, who would have his own reasons to regret Greenwood's appointment, returned to West Brom in time for the new season. Albion's fans had found it easier to warm to him than had his team-mates, and he was idolised among them. If the rest of the squad questioned this as fact, well, the club's annual opening day would have put them right. On a hot August afternoon, hundreds of kids from local schools trooped along to the Spring Road training ground and Cunningham was besieged. At one point, the weight of bodies pressing down upon him hunting his autograph became so great that a policemen was forced to intervene for fear that he'd be crushed.

Cunningham had heard rumblings of there being a new, younger black player at the club, of course he had. Of how he seemed like a force of nature and had so nonchalantly rolled over the indomitable John Wile. But he didn't attach much importance to such things, most often preferring to talk about anything other than football. In any case, he hadn't yet met Cyrille Regis, and out of sight was out of mind.

'The first teamers were the big boys and they walked around the place with a strut, an air of confidence about them, Laurie as much as anyone else,' says Regis. 'Whereas I was still just nineteen years old and had only played three or four games in the reserves. But I was finding my feet and getting into the groove.'

Centre-forwards had attained a special and cherished status at West Brom. The man who wore the number 9 shirt for the club was expected not only to score great and important goals, he was also required to be a kind of mythical figure, one capable of rousing feats. It had been this way since Billy 'W.G.' Richardson had prowled opposition penalty areas in the thirties and forties. A former bus driver from County Durham, Richardson scored 202 goals in just 320 appearances for the club. Four of these came in a dazzling five-minute spell against West Ham United in 1931. He bagged two more that year to win the FA Cup for Albion against Birmingham City.

In the fifties, Richardson's mantle was assumed by Derek Kevan. A hulking Yorkshireman, like Regis, Kevan had come to West Brom as an unrefined teenager. Known as 'The Tank', he used his considerable bulk to bludgeon through opposition defences and netted 157 goals during his ten years at the Hawthorns, one for every 151 minutes he was on the pitch. He left Albion's fans with a lasting impression of him, scoring a hat-trick in his final game for the club against Ipswich Town in 1963.

Kevan's successor, Jeff Astle, was best loved of all and his exploits earned him the grand sobriquet of 'The King'. His extra-time goal against Everton, one of 174 that he notched for the club, won the FA Cup in 1968. With it, he also became the first man to score in every round of the competition in a single season. So feted was the genial and unassuming Astle, it was claimed, perhaps apocryphally, that a piece of graffiti daubed across a canal bridge in the Black Country town of Netherton that read 'King Astle, WBA' was under a preservation order from the town council.

Richardson, Kevan and Astle were also each selected to represent England. This furthered an expectation among the club's fans that as a matter of course West Bromwich Albion would boast the best centre-forward in the land – a conviction that had been shaken ever since Astle's departure in 1974. No one called his replacement, Joe Mayo, 'The King' or indeed anything of the sort. A committed but restricted footballer, Mayo was eventually packed off to Orient, a makeweight in the deal that had brought Laurie Cunningham to West Brom and for which he was most fondly recalled.

The current incumbent was David Cross, about whom there seemed nothing remarkable, despite his averaging a goal every other game since joining the Baggies the season before from Coventry City. The unloved Cross started the first three games of the 1977–78 season, scoring in each of the opening two, a 3–0 home win against Chelsea and a 2–2 draw at Leeds. Yet he was as ineffective as the rest of the team in succumbing 3–0 to the might of Liverpool.

Four days after their humbling at Anfield, West Brom faced a home midweek League Cup tie against Rotherham United of the Third Division. Cross had picked up an injury at Liverpool. Expecting to win, Ronnie Allen decided to pitch Cyrille Regis into the first team for the cup match. Regis walked to the Hawthorns from his digs in Smethwick that evening, past the gaggles of supporters mingling on the streets outside the ground, unrecognised and unknown to them.

'I felt a mixture of fear, apprehension, nervousness and excitement,' he recalls. 'I got into the dressing room and there was Willie Johnston, John Wile and also Laurie Cunningham getting changed. I knew them by sight, but we didn't know each other. There was a television on in the corner and as I started to get stripped off, I felt sure that each of them was looking at me and wondering if I was good enough for their team.

'The biggest crowd I'd played in front of up till that point had been 500. All of a sudden, two months later, there were 15,000 people out there. I was scared, churning up inside. But you know what men are like – I gave off an air of confidence and braved it out.'

In the first half of the game, Regis was full of huff and puff, and he charged round like a young bull. He was playing on nothing but instinct, since all that Allen had told him to do beforehand was go out and enjoy the experience. He had a couple of chances, missed them both, but still he kept showing for the ball and wanting to make a decent impression. West Brom had coasted into a 2-0 lead in the second half when the referee awarded them a penalty.

'Tony Brown, who usually took the penalties, was injured and Willie Johnston had been nominated in his absence,' says Regis. 'For some inexplicable reason, the West Brom crowd started singing, "Cyrille, Cyrille." Willie Johnston had the ball in his hand. He just gave me this knowing look and nodded at me. I'd never taken a penalty before, not even for the school team, but I went up there and scored. Then I scored another goal and we won 4-0. And that was it, the start of my career.'

'The story that night was nothing to do with Albion winning the game, which wasn't surprising. It was all about this kid,' remembers Bob Downing, a reporter for a local newspaper, the *Express & Star*. 'Nobody had known what to expect; Ronnie Allen had even had to tell us press guys how to spell Cyrille's forename. But when this lad came out wearing the number 9 shirt . . . I mean, my God, his physique was incredible.

'You'd have thought that a young kid coming into the side against a team that could put it about a bit would be intimidated, but he scared them. You could see fear in the eyes of their defenders. The crowd took to him in an instant. He could've been black, yellow, bloody polka dot for all they cared. And once you're an Albion centre-forward and the fans have taken to you, you're only going one way.'

After the game, Regis went along with Johnston, Cunningham and half the West Brom first team to the Hawthorns pub sited at the back of the main stand. The landlord bolted the doors and kept the beer flowing until three o'clock the next morning, players and supporters joined together in drinking to their good fortune. Sat among them, Regis didn't say much that night, though he sensed a rapport developing with the diffident Cunningham. Yet deep down, unspoken but undoubted, he knew that his chance had come and that it was now up to him to grasp it.

He retained his place in the side that Saturday for a League match against Middlesbrough. The League Cup was one thing, but now Regis would be pitting himself against First Division defenders. This was the biggest leap up the football ladder he had yet attempted. If he now proved to be nothing more than a flash in the pan, he would have a long, hard fall.

The game was twenty minutes old when Regis picked up the ball on the halfway line, put his head down and ran at Middlesbrough's goal. He shrugged off one, two, three challenges, swatted them aside like flies, and then crashed the ball into the net for the winning goal. During the rest of that game, the Hawthorns crowd sang a new chant. The words of it resounded around the ground for weeks on end: 'Astle is back, Astle is back.'

'He looked like he'd come out of a cartoon strip, like Popeye,' says Dave Bowler, a Baggies fan and author of the book *Samba in the Smethwick End*. 'In that sense, he was a throwback to another era. You could imagine that if you were able to get on the pitch, you'd want to play like Cyrille. There was something Sunday League about him, and I don't mean that in a derogatory sense. You could tell that he loved playing the game.'

'Cyrille was a raw talent on the field, but I tell you what, he was exciting,' says John Wile. 'When he got the ball, he seemed to have just one thought in his mind, which was to go for goal. Nobody scored goals like that in the professional game. If you like, it was a very naive way of looking at it, but it was effective. And because of his strength and size, he physically frightened people.

'With the background he'd had, I think he also appreciated just how much of an opportunity it was for him. He was like a sponge, always wanting to learn. If you told him to run a certain way, he would, he was that keen. But, phew, what a player he was.'

Regis accepted an invitation from Cunningham to go out that evening in Birmingham. They were joined by West Brom's 22-year-old goalkeeper, Tony Godden, another lad who hailed from the south of England. Cunningham took the pair of them dancing. Regis and Godden looked on admiringly as he spun one girl after another around the dance floor, the smoothest operator in the room. Cunningham and Regis hit it off together straight away. Each of them Londoners and just over a year apart in age, they were a couple of black guys on the make.

Once he'd exploded into West Brom's first team, Regis was barely out of it. Ronnie Allen showed so much faith in his young striker that the more experienced David Cross was shipped out of the club that December. The local papers were also quick to extol Allen's new-look side, the *Express & Star* declaring Regis and Cunningham to be the 'deadly duo'. Regis' new team-mates took to him just as fast, whereas Cunningham continued to confuse and confound, as elusive to them as ever.

The rough and tumble atmosphere of the dressing room, with its in-jokes and endless ribbing, held no fears for Regis since he'd come to it from a building site. He took whatever was thrown at him on the chin, and gave as good as he got. It helped too that he was a smoker and had been since he was sixteen. This gave him an instant in with the cabal of senior players who congregated after training each morning to puff on a cigarette and shoot the breeze. These were Willie Johnston, his fellow Scot Ally Brown, another of Albion's strikers, and the Irish midfielder Mick Martin, a man of caustic wit.

Yet Regis was also open and gregarious by nature. He enjoyed the company of others and had a ready laugh. When he was so engaged, the big, broad grin that stretched across his face would light it up. By contrast, Cunningham was invariably a brooding presence in the dressing room, removed from whatever was going on around him. Regis' positive influence did bring him out of his shell on occasion, but not so that most of the other players would ever feel that they got to know or comprehend him.

'Although outwardly he looked flamboyant, with how he dressed and walked, deep down Laurie was shy as a person,' says Regis. 'He was the quietest guy in the dressing room and a lot of people took that to be arrogance on his part. But I think it was much more a form of self-protection. He kept his distance until he warmed to someone or got to know them.'

'Laurie was never very forthcoming and he could be quite

moody too,' says Dave Harrison, who ghost-wrote Cunningham's weekly newspaper column for the Birmingham *Evening Mail*. 'You could go into the ground on Saturday lunchtime and sitting all on his own would be Laurie. You'd be able to tell just by the look on his face whether he was going to have a good game or not.

'He used to get horrendous stick from defenders, who'd kick him off the pitch within the first five minutes of a game. If he was in the mood, he'd just get up and get on with it. If not, he'd vanish. But he was a phenomenal, frightening talent. You went to watch him in training and it would be an education. He could do things with his feet and manipulate the ball in a way that was almost Houdini-like and would enable him to get out of any situation. I think the other players were prepared to tolerate him because of that ability.'

An intensely private man, it was almost as if Cunningham cocooned himself in a suit of protective armour. There were parts of this that even Regis couldn't penetrate. His friends did come to appreciate his droll-but-keen sense of humour. He was an avid *Monty Python* fan and would roar with laughter watching pratfalls or slapstick. Yet his deeper, darker corners were off limits to all but Nicky Brown.

'He loved watching shooting stars, and the joy on a child's face would bring him glee,' she says. 'If he witnessed cruelty, intolerance or abject nastiness of any kind he would react and I wouldn't be able to stop him. Lies made him mad. So did politicians. But also there being bad music at a club, a taxi not turning up at the right time or the fried chicken place not being open when he wanted it.

'There was always dance music on in the house and we read together all the time. He loved the outdoors. If it was raining, we'd go out and get wet, then come back in and spend the rest of the day in bed. If we didn't have to get up, we wouldn't. We'd stay there all day, looking through magazines, watching films. And we'd order out for takeaway food and eat it in bed.'

As he had at Orient, Cunningham gathered around him and Brown a small but tight group of people from the football club. In the stead of Bobby Fisher and Tony Grealish, at West Brom there was Regis, whom he allowed to get closest, Tony Godden and also Derek Statham.

'The first time I met Cyrille we were in a hotel bar waiting to do some kind of interview and Laurie had gone off to the toilet,' Brown recalls. 'This big black guy walked in and looked me up and down in that way that men do. And I looked at him. Then one of the directors from the club came in and said, "Ah, I see you two have met." Cyrille was like, "Don't tell me you're Nicky . . ."

'At the time, Cyrille was very much a ska boy. He loved his reggae and all he wanted to know about was where the black clubs were in Birmingham. He went out with black girls, so he had to adjust to Laurie and me too. Yes, there was an instant thing between the two of them, but I also think the club threw them together to an extent because they were both black.'

Laurie Cunningham became the second Albion player after Jeff Astle to have a piece of graffiti dedicated to him. His appeared on a brick wall at the back of the Hawthorns pub. This was the same pub the players habitually gathered at for a drink after each home game, so there'd be no doubt of them seeing it. Daubed in white paint, it said: 'Cunningham is a black cunt.'

The volume of abuse that had been solely directed at

Cunningham in his first season at West Brom was turned up and intensified now that Regis had joined him on the pitch. If the sight of a solitary black player in the English top division was then unusual enough for him to be exposed, having two together in the same team was tantamount to inciting a kind of fury.

At Newcastle, the week after the Middlesbrough match, a section of the home fans booed and chanted at the pair of them throughout the game. On 17 September, during a typically bruising local derby with Wolverhampton Wanderers at the Hawthorns, away supporters drummed on corrugated iron sheets at the back of the Smethwick Stand and chanted the odious litany that had first been heard in the North East the season before: 'Pull that trigger, shoot the nigger.' And also, 'Nigger, nigger, lick my boots.' Neither incident was referred to in the local or national media during or after the games.

'It was very difficult at that stage for a young reporter to know what to say or do,' contends the BBC's Pat Murphy, then working for local radio in the West Midlands. 'There wasn't a platform for one to stand up and say things on air – to say that the racist abuse was disgraceful. You just didn't do it. That was the culture of the time. You got on with it and did your job, and made sure that you praised the players as much as you could and whenever possible.'

'The abuse directed at them during the Wolves game in particular was foul,' says Dave Bowler. 'I believe that Laurie found it harder to deal with than Cyrille; it cut a lot deeper with him. He took it more personally and, frankly, why wouldn't you? You've got to remember that these guys were just nineteen and twenty-one years old at the time.'

In this regard, football again held up a mirror image to the rest of British society and its predominantly white institutions. There was still then no legal basis to challenge racist chanting, so no action was taken to stamp it out on the spot at football grounds. Had they even had a mind to do so, it would have been pointless for clubs such as West Brom to petition the FA to intervene. The game's ruling association declined to even pass comment on the matter, let alone address it. Both this veil of silence and the collective inertia could be said to be as much to do with sheer ignorance as with blind prejudice or a lack of concern. It was as if it were thought that the mere act of ignoring the elephant in the room might be enough to make it go away.

At West Brom, club director John Gordon took Regis under his wing just as he had done with Cunningham, offering both of them counsel and a sympathetic ear. It was enough to prompt whispers in and around the club about Gordon's motives, though neither player ever thought of him as being anything other than a mentor or father figure. Otherwise at the club, there seemed to be little regard given to, or awareness of, what both players were being subjected to. It wasn't something that was debated in the dressing room, and appeared almost not to have been noticed by the rest of the team. Until, that is, the Baggies travelled to London that November to face West Ham.

The East End of the capital had within its boundaries some of the poorest and most neglected areas of the country, and these were hotbeds of support for the National Front. Party activists were a familiar presence at the football grounds of West Ham and neighbouring Millwall. Fans of both clubs had become notorious for their hostility toward black players. In West Ham's case, the fact that a Bermudan, Clyde Best, and a Nigerian, Ade Coker, had been recent members of the club's first-team squad did nothing to dilute their venom. Regis and Cunningham were welcomed onto the Upton Park pitch that afternoon with a shower of bananas. It was so overt a gesture that no one could have missed it.

'The two lads were very professional about it and tried to shut it out, but it got to them,' says Willie Johnston. 'I got stick for being Scottish, but it didn't bother me. I told big Cyrille to open up a fruit shop. I said to him, "Listen, I'm getting the shit kicked out of me here, you're only getting bananas."'

'There were no black people going to watch football then and we didn't fully realise what these players were experiencing on our behalf,' says Derrick Campbell. 'We thought that Laurie Cunningham and Cyrille Regis were gods. We saw them in that arena, scoring goals, doing something that no other black person that we knew of had ever done or achieved. And yet we had no appreciation of the pressure or stresses acting upon them, of what they had to cope with. Even now, that is why they're held in the very highest esteem.'

Cunningham gave them the last laugh at West Ham, scoring one of Albion's goals in a 3–3 draw. It was a pattern that was followed throughout that autumn and into the first chill of winter. Regis scored goals at Newcastle, Birmingham and Derby County. Cunningham sealed a 4–0 home victory over Manchester United that secured West Brom's position in the upper regions of the First Division table.

On one waterlogged or frozen pitch after another, the two of them also gave lie to the belief that then endured within the game: that black players would baulk when the going got tough or the weather too cold. Regis in particular struck a heroic figure, so strong that opposition defenders bounced off him. With his chest bursting out through his shirt, he looked as if he were hewn from rock.

'Cyrille had a perfect physique and he didn't even have to

work at it,' says Derek Statham. 'He was fast too, but not interested in running more than 100 metres. When we did cross country runs, he used to get one of the local press photographers to give him a lift back to the training ground. The rest of us would all come in knackered after doing eight miles and he'd be showered and ready to go home.'

'I always thought that Cyrille looked like a god,' says Pat Murphy. 'The torso, the rippling physique and brave with it. He seemed a very happy soul, polite and well mannered, but there was a fire in his belly. He was sharp enough to see the game as a social release, like it was for the West Indian cricketers. He didn't have Cunningham's confidence, far from it, but he scored the kind of goals that we fantasise about. He realised your dreams for you.'

On the pitch, Cunningham's disposition was almost regal, as if he saw himself as being above the more mundane and rudimentary aspects of the game. Off it, he looked the part too in his fine, flash clothes and cruising around in the new white MG sports car that was his pride and joy. The junior partner of the two, Regis appeared more modest by comparison, but he'd also begun to enjoy the fruits of his new life. He liked a drink and enjoyed Birmingham's abundant nightlife. He revelled in the attention it afforded him, since he was something of a ladies' man and quick to charm.

'Cyrille might seem a little bit quiet and laid-back at first, until you got to know him, but he's very much a man's man,' says Tony Godden. 'A lot of the things that I got up to with him would curl your hair, but we had tremendous fun. I remember going round to his place one morning after a night out and he was asleep in his car in the garage. He said he hadn't been able to get into the house. I walked round to the back door and opened it. Turned out, he'd been pulling the handle the wrong way – that was just how he was.'

As Christmas neared, West Brom suffered an alarming wobble in form. They won just one of eight games, coming out on the wrong end of three-goal defeats against Aston Villa, Bristol City and Arsenal. The club was also dumped out of the League Cup by lower league Bury. As this wretched run progressed, rumours began to circulate in the local press that Ronnie Allen was preparing to resign as manager.

In fact, Allen had been negotiating a lucrative contract to advise the national team of Saudi Arabia. This was much the same set of circumstances for which Don Revie had been so widely condemned. Yet Allen escaped opprobrium, largely because the London-based national media attached such little significance to events at provincial football clubs. However, Allen had also baulked at West Brom's failure to offer him a longer-term deal. The story was broken in the West Midlands by Bob Downing of the *Express & Star* and the *Evening Mail*'s Dave Harrison, the pair of them having learned that Allen had flown out to the Saudi capital of Rijad.

'Bob and I went down to Heathrow on the train and met Ronnie off his plane,' recalls Harrison. 'He actually offered us a lift home, and on the way back told us that he was going to leave. He said he was going to let his head rule his heart for once and make some good money. I had to ask him to stop off at a phone box so I could call in the story.'

'Ronnie had lost the dressing room too,' insists Downing. 'At half-time in the cup match at Bury, John Wile was berating Willie Johnston for not going past their full-back and Ronnie stood up and agreed. I heard on the team bus afterwards that Willie had told him to fuck off.'

Allen's successor wouldn't be announced until early the next year. He was Ron Atkinson, who'd previously been in charge of Second Division Cambridge United, and about whom Cunningham, Regis and the rest of the Albion team knew not the slightest thing.

Chapter Five: Big Ron

Nothing much was great or glorious about the playing career of Ronald Frederick Atkinson. He was born in Liverpool on 18 March 1939, but within a matter of weeks had moved with his family to Birmingham. As a seventeen-year-old, he signed on as a trainee with Aston Villa, which was his adopted hometown's most prominent club. During his three years at Villa Park, he failed to make a single appearance for the senior side. Yet Atkinson did at least benefit from the tutorage of Villa's youth team coach, Jimmy Hogan. It was Hogan who was to have the most lasting influence on how he came to think about the game.

One of the sport's first true visionaries, Hogan initially studied for the priesthood in his native Lancashire. He instead went on to become a professional footballer, playing for Rochdale, Burnley and Bolton Wanderers in the years leading up to the Great War. However, it was as a coach that he secured his lasting reputation as a trailblazer. In 1936, he took the Austrian national side to the final of the Olympic football tournament, and he also had productive spells managing in club football in both Switzerland and Hungary. The principles he established during his time in Hungary became the foundation for the 'Magical Magyars' side of Ferenc Puskás, which famously humbled England 6–3 at Wembley in 1953. Hogan's maxim was simple and he drilled into his young charges at Villa: 'Wherever you are on the field, if you've got the ball, you're always attacking. And if they've got it, you're defending.'

Upon being released by Villa in 1959, Atkinson was picked up on a free transfer by Oxford United (the then non-league outfit were known as Headington United at the time). He went on to play nearly 400 games for the club, captaining the side through their rise from the Southern League to Division Two of the Football League. He was a stocky wing-half who was powerful but had little panache. In 1971, aged thirty-two, he returned to non-league circles to join Kettering Town as their player-manager, enjoying success and subsequently attracting the interest of Cambridge United in the Fourth Division. Atkinson took Cambridge up to the third tier of English football in 1977, and the team was chasing a second successive promotion the next season when the post of manager at West Bromwich Albion became vacant.

At Cambridge, Atkinson made no secret of his ambitions to work at the top level of the game. He didn't lack for assurance in his own abilities, telling anyone who listened that he was destined for greater things. Yet he was also astute enough to court more experienced football managers and acquire knowledge from them. Senior figures such as Bill Nicholson, who in 1961 had led Tottenham to the first English League and Cup double of the twentieth century, often came to Cambridge's Abbey Stadium to scout for talent. Atkinson made sure to invite them into his cramped office after the game for a cup of tea and a chat. He was a regular visitor to Wembley for international fixtures and ingratiated himself with higher profile coaches such as Malcolm Allison, then with Crystal Palace, and John Bond from Norwich City.

From this flamboyant pairing, Atkinson cherry-picked the accoutrements with which he was able to create his very own persona. From Allison and Bond he cultivated a fondness for flash clothes, gold jewellery and big cigars. Since Allison was known as 'Big Mal', Atkinson became 'Big Ron', a mover and a shaker in the game. This also somehow seemed to grow him in stature, though he stood much less than six-feet tall. It also concealed a keen brain and a burning passion for football, but it did what was intended and got him noticed.

Atkinson wasn't the first manager Albion approached to replace the departed Ronnie Allen. Their original choice had been an even younger man, 33-year-old Graham Taylor, who in 1976 had won the Fourth Division title with Lincoln City. The bespectacled Taylor had a studious look about him and took a scholarly approach to the game. However, he unexpectedly snubbed the First Division side's offer in favour of one from another of the Football League's basement clubs, Watford. The Hertfordshire club had just then been bought by rock star Elton John, and Atkinson was left to step into the Hawthorns' breach.

'I got a call from one of the West Brom directors, Sid Lucas, asking if I'd meet up with him and the club chairman, Bert Millichip, at a hotel near Coventry,' Atkinson recalls. 'It was all very much a done deal, but I was only being offered a £500 rise in salary from what I was on at the time.

'When I pointed this out to Sid Lucas he said to me, "Come and have a look out back. I think you'll like what we've got for you." Sat there in the car park was a big blue Jag. I told him it was nice, but that I'd already got one at home and that mine had a bigger engine. Coming from Cambridge, they assumed I'd be driving a bloody Mini.'

Atkinson seized the chance to step up and swept into West Brom in the second week of 1978. If he was afflicted with even a shadow of doubt about the challenge now facing him, he didn't allow it to show. He turned up for his first day in the job resplendent in a long, black leather coat that made him look like nothing so much as a Gestapo staff officer. Dave Harrison from the Birmingham *Evening Mail* had been dispatched to Cambridge the week before to interview the newly appointed Atkinson and was again waiting for him outside the Hawthorns.

'Ron got out of his car, bold as brass and recognised me straight away,' says Harrison. 'First thing he did was hand me his bag to carry into the ground. He said to me, "Here you go, that's your job now, Scoop."'

The impact Atkinson had on the Albion players was just as instant and forceful. Laurie Cunningham and Cyrille Regis were the first he encountered during that initial afternoon. They were coming out from one of the first-team squad's favourite haunts, the Europa Hotel, just down the road from the Hawthorns. The pair of them sauntered past Atkinson, bidding him, 'Alright, Ron.' He stopped them in their tracks, called them back and told them in future to address him as 'Boss', before sending them on their way.

He soon enough bowled up to the rest of the team. Being so ebullient, wise-cracking and self-assured, he caught each of them off guard. This went for the younger players and their older, more cynical colleagues alike. All, that is, except for one of the Irish contingent, Paddy Mulligan. A long-in-the-tooth full-back,

Mulligan dismissed Atkinson for his bluff manner and modest credentials as a player. He referred to him not as Big Ron, but rather as the 'Towering Inferior'. This got a laugh in the dressing room, but it marked Mulligan's card with the new manager.

Atkinson had arrived with grand ideas of how he intended to mould and shape the team, but he was quick and canny enough to realise that little of the blueprint Johnny Giles had first laid down at the club needed fixing. Like Ronnie Allen, he retained Giles's model for training sessions. These were kept to fast, competitive five-a-side games that honed and encouraged the players to pass and move, and to do this over and again at speed. It was precisely this that Atkinson wanted from his side.

The squad was split by Atkinson for these matches into the English group, known as the 'Cream', and the Irish and Scots, who were branded the 'Scum'. Adopting for the occasion the identity of one of the game's great players, perhaps George Best or the German maestro Franz Beckenbauer, Atkinson joined in on the English side alongside the likes of Cunningham, Regis and Bryan Robson. The games were further enlivened by the manager betting money on their outcome and the players tore into them as if there were a great prize at stake, kicking lumps out of each other. In any event, Atkinson invariably kept them going until his side had scored the decisive goal.

'Ron set out to make an impression on us and that he certainly did,' says John Wile. 'But he was also able to take us on to the next level as a team. All he basically said was that he wanted us to play at a quicker tempo, to hit the front men a bit earlier and push higher up the field. He injected pace into the side and gave each of us confidence as well, because he exuded it.'

★

Atkinson's methods had the immediate effect of improving team spirit, which had dwindled under Allen. Yet to begin with at least, the new manager wasn't able to have such a marked effect on results and West Brom's poor run of form continued. Their first game after his appointment resulted in a 1-0 home defeat to Liverpool and the side lost again the next week by the same score at Middlesbrough. Indeed, Atkinson's team recorded just one win in his first seven League games in charge.

If nothing else, the Middlesbrough encounter gave Atkinson a proper insight into the complicated character of Laurie Cunningham. Prior to leaving the Midlands for the North East, he'd berated Cunningham, and also Regis and Tony Godden, for failing to turn up for the trip in a shirt and tie. Cunningham brooded on the long journey up to Middlesbrough, confiding to Godden that this was going to be one of those days when he was incapable of rousing himself to play.

He was as good as his word, being a spectral presence during the first forty-five minutes of the game. Hugging tight to the touchline, he appeared unconnected to or unconcerned with what was going on elsewhere on the pitch. Not that much was happening, since the match was proving as drab and unappealing as the January gloom. When the players trooped into the dressing room at half-time, Atkinson at once set about trying to goad them to action. The sour expression on Cunningham's face pulled him up short.

'Big Ron said to him, "Listen, son, if you don't fancy going out for the second half, get yourself in the bath,"' says Derek Statham. 'He was being sarcastic and obviously so. But Laurie said, "Okay, boss," and then stripped off and disappeared to the showers. The rest of us were a bit shocked, because we were about to go and battle on through the game.

'Laurie could be like that, a bit of a boy at times, and that incident summed up his character. There were one or two other situations like it later on, but in general with him, the good outweighed the bad.'

Cunningham was dropped to the bench for the next match, a home fixture against Coventry, and also omitted from the five games that followed it. Regardless of this, Atkinson now claims that his first key act at West Brom was to restore Cunningham to the side, suggesting he was being shunned by his predecessor. In truth, Cunningham was a regular starter in Allen's team. It was only during the final weeks of his reign that the manager wearied of his erratic form and left him out, hoping to provoke from him a positive response.

Like Allen, Atkinson took a paternal attitude towards his most enigmatic player. He nurtured him, but also suffered the pangs of a frustrated parent at a wayward child. He had an easier relationship with Regis, one that was based on mutual respect. Of the two of them, it was the big striker he felt most able to rely on whenever the going got tough. The fact that Regis had been an electrician was a standing joke between the pair of them. Whenever he had a poor game, Atkinson would threaten to banish Regis back to his former trade.

'Both of them were good lads, but Cyrille was more outgoing,' says Atkinson. 'You could talk loudly with him across the group, whereas with Laurie, you were better off taking him to one side and doing it on the quiet.

'I spent a lot of time after training with Laurie, which is when I got closest to him. He'd stay out on the pitch with me and bang balls about, taking free kicks at the goalkeepers. I thought he was very much misunderstood. People formed an impression of him, because he would turn up to a disco in a white suit, but I found him to be a terrific guy.'

A shrewd man-manager, Atkinson recognised how close Cunningham and Regis had got to each other and created a sense of competition between them. Sidling up to Regis before a game, he'd glibly suggest he go out and see if he was as good as Cunningham. To Cunningham, Atkinson would dangle the carrot that Regis's all-action performances were showing him up. The two of them invariably rose to the bait, one being as proud as the other.

'Big Ron would wind Cyrille up in particular,' says Ally Robertson. 'After training, he and Laurie would whack balls at each other for extra practise. Laurie controlled the ball without seeming to try, whereas at first it would be bouncing everywhere off Cyrille. Big Ron would be bawling at him, "Control the frigging thing." But Cyrille kept working at it and you should've seen the difference in him.'

'I believe I only ever played with one black lad, but when I was younger I did some training with the coach of the British weight-lifting squad,' says Atkinson. 'I'd be in the gym with all the black lads on that team, like Precious McKenzie and Louis Martin, the world champion.

'This was 1960 and none of us then knew much about the black lads, but I was amazed at how they would laugh and joke about everything. There were no inhibitions and everything was treated with humour. That's how we used to go about it at West Brom as well.'

As Atkinson was settling to his task that January, the social divides then running through the country continued to crack and yawn. The former chairman of the National Front, John Kingsley Read, was sent to trial at the Old Bailey in London on a charge of inciting racial hatred. Read had given a speech eighteen months earlier in Newham, East London, in which he'd referred to 'niggers, wogs and coons'. He had also brought up the recent murder of an Asian man in nearby Southall, telling some 300 supporters, 'One down, a million to go.'

In his summing up, the presiding Judge, Justice Neil McKinnon, questioned whether 'nigger' was an offensive term. As evidence against this he cited the antiquated nursery rhyme, 'Ten Little Niggers'. He went on to state that, although Read had insulted a murder victim, this was not in itself an offence. Read was acquitted by the jury, prompting a storm of protest. A total of 133 MPs subsequently signed a petition to have McKinnon de-wigged.

The same month, Leader of the Opposition Margaret Thatcher gave an interview to the TV current affairs programme *World in Action* in which she claimed that Britain was unable to take in any more migrants. Thatcher's comments resonated with a portion of the electorate, resulting in a surge in the opinion polls for her Conservative Party and staking out a territory that she would fight on during the General Election of the next year.

As winter passed into spring, fortunes improved for West Bromwich Albion on the pitch. Atkinson's team gathered momentum around the speed of Cunningham, now restored to the side, and that of Regis, Willie Johnston and Ally Brown, the one player he had rescued from the reserves. He'd also revived the career of the club's longest-serving player, Tony Brown, who'd clashed with Allen but was now once again a pivotal point of the team.

Between then and the end of the season, the Baggies suffered just two further defeats in the League. Atkinson and his team grew in stature. Bryan Robson and Derek Statham flowered into exciting talents, and Regis and Cunningham shared sixteen goals between them. There was nothing complicated about Atkinson's approach to management: he got the best out of his players by keeping his message to them as basic and concise as possible.

'Ron was full of life and had such great enthusiasm for the game, and that rubbed off on the players,' says Robson. 'He wanted people to enjoy themselves around the football club and for us to express ourselves in every game. There were no unbelievable tactics in his team talks he'd just tell us to go out and play attacking football.'

'If we won 5-4 or 4-3, Ron was over the moon,' says Johnston. 'Before a game he might mention which player he expected you to mark, but all he really talked about was scoring goals. That was his one measurement, were we entertaining him and the punters.

'Aye, he was a flash bugger too. A neighbour of mine at the time was a jeweller and I used to pick up loads of gear off him, things that were worth a fortune. Laurie and Cyrille were into it and then Ron started to take stuff off me as well, bracelets and gold ingots that he wore round his neck.'

After the withdrawn Allen, Atkinson's outsize personality was a gift to the local media. He would always take a call from a reporter, was never short of a quote and he revelled in the attention it brought him. Outwardly, and as much among the players, he didn't discourage the view that he was a big-time Charlie and the life and soul of the club. But in seeing him up close, one was allowed an opportunity to peer behind this mask.

'Ron was a great one for filling up people's glasses, especially if the chairman was paying for the drinks, but he wasn't a boozer,' says Pat Murphy. 'He'd work the room, but would only sip at a champagne or white wine. I never once saw him worse for wear.'

'We often used to travel on the team bus in those days and that season I remember being sat with Ron for an overnight trip to Ipswich,' recalls Bob Downing. 'He got out a copy of the *Rothman's Football Yearbook* and told me to open it at random. He asked me to pick out any player from it and read out his statistics to him – the number of games he'd played, how many goals he'd scored and so on. Straight off, he told me the name of the player and he did that over and again for the next two hours. I couldn't believe it. But that was what he was like. He loved football.'

The real making of Atkinson and his West Brom side was the FA Cup run they went on through the second half of that season. Albion had already eased past Blackpool in the Third Round of the grand old competition before Atkinson joined them, but he was in charge for their next tie, a clash against Manchester United at Old Trafford. The Red Devils were by then a shadow of the glorious team assembled by Matt Busby in the 1960s, the one of George Best, Bobby Charlton and Dennis Law. In 1974, they had even suffered the ignominy of relegation to the Second Division. However, they had reached the final of the competition in each of the last two seasons, winning it in 1977, and they were still formidable opponents on their own ground.

On a miserable January afternoon, 57,000 supporters watched the two teams fight out a 1-1 stalemate in driving rain. United were kept in the tie by their England international winger, Steve Coppell, who grabbed an equalising goal in the last minute of the game. The replay took place four days later on an even wetter night at the Hawthorns. In a deluge, a near-38,000 full house was held captivated by one of the defining games of

Atkinson's regime. Played on a glutinous pitch, it witnessed their irrepressible manager urging his West Brom team to a death or glory charge.

Tony Brown put Albion ahead in the fourteenth minute, but United reeled them back in before half-time. Early in the second half, Regis was first to react after Willie Johnston had thundered a shot against the crossbar, and he hustled the ball over the line to claim the lead again. Still United roared and again they got back on level terms in the final seconds of the game through another of their England players, Gordon Hill. With rain still lashing down, Atkinson stirred his exhausted players to one more titanic effort in extra time. He was rewarded with a second Regis goal, a towering header, less than a minute after the restart. United came once more and pounded at the sagging Albion defence, but to no avail. The cup holders were conquered.

'I have never been involved in anything like these two games,' Atkinson told reporters after the match. 'There was so much drama and atmosphere that anyone who saw them will remember them for a lifetime.'

This was just the start of things. Three weeks later, West Brom's Fifth Round match was almost as thrilling, a 3–2 victory over Derby County, with Regis helping himself to another two goals. By then, Atkinson had turned his attention to the future beyond that season. The following week he announced his first signing for the club, a full-back plucked from his former side, Cambridge United.

Brendon Batson had just turned twenty-five and the size of the fee Atkinson paid for him – £30,000, a trifling sum even then – spoke of his standing in the game. An unheralded Third Division footballer, he would nonetheless prove to be Atkinson's shrewdest investment. He was bought to replace Paddy Mulligan, who'd entered into a battle with Atkinson he couldn't win.

'I'd had a lot of very promising young players at Cambridge, all of whom were eighteen, nineteen years old,' says Atkinson. 'Everybody expected me to go back to the club for one of them. It wasn't until I got to West Brom and saw Paddy Mulligan playing at right-back, and quite well as it happens, that I thought, "Blimey, Brendon can do everything he can, but he's quicker and a lot younger." Until then, it had never entered my thoughts to sign Brendon.'

Chapter Six: Batman

L ike Cyrille Regis's family, Brendon Batson's took root in the Caribbean. He was born on 1 February 1953 on Grenada. The island's origins were volcanic and the rich fertility of its soil allowed it to produce an abundance of such spices as nutmeg and mace. Batson and his brother and sister were raised in this idyll by their mother who was estranged from their father, a man the three children barely knew. The first memory Batson has of his childhood is that of running along a beach, an azure sea lapping at the sand.

When he was six years old, Batson's mother nonetheless moved her three children to their father's home island of Trinidad. Compared to the more sedate Grenada, it was a bigger and more bustling environment in which to grow up. They went to live with their godmother in San Fernando, a coastal town that lies to the south of the island's capital, Port of Spain.

'I had a very happy time on Trinidad being around my cousins,' Batson recalls. 'Port of Spain was a hive of activity and I remember seeing a lot of cricket and hockey out in the savannah. Yet my mom always felt there was something better out there for us. Her older brother and sister had gone to live in England and it was explained to us that the streets over there were paved with gold.'

In 1962, Batson's mother decided to send her two sons off to this supposed land of promise to live with their uncle and his wife. Lacking the funds for four air tickets, she was forced to remain behind on Trinidad with their sister. She swore to her sons that the pair of them would join the brothers in two years, an undertaking that she kept to the day.

The two boys flew into London and from there went to live with their extended family in Tilbury, the Essex town from which the original Caribbean immigrants to Britain had dispersed across the country. It was April and Britain was emerging from an especially frigid winter. Batson's aunt was a midwife and it was said that she had delivered over half of the town's children. Yet the Batson's were made more conspicuous by being the only black family to be then living in Tilbury.

'We never had to introduce ourselves to anyone,' says Batson. 'Whenever people in the town saw a couple of little black boys, they knew we must be Batsons. My mom had really sold coming to England to us as a full-blown adventure, but then reality started to kick in. My brother and I were looking forward to seeing snow, but it was freezing cold. I've hated winter in England ever since. We were used to living in big houses with verandas and wide-open spaces, but Tilbury was very small and cramped.

'Trinidad was a very cosmopolitan country too. I've got lots of mixes in my family, Indian and Chinese bloodlines. By contrast, England seemed to me a very white country. I'd never experienced racism before, but I suddenly found as a nine-year-old at primary school that I was being called all these names that I didn't fully understand. I learned to fight then and carried on fighting until I was well into my teens. It certainly taught me how to grow up.'

Batson attended the local Catholic school, St Mary's, which prided itself on the strength of its football teams. Before coming to England, he'd never even seen a football match. But a fellow pupil named Dennis Sheridan coaxed him into joining in with the massed games that were a feature of life at the school.

'There was a big field full of daisies round the corner from us and that's where we went to play,' says Batson. 'You'd go across with your mates, three or four of you. And then another group of four would come and join in, and then another. Before you knew it, you had a twenty-a-side game going on.

'Everyone would bring along a ball and we'd pick the best one to use for the game. One of the things I most remember is seeing all these footballs lined up in a row alongside our makeshift pitch. When it fell dark, you had to scramble for your ball if it was decent, otherwise some other kid would run off with it.'

The St Mary's school side was run by a Mr Fitzgerald, who taught maths and English. At the start of the next school year, Batson put his name down for the open trials that Fitzgerald ran for the team. In several regards he was ill-prepared for such a test, most notably in that he didn't own a pair of football boots and still knew next to nothing of the rules of the game. In fact, the sole position on the field he could name was goalkeeper – and this was only on account of his classmates having told him not to volunteer for that slot, since in their opinion it was the worst place to be stuck in to play.

It was therefore no great surprise that the trial game turned out to be a disaster for him. He seemed so befuddled during it that Fitzgerald approached him afterwards and suggested to him that cricket might be his game after all. Seeing he was now on the verge of tears, Fitzgerald offered Batson the comfort of a second chance the week after. He loaned a pair of boots in the interim and did well enough on this next occasion to be selected for the team.

This rapid rate of improvement continued through his school years. It was as if he were meant for the game. He found his niche as a defender and, being a fast learner, soon excelled in the role, gravitating from the school side to the Thurrock district team. When he was eleven, Batson's mother and sister arrived at last in England. The reunited family moved from Tilbury to the London district of Walthamstow, in the north-east of the capital. This change in circumstance did nothing to interrupt his progress at football. He turned out for his school and district sides and also a Sunday league team, Rippleway Rangers.

It was while representing his London district that Batson was spotted by George Male, a scout for Arsenal. Male had played at full-back for the all-conquering Arsenal side of the pre-war era, which had won the League title five times between 1931 and 1938. He invited Batson, then aged thirteen, along to train with the club's schoolboys twice a week, on a Monday and Thursday evening.

Arsenal was a club of rich traditions. The grand marble entrance hall of their Highbury stadium in north London reeked of class and distinction. It had as its centrepiece a bronze bust of Chapman, the man who'd first given rise to their sense of entitlement. Yet the 1960s had up to that point been a fallow decade for the club. The former captain of England, Billy Wright, had failed to recapture the glories of his own playing career while serving as the club's manager, and Arsenal's recent trophy cabinet was baren.

In 1966, the year that England won the World Cup and Batson

signed schoolboy forms with the club, Arsenal appointed Bertie Mee to replace the underachieving Wright. The 48-year-old Mee had played for Derby County and Mansfield Town, but his career had been cut short by injury in 1939. He joined the army, rising to the rank of sergeant in the Royal Medical Corps where he also trained as a physiotherapist. After the war, he took the new skills he'd acquired in the forces into professional football, working at a number of clubs before coming to Arsenal in 1960. A man of sharp intelligence, Mee set about re-organising the club as if he were engaged on a military exercise.

Batson settled in well at Arsenal over the next three years, but in June 1969 was given an ominous warning of things to come. He was playing for the club's junior side in a South East Counties League game when he felt his knee buckle in a tackle. He'd ruptured his cartilage, an injury of sufficient seriousness to keep him out of the game for a year. On this occasion he was able to heal, and he returned in time to participate in a vintage season for Arsenal. In that splendid year of 1970–71, Mee led the club to a League and Cup double, and Batson's youth team also went on to lift the FA Youth Cup.

'After we'd won in the semi-final, Bertie Mee took all of the youth team and the coaching staff out for meal,' says Batson. 'We went to a restaurant called the Hunting Lodge in Haymarket. I was a London boy and a bit of a Jack-the-Lad, but it was by far the best restaurant I'd ever been to. Bertie Mee's philosophy was that some of us were hopefully going to go on to have successful careers in the game, so we needed to know how to behave in such an environment.

'He was one of the most astute men I've come across. He had a motto: "Remember where you are, who you are and what you represent." He wasn't just thinking of us as footballers, but as young men growing up. He knew a lot of us weren't going to make the grade. In the meantime, he wanted to give us a good education in not just football, but also in life in general.'

In all, 1971 was an eventful year for eighteen-year-old Batson. At Arsenal, he successfully graduated from the youth team and was offered a full contract by the club. He also met his future wife, Cecily. The couple were introduced to each other through mutual friends and were to be married three years later. Through all the tribulations to come, Cecily would be Batson's rock, and her faith in him was deep and unwavering.

Soon he was on the verge of the Arsenal first team, his passage through the ranks as smooth as it had ever been. He made his debut the following March in a 2-0 defeat at Newcastle. No fanfare surrounded this game and for years afterwards Batson remained ignorant of the fact that he'd become the first black player to represent the club in the Football League. He made a further nine appearances for the senior side during the next eighteen months. But he was always there as understudy to the club's regular full-back, Pat Rice. It was the first time since taking up the game that Batson felt as if he had stalled.

'I began to realise that things weren't going as well for me as they should have been and I was losing ground to other young players that were coming through,' he admits. 'I didn't like the idea that I was being overlooked. The club had also brought in another defender, Jeff Blockley from Coventry, and for a lot of money. I thought that if I wasn't better than him in their eyes, then I'd be better off going elsewhere.

'To be honest, up to then I'd taken football a bit too lightly. It was all relatively new to me and I didn't see the significance of it as being that great. It was just something that I enjoyed doing. I jumped at the first offer that came my way, because I was so flattered that somebody else wanted me in their team.'

In January 1974, Batson left Arsenal for Cambridge United. In doing so, he dropped from the First Division to the Third. Cambridge had only been elected to the Football League as recently as 1970, but had won promotion at the end of the previous season under the management of Bill Leivers, who'd been a rugged defender for Manchester City and Doncaster Rovers in the fifties and sixties. However, the club was struggling to compete in a higher division and the signing of the new young full-back did nothing to reverse their fortunes. At the end of Batson's first season with them, Cambridge were relegated back to the Fourth Division.

'Within a few months, I'd gone from the top of the game to bottom,' says Batson. 'We started off the next campaign disastrously as well. The chairman gave Bill Leivers a vote of confidence and two weeks later sacked him. The lads were running a book on who was going to replace him as manager. No one put a bet on Ron Atkinson, because none of us had heard of him.

'He turned out to be a totally different manager to both Bertie Mee and Bill Leivers. Neither of them got involved in the hurly-burly of the club, but Ron genuinely believed that he was the best player at Cambridge. He got involved in everything from picking himself for the reserve team to playing cards with the lads at the back of the coach. We did wonder what the hell was going on, but he was infectious and also nakedly ambitious.'

At Cambridge, Atkinson acted fast to turn the team around. He got rid of the older players he presumed had been idling and brought in a group of younger, hungrier recruits for little or no money. Results soon improved, but it took him longer to resolve his opinion of Batson. In Atkinson's mind, Batson was still swanning around the place as if he was at a big club and he made it his job to knock him down a peg or two.

'I fell out with him on a regular basis,' says Batson. 'He thought I had a chip on both shoulders and I disagreed. I probably did hark back too much to my time at Arsenal, but because that was my benchmark. However, I think he had an ulterior motive. He saw that I was one of the main players at the club and if he could dominate me, then he'd be able to dominate the whole dressing room.'

'It was entirely his fault,' counters Atkinson. 'I had to have a right blast at him. He thought the manager himself was untouchable, because apparently he had been under the previous regime.'

Atkinson dropped Batson from the first team and into the very reserve side for which the manager himself was then turning out. On the bus to their subsequent games and also on the pitch, Atkinson pointedly ignored him. The pair of them didn't exchange a single word for the next three weeks. At which point Atkinson summoned Batson to his office and told him he was re-instating him in the Cambridge first team. Even so, he still hadn't finished pricking at Batson's ego.

'He said to me that he'd liked my attitude and then, bugger me, he made me substitute,' says Batson. 'If he hadn't been so big, I'd have taken a swing at him. It was my dear wife who gave me the advice that I needed and I kept my head down. After that, he pulled me in again out of the blue and told me I was going to be his next captain.

'From then on, Ron and I got on famously. Ever since, he's had this name for me – Batman. And without him, I don't think I'd have ever got back into the top flight of the game.'

'Brendon would be the first to admit that his outlook to the game, and to life in general, changed completely,' considers Atkinson. 'He was only young, I suppose, and he thought he was Billy Big Time having come down from London. We quickly agreed that he wasn't and got on with it.'

There was another aspect of playing for a smaller club that Batson also became accustomed to. In the tight grounds of the Fourth Division, he was able to hear each word of the vitriol being directed at him from the terraces. To begin with, his wife came to see the games. She was accompanied by one of his cousins, who stood six foot six and would stand glaring at the perpetrators until they fell silent. But Cecily Batson soon sickened of the shouts of 'nigger' and the monkey noises being directed at her husband and thereafter stayed away.

On the pitch, Batson couldn't and wouldn't turn the other cheek. Just as he'd done ever since he was at school in Tilbury, he hit back at his tormentors. During a game at Bradford, Atkinson's assistant, John Doherty, had to restrain him from jumping into the crowd to confront a fan who'd thrown the ball back at him. His temper also never failed to flare when he was goaded by opposition players. He was sent off three times in Atkinson's first two seasons at the club.

The first of these occasions was against Stockport County. He was up against a senior Stockport player. According to Batson, the player directed a stream of racist invective at him throughout the game. In the fifty-fifth minute, his tolerance broke and he lashed out, his fist flashing past the referee who'd come between the two of them and striking the player on the jaw, knocking him to the turf. Batson then turned and walked off the pitch, not bothering to wait on the official's judgement.

Atkinson appealed against this dismissal and the referee

also intervened on Batson's behalf. His hearing was held in Birmingham the following week and before the FA's disciplinary committee. By coincidence, sitting at the head of this was the West Bromwich Albion chairman, Bert Millichip. Speaking in a plummy baritone, as if presiding over the highest court in the land, Millichip told him: 'Mr Batson, we do not wish to see you here again.'

'The following season, we were again playing Stockport and winning 4-0 with two minutes to go,' says Batson. 'That same Stockport player kicked out at me and said something, so I hit him again. Ron came into the dressing room afterwards and said, "Well, Batman, I don't think we'll be appealing this time."

'It was a real shock to me. I'd got a bit of abuse as a schoolboy, but up till then I don't recall ever getting it from fellow pros. The other lad was Robin Friday – bless him – who was playing for Reading at the time. I lashed out at him too. He came up to me in the players' lounge after the game and said, "Bren, I'm so sorry, but I was told to wind you up because you're a bit hot-headed." He thought the best way to do that was to call me all the racist names under the sun. I nearly hit him again.

'I also had a set-to with one of our own players at Cambridge. Ron called me in for a cup of tea and read me the riot act. But he also gave me a lot of good advice. I seemed to calm down after that and never got sent off again.'

With Batson as his skipper, Atkinson took Cambridge to the Fourth Division title in his second full season at the club. He left them the next year sitting on top of the Third Division. Four weeks after he'd gone, Batson followed him to the Hawthorns.

To begin with, Batson got a mixed reception from his new team-mates. His arrival at West Brom stirred up undercurrents in the dressing room, a complex environment at any football club, and one where fear and paranoia are never far from the surface. This was especially the case whenever there had been a change of manager, since the existing order was now under threat and no one was certain of their place in the scheme of things.

Coming from Cambridge and as Atkinson's erstwhile captain, the other players viewed Batson with suspicion, surmising that he was the manager's agent. It was also evident that he'd been brought to the club to replace Paddy Mulligan, an eccentric but popular figure in the team. More often than not, players meet such a challenge with either grace or dull acceptance, but Mulligan seethed.

'Paddy Mulligan was a loony,' says Tony Brown. 'A typical Irishman, I think. A bit of a lad, loved the women. He made it clear that he was upset about Brendon coming in. The lads take notice of that kind of thing and Brendon took a bit of stick. But if you go under in the dressing room, then you've got no chance. Brendon could look after himself. He was very well-spoken and he knew what it was all about.'

'A dressing room is a dressing room,' says Batson. 'Some are good, some bad and some are indifferent. The one at West Brom was typical. You had very strong characters in there like Len Cantello and Ally Robertson. John Wile was an imposing figure. Then there were the quieter lads like Bryan Robson. Laurie was shy, but charming. He spoke in a very soft voice. I'd seen Cyrille on the TV ploughing through the mud, but he was even bigger in the flesh.

'As the new boy, it's up to you to integrate and the one thing you've got to be able to do is prove that you can play. I had to win them over that way. Without doing that, I was going to get slaughtered.'

Atkinson immediately threw Batson to the lions. He allowed him just the one training session before pitching him into the first team at Mulligan's expense for a midweek match at Birmingham City. Being a local derby, there was an extra tension surrounding the game. This was further heightened by the storm that raged in the Midlands that night, the rain coming down in torrents and a howling wind blowing through the creaking St Andrew's ground.

In the minutes before kick-off, Batson was suffering his own, quieter tumult. In the changing room under the main stand, he sat shrunken in his seat. He absorbed nothing of Atkinson's pre-match team talk, but for the sight of the manager's mouth opening and closing. He didn't even sense Mulligan's eyes boring into him. The Irishman was sitting across from him, right next to the door. At that moment the two of them had everything to lose.

As the players filed out onto the pitch, Mulligan bid each of them good luck and best wishes. He met Batson with a warm smile. 'All the best, Brendon,' he said airily. 'Hope you have a fucking nightmare.'

'Brendon was terrible that night,' recalls Albion supporter John Homer. 'His positional sense seemed to be all over the place and he couldn't control a ball for love nor money. He'd come out of the Third Division and he looked lost.'

'I think that debut was probably the worst I ever saw,' says Bob Downing. 'All of us reporters went up to Ron's office the next day and asked him for his thoughts on Brendon. He told us he'd come good. I shot back that he hadn't been good last night, because you could talk to Ron like that. He said, "Brendon will be alright, he'll prove himself." And he did.'

For all Batson's woes, West Brom battled to a 2-1 win at Birmingham. He retained his place in the side for the next match at Ipswich. Following his mischief at Middlesbrough two months earlier, Cunningham was still exiled from the starting team for this game, but Atkinson introduced him as a second-half substitute. It was the first time that Batson, Cunningham and Regis found themselves together on the pitch.

In due course, Atkinson fielding an unprecedented three black players in his West Brom team would be unmissed and unforgettable. It would not fail to provoke one form of reaction or another, good or bad. Yet no mention of it was made in the press reports that followed the game, a 2-2 draw. For now, at least, it was a minor issue to the wider world.

However, it didn't go unnoticed within the West Brom dressing room. In his own autobiography, Atkinson claimed that a number of the other players were initially resistant to this influx to the team and that he had to quell an uprising. He now modifies that statement.

'No, the three of them were popular lads at the club,' he says. 'And in that regard, I only ever had a problem with one player. He told me that it was clear you had to be black to get into the team. I said to him, "Well, it makes a change from being Scottish or Irish, doesn't it?"'

Chapter Seven: Melting Pot

The ways in which Ron Atkinson got under the skin of his players were as many as they were unorthodox. To switch them on to the task at hand, he'd have them submerge their heads in buckets of ice-cold water, or smear Vapour Rub in their faces. Each West Brom player also got used to having Atkinson inform him in a conspiratorial whisper that he was the team's main man.

Before a game, Atkinson prowled the dressing room like a caged lion. He regaled the players with his musings on the strengths of the opposition that day and then told them that they were better, that it was a matter of fact that they were going to win this game and all others. Or he'd ask them to look around the room and tell him which of their team-mates they'd swap for someone from the other side, knowing full well the answer. 'No one, Boss,' they chorused back.

When the players at last lined up to leave the sanctuary of the dressing room, Atkinson blocked their path. He barged into each of them, one after another and with his chest barrelled out. As he was doing this, he beseeched them all to go out there and excite both him and also the people who'd paid good money to see them. By then, even the meekest among them walked onto to the pitch feeling ten-foot tall.

'Back then and in his pomp, he was a terrific manager,' says Martin Swain, now chief football reporter with the *Express & Star*. 'He was young, on the make and on the way up. His great mission statement was that he didn't ever want to put out a team that bored him. Because if it bored him, how the hell could it be expected to entertain the crowd? And that West Brom team was the embodiment of his ideal.

'All the journalists of the time also loved Ron. Each of them looked forward to doing their match previews with him on a Friday morning. He'd sit there in his office, pouring the tea, cracking jokes and feeding them lines. Clearly, that spirit flooded into the side because they began to play with a freedom that broke the mould of English football in the seventies.'

As well, Atkinson was able to manage effectively such contrasting personalities as Laurie Cunningham and Cyrille Regis. In their case, this was perhaps because the extremes of his character were such close echoes of theirs. He was a flash dresser like Cunningham. Yet to both of them there was a quieter, more reflective side. Neither of them was a big drinker and each guarded their hidden depths with degrees of intensity.

With Regis, he shared a charming and engaging manner. People warmed fast to the pair of them and both men came to life among others in a way that Cunningham never did or could. Each of them was also mindful of the lower station in the game that he had come from, and as a result both were compelled to seize the opportunity afforded them at West Bromwich Albion.

It was Atkinson's intention to put the club on the map, since by doing so he would also make his own name. As such, he welcomed the attentions of the media and threw doors open to reporters. Regis was comfortable in this carefree environment, whereas Cunningham retreated into his shell.

'If it was an away game, I'd be at the ground at 9 a.m. to get on the bus with the players,' recalls Bob Downing of the *Express & Star*. 'They had a card school running on the coach going to matches, but Laurie was never part of it. He was always very quiet, never went looking for publicity. It was very difficult to get him to open up. He might well have done to Cyrille, but he certainly didn't to the press guys and I don't believe he did to the other members of the team either. I don't suppose the rest of them ever really got to know him at all.'

'There was no such thing as agents in those days and you'd have to ring the players at home to get a story,' says Dave Harrison of the *Evening Mail*. 'If you didn't have their phone numbers, then you weren't doing your job. I'd often call Cyrille up. He lived round the corner from me and we'd meet up in the pub at the end of our street, the Star & Garter.

'He was totally different to Laurie. He'd had a tough upbringing and I think he was more appreciative of what the game offered him. He was great company too. He had charm, good looks, personality, but without being in your face or over the top. He did also like the ladies and a night out. If you were ever struggling for a piece for the paper, you could go down to a club called Holy City Zoo in Birmingham on a Saturday night. Cyrille and some of the other Albion players would be in there more often than not.'

More so than either of his immediate predecessors, Atkinson encouraged a sense of togetherness within the team, and if that meant them going out for a skin-full, then so be it. It wasn't that

Johnny Giles hadn't allowed the players a drink. It was just that, when he did, he would tell them to enjoy their first beer because it would also be their last. Even this relaxing of the reins was anathema to the temperate Ronnie Allen, who frowned upon the slightest suggestion of excess.

Under Atkinson, the West Brom team played as hard off the pitch as on it. Wednesday was the big night out for them in the week. However, some of them would bend club rules that forbade drinking forty-eight hours before a game and sneak out on a Thursday too. The other great social occasions were after the match on a Saturday, when they were most able to cut loose.

In the week, the players would gather first for a couple of pints in one of the spit-and-sawdust pubs near the Hawthorns. Older heads such as John Wile and Tony Brown soon called it a night and went home to their wives and families. Brendon Batson, temporarily withdrawn from the team by Atkinson after his first two appearances, invariably followed. The others would go on to a nightclub in Birmingham. The next morning at training, the worst afflicted of them wore bin liners under their football shirts to better sweat out the alcohol.

'Yes, we did like to party,' says Regis fondly. 'After a game, win, lose or draw you'd also have a drink with the opposition in the players' lounge. It's Corinthian, isn't it? Nowadays, none of that sort of thing goes on. The players are straight on the coach and off home. They don't even talk to each other. To me, that wasn't what football was about. It was a social entity and having a night out was a big part of the whole thing.

'Of course, Ron would also join us from time to time. We used to run into him in a club in Birmingham called Maximillian's.'

'Ten of us would all be out together, and it was so wrong and yet so right,' says Ally Robertson. 'The laughs we used to have, I can't even begin to tell you some of the stuff that went on. Big Ron was forever receiving complaints about all the players being in nightclubs and getting up to this, that and whatever. He used to show us the letters that were being sent in to the club. He'd tell us, "So long as you're not getting beaten, I'm not bothered. Start losing and I'll do something about it."

'At times, people would pick on the black lads if we were in a club, but all of us stuck together. No one ever got in trouble or into a fight, because there'd always be someone from the team there to pull you away. It showed on a Saturday as well. We all looked out for each other during a game.'

Just as he would when the mood took him on the football pitch, Laurie Cunningham would delight on such nights in being among his team-mates and a crowd that was his for the taking. He might have shunned small talk and other social niceties, but he was never able to resist a chance to perform.

Says Tony Godden: 'My fondest memories of Laurie are from those nights. Give him a bit of music, any music, and he'd be there. That's when he'd come out.

'The club would be packed and he'd go off and dance on his own to the middle of the room. Within thirty seconds, everyone else would have stopped dancing and be standing around the edges of the dance floor watching him. I'm telling you, he was the black man's John Travolta.'

While out with the rest of the team, it was unusual for Cunningham and Regis to attract more unwanted attention. There might be the odd comment made, or someone who didn't like the way his girlfriend was looking at one or the other of them. But it was nothing too serious. It could be a different matter if they went out on their own and were unrecognised.

One night, Cunningham was with Nicky Brown at a club in

Birmingham and waiting in line for a drink. A white guy jumped the queue, shouting out that he wasn't able to stand behind Cunningham on account of the smell. The watching bar staff served him, ignoring Cunningham and Brown's protestations. In these earlier days at West Brom, both Cunningham and Regis also got used to being refused entry to clubs in the city centre.

'At that time, you couldn't get into a nightclub in Birmingham if you were black,' Regis says. 'It was a nightmare for me. Later, I never knew if I was only being let into a place because of who I was. If you're good at football, it crosses those barriers and you get a bye. "Cyrille Regis? Oh, come in!"'

'Whenever Laurie was injured, I'd go out with Cyrille,' says Brown. 'And I'd step up and get him in. It got to the stage where I could get both of them in anywhere. Very young, I learned to have a set way about me and it was an act. I'd always get in the face of whoever was responsible and fight it. But then, in his own quiet way, Laurie was also belligerent about it and so was Cyrille.'

There were also the occasions when Cunningham was given no choice but to confront such prejudice head on. Another evening, the Saturday after a game, he and Brown had decided to make a quiet night of it and were walking to their favourite Indian takeaway in Birmingham. Four white lads were coming the other way. One of them sneered at Brown as they crossed paths and spat out, 'Nigger lover.'

Cunningham drew up. Brown begged him to keep walking, but he told her he had no option. The four lads had stopped too and were coming back to confront them. The leader of the group again directed his insult to Brown, stretching it out as though it sounded better to him second time round. Cunningham walked right up to the guy and told him to apologise to Brown. He responded by drawing his head back and moving to butt

Cunningham. Being so fast on his feet, Cunningham ducked to one side like a boxer and knocked his would-be assailant to the ground in the next movement.

One of the others rushed him next and he cuffed him to the floor as well. By this time, Brown had run into the restaurant to fetch help. When she came back out, dragging several waiters with her, a third man was on his knees and Cunningham had the fourth in a headlock.

'Laurie was going to him, "See what you made me do? How ridiculous do you look now?"' says Brown. 'One of his mates had just then recognised Laurie. He was getting up, his face bloodied and he was shouting about how Laurie Cunningham had broken his nose and that he loved him. It turned out that all of them were Albion supporters.

'After that, the four of them couldn't apologise enough. They offered to pay for our taxi home and for Laurie to have his new silk shirt cleaned. Laurie ended up inviting them to a game and speaking to them about their attitude.'

It was better and safer for all of them to go to the reggae clubs in Handsworth. Not to the Hole in the Wall, since it was known to be wild and sometimes dangerous. But to places like the Rialto, the Georgian or the Santa Rosa, which each operated a dress code and where the music was good and the mood mellow. No one ever bothered them at such places.

'I used to go with them to Handsworth,' recalls Godden. 'The clubs would be full of Jamaicans and the boys would go into their own little lingo. I used to pull them up. I'd say, "Laurie, Cyrille, hold on, you've got a white man here."

'Because I was the only white face in the place, I'd get stared at. But I made a lot of black friends through being with the guys, good mates who'd look after you. I was just taken as a pal of Laurie and Cyrille's. In my experience, colour never came into it with the black man. I loved the music too: I was brought up on ska and reggae when I was kid. It still makes me feel happy.'

The music of the Caribbean had then begun to percolate out of its natural inner-city strongholds and through to a generation of white kids who were growing up in Birmingham and the West Midlands. It would be this and not football that struck the first great blow towards advancing a sense of multiculturalism in the region.

The previous year, Bob Marley had become an international star through the unprecedented success of his *Exodus* album, and this had also progressed reggae onto a global stage for the first time. During that spring, there was no escaping the loose-limbed sound of Marley's follow-up record, *Kaya*, in the clubs and joints of Handsworth and Balsall Heath. In both of these districts, sound systems also boomed out from the house parties, or 'shebeens', that came to vibrant life at the weekend. These would spring up in backyards or derelict houses. The local communities came out for them to drink, smoke and dance through to dawn, and often as not on into the next night as well.

There were very few British reggae bands at this point, but two of the most notable sprung up out of Birmingham. The first of these was Steel Pulse, who'd formed in 1975 and cut their teeth in Handsworth clubs such as the Santa Rosa. Later that year their first single, 'Ku Klux Klan', was released through Island Records, the label that had brought Marley to a bigger audience.

Steel Pulse had been moved to write the song after reading newspaper reports about a planned visit to the area by David Duke, the Klan's Grand Wizard. Duke, a 27-year-old from

Jefferson, Louisiana, was due to address a meeting in nearby Wolverhampton on 6 March 1978. However, he was banned from entering the town by the local council and at the urging of its newly formed Anti-Racist Committee.

'The other part of that story was that Duke had also come to Britain to meet with John Tyndall, who was then running the National Front,' says Steel Pulse frontman, David Hinds. 'I wrote the song imagining these two guys coming together and creating havoc around us.

'Oddly enough, there was a faction of people who thought that the band was supporting the Klan. One of the guys who helped to put reggae on the map in the Midlands was a black DJ named Barry Curtis, and he refused to play it on his Sunday night radio show. I remember going down to the station and literally waiting outside to confront him.'

UB40 even better highlighted the extent to which music was crossing into and merging communities in Birmingham. A collective made up of eight friends drawn from various schools in Balsall Heath, the group took its name from the signing-on document issued at the dole office and it's members were variously black, white and an Arab. They came together in, of all places, a city centre folk club run by the father of the band's two brothers, singer Ali and guitarist Robin Campbell. Campbell Sr. began putting on a weekly reggae night at his club, booking among others Steel Pulse as a headline act, and he corralled the UB40 boys to tend the bar and sweep up.

'That period was an awful time in the Midlands,' relates Ali Campbell. 'We were a disenfranchised youth. We'd started off trying to get jobs and then realised there weren't any. Each of us in the band was on the dole, surviving on £8 a week. We pur-loined and stole instruments and then spent six months rehearsing in a cellar that we'd cleared out. On my seventeenth birthday, I got glassed in the face in a bar. I received some compensation money for criminal injury and we used it to buy our first proper gear.

'The scene around the south of Birmingham was very multicultural and our audience was as mixed as we were. We'd play at all these garden parties, where they'd have a reggae band like us on and then a folk act or a heavy metal group. My wife-to-be lived in Fulham and she used to come up to Birmingham and be constantly amazed at how relaxed the atmosphere was in the city. She said things were much heavier in London at the time.'

Other groups began popping up out of this fertile ground. Some of these mirrored the make-up of UB40 and each owed a huge debt of influence to black music. From Birmingham and taking their cues from American soul music came Dexy's Midnight Runners and also the Beat, who looked back beyond reggae to the ska sound that had preceded it in Jamaica. Fifteen miles down the road in Coventry, another group of lads picked up on ska and also approximated its 'rude boy' look of sharp-fitting suits and porkpie hats. Known at first as the Automatics, they soon changed their name to the Specials.

'We started to see white people using our music,' says Derrick Campbell. 'It was technically well designed, but it didn't have soul. You could clearly hear that it was a white boy trying to sing black man's music. Yet it was also important to changing social attitudes. In that respect, music was definitely a meeting point and it brought people together.

'A lot of poor white kids were living on the same run-down council estates that I grew up on, and they had similar life experiences with regard to social stigma. Like we did, they lived in damp homes and had to go to the second-hand shops to buy their clothes and shoes. Lots of these kids started to listen to reggae and smoke weed and that was how we became mates.

'However, there were still some cultural differences. When they went home for tea, they had faggots, chips and peas. Black kids like me went home to rice, beans and chicken. That was a divide that was never bridged.'

On 11 March, West Brom played Nottingham Forest at the Hawthorns in the quarter-finals of the FA Cup. Promoted the previous season, Brian Clough's Forest side were the surprise run-away leaders of the First Division. Up to that point they had lost just three games, their last defeat coming at Leeds in November. They would remain unbeaten in the League through to the end of the season, when they would be crowned champions.

Clough had first won the First Division title six years earlier, with another unfashionable club from the East Midlands, Derby County. At Forest, he had followed the same blueprint as then in assembling what looked like a ragbag collection of misfits, well-travelled old pros and young hopefuls and fashioning them into an outstanding team. Like Atkinson, he was also a strident personality and a devotee of attacking football. Clough too had a simple mantra. He told his players that if the game were meant to be played in the air then there would be grass growing up there.

Yet Clough stood out from the game in another sense. He took a public stance against racism. In 1977, he endorsed the founding of the Anti-Nazi League and the organisation was thereafter given free advertising space in the Forest match-day programme. He had also nurtured a young black player through the ranks at the club. A Nottingham-born lad, full-back Viv Anderson had joined Forest from school, and as a teenager in 1975 became a first-team regular under Clough.

'I vividly remember one of my first games for Mr Clough,' Anderson says. 'We were playing up at Carlisle and I was substitute. At one point, he told me to go and warm up. As soon as I got out of the dug-out, the crowd began throwing fruit at me. After five minutes of this, I went and sat back down on the bench. Mr Clough glared at me and said, "I thought I told you to warm up." When I told him what had happened he just said, "Get back out there. And bring me back a couple of pears and a banana."

'Afterwards, he called me into his office and told me I couldn't let people like that dictate to me. Because I wouldn't be any good to him if I did and he'd be forced to put someone else in the team. I wanted to play football for a living. And you couldn't let racist abuse affect you if you wanted to get on in those days. So I shut it all out and it became water off a duck's back.

'It was a bit different for Laurie and Cyrille. I was a defender and to an extent got under the radar. They were both flair players and caught the eye. People look at the stereotype, which was to be flash, and that was Laurie.'

Anderson was injured for the cup-tie and didn't play. Regis led the West Brom forward line, but Cunningham was still being used as a substitute. Having turned out for Cambridge in the competition earlier in the season, Batson was ineligible for cup matches. The game began at a furious pace and on a bright, crisp afternoon. Forest, the favourites, looked ominous from the start and pegged Albion back into their own half. In the home team's goal, Tony Godden was soon being forced into a string of fine saves.

However, in the fifteenth minute and against the tide of the match, the Baggies took the lead. Their Irish midfielder, Mick Martin, latched onto a looping ball on the edge of the box and lifted it over the onrushing England goalkeeper, Peter Shilton. Forest continued to press forward, but now West Brom matched them and the game veered from one end of the pitch to the other, both sides attacking with speed and verve.

There was something gladiatorial about the movement of the contest, each team taking guard and then lunging for the throat of the opponent. Regis landed the killer blow three minutes into the second half. He chased a long punt down field from Godden, shoulder to shoulder with Forest's imposing centre-half Kenny Burns. Muscling past Burns, Regis took the ball on its first bounce and struck it from the edge of the penalty area and beyond Shilton's grasp. It was a strike that was as bold as it was thrilling.

'Right then, Regis was rewriting the rulebook on centre-forward play,' opines Martin Swain. 'He had everything, explosive pace but also a deft touch, grace and intelligence. He was exhilarating to watch. If he'd have been an album, Regis would have been the Beatles' *Sgt. Pepper's*.'

In his first season as a professional, Regis found himself within one victory of the FA Cup final – in those days still the English game's showpiece occasion. Albion's semi-final opponents the next month were Ipswich Town, who were managed by Bobby Robson, a former West Brom player of the fifties and sixties. The Suffolk side were battling against relegation and a fairy-tale script appeared written for the young Baggies striker. The week before the game, Atkinson's confidence was such that he was filmed by the BBC's *Football Focus* show walking up to the Royal Box at Wembley Stadium to collect the cup.

Atkinson also changed his team for the match. Despite being

back in the side in the League, Cunningham returned to the bench, and Bryan Robson was also dropped. Such hubris proved costly. The game was played at Arsenal's Highbury stadium and West Brom had lost it within twenty minutes of the kick-off. By then, Ipswich had scored two goals without reply. Mick Martin got himself sent off and John Wile sustained a head injury trying to defend the first goal. His head swathed in bandages, Wile played out the rest of the match with blood streaming down his face. Yet his team-mates appeared just as dazed as he did in limping to a 3-1 defeat; no one more so than Regis, who froze for this, his biggest game.

'It was painful, very painful,' he says. 'We'd been playing great football and we were on a hot streak, but we didn't perform on the day. It was my first real taste of disappointment. Ron also did that TV programme and Ipswich didn't need any more motivation after that, watching him walking around Wembley.'

'Ron lost us that game,' insists Godden. 'We were all sitting there in the hotel on the morning of the match and there he was on the telly, picking the cup up. We all went, "Oh, shit." I spoke to a couple of the Ipswich lads after the match. They said Bobby Robson had walked into their dressing room and told them not to worry about the game as we'd already won it.

'In his early days as a manager, that was an example of Ron's naivety. I think he'd also begun to believe his own self-importance. But he was learning as he went along and he came down a peg or two.'

There was a second significant event that took place in the capital that month. A crowd of 82,000 gathered in Trafalgar Square on 30 April and marched from there to Victoria Park in Hackney for an outdoor concert organised by Rock Against Racism. Britain was doubtless a divided nation, but this mass, the majority of them white, at the very least indicated that the cracks along social and racial lines were not as uniform as they might have first appeared to be.

Among the artists on the bill that afternoon were the Clash, X-Ray Spex, the Tom Robinson Band and Steel Pulse. Roger Huddle and Red Saunders from Rock Against Racism had only managed to obtain a licence for the event by telling the local council that they expected no more than 500 people to attend.

'Otherwise, we'd have had to get Portaloos and we couldn't afford them,' says Huddle. 'The National Front twice tried to burn the stage down in the days beforehand. I remember the Clash and their dreadful manager, Bernie Rhodes, being very, very awkward. We bought a bottle of Red Label whisky for the park keeper and introduced him to Steel Pulse. My abiding memory is of him sitting with their road crew, a great cloud of dope smoke enveloping them.

'It had been raining all week, but the sun broke out when the demonstration arrived from Trafalgar Square. It was almost Biblical. The people who've since written all the punk rock books have said that the kids were just there for the bands, which is total crap. This perception that everyone who was white and working class was then a racist is an absolute nonsense.'

'That show galvanised all the cultures that were happening in Britain at the time,' claims David Hinds of Steel Pulse. 'It turned on its head the idea that all of Britain was racially divided. The country was seen as being very right-wing, but the punk guys were all about trashing the system and saying they weren't down with the programme. Reggae music got on board with that.

'After that, we started to perform at universities. That was to predominantly white audiences, because not too many black folks were able to pursue that level of education at the time.'

★

The semi-final defeat exposed a weakness in Atkinson's West Brom team: an inability to deliver when it mattered most. This was their Achilles heel and it would come back to disable them time and again during the next year. However, they recovered their sense of purpose in the immediate aftermath of the Ipswich game and picked up a head of steam in the League.

The next Wednesday night, they beat Newcastle at the Hawthorns. Regis opened the scoring and Paddy Mulligan, now on borrowed time, added a second. The following Saturday, they saw off Manchester City 3-1 at their Maine Road stadium with Cunningham once again in the starting line-up. Regis scored the first goal that afternoon too. Picking up the ball on the halfway line, he barged through the entire City defence. Goalkeeper Joe Corrigan advanced to meet him, but Regis didn't break stride, lifting the ball up and over Corrigan and into the net. He was perhaps never greater than he was in that one moment, never again appearing so much a force of nature.

'I was sat among the City fans in the main stand that day,' recalls Albion supporter John Homer. 'Cyrille ran through most of their team to score his goal. I couldn't help but jump up it was so exciting. There was an old guy sat next to me with a broken leg. He hit me over the head with his crutch.'

'That goal showed just how quick and powerful Cyrille was,' says Bryan Robson. 'He had all the attributes to go on and become even better, but he was laid-back and I thought that held him back a bit. I used to tell him that if I'd have been his size, I'd be smashing people out of the way left, right and centre. He was definitely too nice for his own good.'

In all, West Brom lost just one of their remaining seven games and finished the season in sixth place in the League. Atkinson brought Batson back into the team for the final three matches, sealing Mulligan's fate and setting in place the foundations for the next season. Thereafter, the three black players would be picked out and held up as a self-contained unit within the team. Yet Batson, the elder of the three, gravitated more to such senior members of the side as Tony Brown, Ally Robertson and Ally Brown.

'Brendon is intelligent, astute, well-read and principled and we were all great friends,' says Regis. 'But Laurie and I were single guys and very tight. Brendon was five years older than me and he had a wife and kids, so he couldn't hang around as much with the two of us.'

At its end, another drama was also played out that season. A couple of Frenchmen turned up at the Hawthorns one afternoon purporting to be journalists and requesting an interview with Regis. Atkinson checked out their credentials and discovered that both were working for the top French side St Etienne, who'd won their national title in three of the last five seasons and had also reached the European Cup final in 1976.

Their interest in Regis was two-fold. In the first instance, St Etienne was seeking to pair him with the club's emerging young French striker, Dominique Rocheteau, for the next season. The French Football Federation also wanted to fast-track blossoming talent into its recruiting system in time for the 1978 World Cup finals in Argentina. Since Regis had been born in French Guiana and had dual nationality, he fitted the bill. He was also coming to the end of his one-year contract with Albion.

'As soon as the story broke, I was dispatched to the Hawthorns,' says Bob Downing. 'I parked at the Europa Hotel and as I was getting out of my car, Cyrille was coming out of the front doors and Ron was pulling up in his Jag. Ron wound the window down and shouted at Cyrille, "Tell him fuck all." Cyrille shouted back, "But I don't know fuck all."'

'We were being offered £750,000 for a kid who'd had only a handful of League games for us,' says Atkinson. 'At the time, the record fee for a British player was the half-million quid Hamburg in Germany had paid Liverpool for Kevin Keegan the previous year.

'Anyway, I knocked it on the head. I gave him a better contract with us and that was Cyrille settled. On top of that, I gave him an extra couple of grand as a signing-on fee because he'd been up front with me. What I didn't know, John Gordon had already then handed him £10,000 over and above what he was getting to stay at the club. He didn't tell me that, the cheeky sod. To be fair, had he gone to France, Cyrille would have made an absolute fortune.'

The most important result of that season for Regis and the rest of the West Brom team occurred in a game in which they weren't even involved. On 10 May, Liverpool beat the Belgian side Club Brugge 1-0 at Wembley to retain the European Cup and secure their place in the competition for the next year. Then in its purest form, European Cup qualification was dependent upon a club winning its national League or holding the trophy. Liverpool's continued participation in it allowed West Bromwich Albion to claim the fourth slot allocated to English sides in the second European club tournament, the UEFA Cup, and in what would be the club's centenary season.

Having held on to their talismanic striker, there was a growing sense at West Brom of something special looming on the horizon. Atkinson and his board of directors doubtless suspected it might be measured in the accumulation of trophies. Yet ultimately, it amounted to something more lasting and profound.

Laurie Cunningham already standing out as a 13-year-old in the Regent's Park Junior League's representative team.

The first black player to be selected for Arsenal's first team, Brendon Batson in action for the Gunners against West Ham in 1972.

'He wasn't an archetypal footballer ...': Cunningham in his finery at Leyton Orient, 1975.

'He kept his distance until he warmed to someone …': Cunningham finds a soul-mate at West Bromwich Albion in Cyrille Regis.

(right) 'Brendon thought he was Billy Big Time. We quickly agreed he wasn't …': Batson becomes Ron Atkinson's first signing at West Brom, February 1978.

(below) Regis scores the decisive goal against Nottingham Forest that took West Brom into the semi-finals of the FA Cup in 1978.

Regis and fellow goal-scorer Mick Martin *(left)* toast the FA Cup quarter-final victory over Brian Clough's Forest.

Cunningham shows off his pride and joy – his MG car.

'He was getting hacked to pieces …': Cunningham was often targeted for special treatment by defenders as is shown here against Derby County.

'He was perhaps never again so much like a force of nature …': Regis' stunning goal against Manchester City, 15 April 1978.

West Bromwich Albion's first team squad, 1978. Back row *(from left)*: Physio George Wright, Paddy Mulligan, Ally Robertson, Ally Brown, John Osborne, Mick Martin, Tony Godden, Cunningham, Batson, Regis, Atkinson. Front row: Bryan Robson, Tony Brown, Len Cantello, John Wile, Derek Statham, John Trewick, Willie Johnston.

Cunningham with his parents Mavis and Elias after a match at the Hawthorns. The champagne was courtesy of Ron Atkinson.

(right) Cunningham, Regis and substitute Wayne Hughes after the UEFA Cup tie in Spain with Valencia which first put Cunningham on Real Madrid's radar.

(below) Cunningham in action during the victorious second leg of the UEFA Cup contest with Valencia at the Hawthorns, 6 December 1978.

'He was so good he could run on snow without leaving footprints …': Cunningham torments Bristol City on New Year's Day 1979.

Regis scores the goal against Norwich City that took West Brom to the top of the First Division, 13 January 1979.

Two-thirds of West Brom's 'Three Degrees' enjoy a night out in Birmingham with their pop group namesakes. The missing Batson had 'gotten embarrassed' by the association. 'It was just so contrived,' he says.

Batson with 'my rock', his late wife Cecily.

Regis with the only trophy won at the end of the 1978/79 season – his PFA 'Young Footballer of the Year' award.

Regis in excelsis – scoring a winning goal against Manchester United, 5 May 1979.

Cyrille Regis' 'All Blacks' team line up for Len Cantello's testimonial game at the Hawthorns on 16 May 1979. 'It was anything but divisive,' said Batson.

Chapter Eight: Perfect Storm

Nine days after playing their final game of the 1977–78 season, Ron Atkinson and his West Brom players left the West Midlands for China. The seeds of this unlikely post-season jaunt were sown when the Football Association declined an invitation from the Chinese government for the English national side to be the first Western team to visit the country. West Brom was volunteered in its stead by the club's chairman, Bert Millichip, a solicitor by trade and also an influential member of the FA Board.

The West Brom party arrived in the capital of Peking on 11 May to begin what was dubbed the 'Friendship Tour'. They were accompanied by a couple of journalists from the Midlands and a BBC documentary crew fronted by the reporter Julian Pettifer, who'd made his reputation a decade earlier covering the Vietnam War. It was less than two years since Chairman Mao's death and China was still finding its way out from under the rigid strictures imposed upon it by his Cultural Revolution. To the visiting footballers, the country seemed bleak and unremitting. As Bryan Robson bemoaned to Pettifer, this was nothing like their preferred destination – a beach in Spain.

Prior to leaving, the players had been ordered to the Foreign Office in London and informed that the trip was to be an important diplomatic exercise aimed at gilding China's re-emergence into the world. In other words, they were to behave themselves. As they were being paraded at a succession of official engagements in China, their mood remained as sombre as that of the various Communist Party 'minders' who tailed them for the next three weeks. Atkinson laid a bet with his players that before leaving the country he'd have coaxed one of these shadows into joining him for a glass of champagne and a Havana cigar. He never even came close to succeeding.

There were occasional moments of levity. During a visit to the Great Wall, midfielder John Trewick was filmed affecting disinterest at the sight of the vast man-made structure. 'Once you've seen one wall, you've seen them all,' he dolefully concluded. It was an example of Trewick's bone-dry humour, but in *The World About Us* documentary film that resulted from the trip it was made to seem like the kind of witless remark expected of a footballer. Edited out of the footage by the BBC men were a succession of like-minded wisecracks from Trewick's team-mates, among them Mick Martin's assertion that he'd bent balls around bigger walls. The players had laughed especially hard at that one. Laughter was otherwise the rarest of sounds on this groundbreaking foray.

'China remained in Mao's grip and it was very austere, everything that Big Ron in particular hated,' says Dave Harrison, covering the trip for the *Evening Mail*. 'We visited all these cultural sites by day, but there was nothing to do at night. And Ron loved a night out. He described those three weeks to me as the longest three years of his life.

'I remember aimlessly walking around the hotel one evening and going by Ron's room. The door was open and he shouted out to me, "Oi, Scoop – in here!" He told me I had to take away his belt, shoelaces and razor blades, because he was considering topping himself. I sat there and chatted with him for the next hour about all sorts of things – football, home, family. After that, he always referred to me as the man who'd saved his life.'

'Cyrille and I went to see Mao lying in state in what was then Red Square,' adds Tony Godden. 'It was more for something to do, because we were absolutely bored shitless. We were being chaperoned and filmed everywhere we went, and having to be suited and booted to go around the embassies.'

For the most part, the majority of the West Brom side shunned the many cultural excursions laid on for them by the Chinese authorities. They instead occupied themselves with either playing cards, tennis at the British embassy or cricket in the grounds of their hotel. As was his habit, Ally Robertson skulked around the hotel armed with a bucket of water intent upon drowning one team-mate or another. However, his roving was brought to an abrupt end when he leapt out from behind a door and inadvertently doused a passing Bert Millichip. Normally a man of great reserve, the Albion chairman's outraged response was heard several floors up.

The exceptions to this rule were Cunningham, Regis and Batson. Alone among the party, the three of them visibly welcomed the Chinese experience. They went off together on each of the organised trips, they sampled the local dishes laid on at the various official functions and enjoyed the attentions of a curious public. Harrison says he asked Regis about this 'and he told me that, as far as he and Brendon were concerned, both of them had come from outside of England, so they were used to embracing a new culture. The other thing was that no one in China had seen a black person, so they were a bit of an attraction themselves. Wherever they went, there was interest in them.'

'The thing that stood out for me was how smart the three lads were,' says Trewick. 'We were all the rest of us scruffy so-and-sos and there they were, immaculately turned out in their beautiful shirts and well-tailored suits.'

West Brom played four matches while in China. The first was against a club side from Peking on a bare, hard pitch and in sweltering heat. Despite 80,000 people packing the city stadium, the game took place in silence. Before kick-off, an announcement was made over the PA instructing spectators to remain quiet and seated. During the half-time interval, the Albion players were further taken aback by having a retinue of officials enter their dressing room and serve them bowls of ice-cream on a trestle table.

The match was won at a canter, 3-1. It was a story repeated in the subsequent games in Shanghai, Kwantung Province and against the Chinese national side. In Shanghai, the oppressive air appeared to have been lifted as 40,000 shirt-sleeved fans peppered the local stadium with splashes of colour. It was a stark and welcome contrast to the sea of grey tunics that had confronted them in Peking.

Returning home via Hong Kong, Atkinson arranged for the grateful party to have a night out at the horse races on the then British colony. Here, at last, the manager was again in his element, playing the role of ringmaster and keeping everyone's glass but his own filled with champagne. There was a horse called Cambridge Lad running in the last race of the evening. A delighted Atkinson harangued everyone into betting on it and it romped home at odds of 20/1.

Willie Johnston hadn't gone to China. Rather, he'd joined up with the Scottish squad to prepare for that summer's World Cup in Argentina. Played to the rhythm of a tango and against the backdrop of swirling clouds of ticker tape, the tournament itself was a spectacle so unfamiliar to the watching audience back in Britain that it could have been taking place on a different planet, albeit one under the rule of a brutal military junta. Compared to the game at home, there was something otherworldly about the football that was served up too. The best of it – which is to say when the leading nations rose above blatant gamesmanship and physical intimidation – was a carnival of skill and daring.

The Scots travelled to South America flush with a misguided sense of optimism. In the event, they were beaten by unfancied Peru in their opening match and crashed out of the competition at the first group stage. Even before then, Johnston had been sent home in disgrace, having failed a drugs test that was administered after the game with Peru. The substance in question was nothing more sinister than a hay fever remedy, but Johnston's reputation doubtless counted against him at the Scottish Football Association. It offered up no challenge to his exclusion from the tournament, or the subsequent twelve-month ban that FIFA handed him down at both international and club level. This ruled Johnston out of West Brom's upcoming UEFA Cup campaign and hastened his exit from the club. It also meant Cunningham was now unchallenged as the team's wing man.

'After Argentina, that was me done,' says Johnston. 'At every ground I went to the next season, I was getting booed or having 'junkie' chanted at me, and it was all for a load of shite. Big Ron told me I wasn't going to get in the team and also that the chairman didn't want me at the club. Eventually, Vancouver Whitecaps in the American Soccer League came in for me. I'd not been to Canada, so off I went.'

Back in Britain, Johnston's troubles amounted to no more than a footnote next to the dominant story of that summer. This was that of the former leader of the Liberal Party, Jeremy Thorpe, who was facing a committal hearing on a charge of conspiracy to commit murder. An extraordinary saga, as it was played out it became as much to do with the morals and mores of the country's privileged – and white – upper classes as with any alleged crime.

Educated at Eton and then Trinity College, Oxford, Thorpe was born to be a high-flyer and a pillar of the establishment. His rise appeared inevitable and unfettered, but in the background there had lurked persistent rumours about his sexuality. In 1961, when his political career was still in its infancy, Thorpe had struck up a friendship with a former petty thief and male model named Norman Scott. When Thorpe broke this off, Scott filed a police report in which he claimed to have had a homosexual relationship – at that time an illegal act in Britain – with the politician.

Since Scott appeared to be a habitual liar, no charges were brought against Thorpe, and in 1967 he was elected Liberal leader. However, Scott continued to haunt the shadows of his career. During the ensuing years, a series of payments were made to Scott through a fellow West Country Liberal MP of Thorpe's, Peter Bessell. Thorpe intimated to Bessell and other close friends that he was being blackmailed. Scott later alleged that it was his silence that was being bought.

This chapter of the story came to an outlandish climax in October 1975. Scott was then living near to Thorpe's constituency home in north Devon and was contacted by an Andrew Newton, a former airline pilot masquerading as an MI5 agent. Newton persuaded Scott into his car one evening and drove him and his Great Dane dog onto Exmoor. Pulling a gun, Newton forced Scott from the vehicle and shot his dog dead at the roadside. In his evidence to police, Scott claimed Newton had then attempted to shoot him, but the gun had jammed and he was able to flee on foot across the moor.

The resulting two-year police investigation first connected Newton to a pair of businessmen, George Deakin and John Le Mesurier. From them the trail led to David Holmes, then the Deputy Treasurer of the Liberal Party and a good friend of Thorpe's. Police concluded that these three men, acting at Thorpe's behest, had hired Newton to kill Scott. Thorpe's political career was in ruins and yet he continued to conduct himself as though men of his standing would ultimately not be failed by the British judicial system.

'Thorpe always had this raffish look,' says David May, a reporter who covered the story for the *Sunday Times* and later co-wrote a book about the case. 'He really was an upper-class Edwardian gentleman and to me seemed like he'd stepped out of another, earlier era. I met him a few times and he was charming and a very sophisticated political operator.

'As journalists, at the time we were obsessed with finding the British equivalent of Watergate. We all wanted to be Woodward and Bernstein, and the Thorpe case seemed to have pretty much everything one could want for in a sensational political story: allegations of illegal sex and the political and financial corruption in covering it up, personal betrayals and a byzantine incitement to murder conspiracy, the only victim of which was Norman Scott's dog, Rinka.'

The week Thorpe went to court, another story just as

representative of the period slipped by almost unnoticed. This was a rallying cry from the National Council for Civil Liberties against proposals then being put forward by the Metropolitan Police Commissioner, Sir David McNee. McNee wanted his officers to be granted sweeping powers of stop and search. Bald statistics later confirmed that no one was likely to feel the brunt of this measure more than a young black man living in an area such as Handsworth.

Such were the unsettling and oppressive currents stirring the British air in the August of 1978. To be sure, there seemed an ill wind blowing. It was one that even penetrated the bubble inside which the game of football often appeared to take place. As the new season approached, the *Express & Star* reported that police in the West Midlands were drawing up undercover plans to combat the growing menace of football hooliganism in the region.

The World Cup had given Ron Atkinson a new crop of characters to adopt during the pre-season training games at West Brom. He now swaggered about the place in the guise of the dashing Argentine striker Mario Kempes or Rainer Bonhof, the West German midfield powerhouse. Playing as either man, Atkinson's big trick was the self-styled 'lollipop', which comprised of him throwing his leg over the ball in a dummy feint. The players joked that they could see this coming from the other side of Birmingham.

Going to China had at least served to bond Atkinson and his team tighter together. The spirit that pervaded at these sessions was entirely at odds with the temperature in the rest of the country, as a feeling developed among the players that these were the best of times. This soon enough carried over on to the pitch.

In the first week of the new season, West Brom recorded three straight victories in the League: their FA Cup conquerors Ipswich were beaten 2-1, Queen's Park Rangers 1-0 and Bolton were hammered 4-0 at the Hawthorns.

The side that gelled through these games was to remain almost unchanged for the next nine months. In goal, there was Tony Godden. Across the back line, Brendon Batson and Derek Statham as full-backs, John Wile and Ally Robertson as centre-halves, as obdurate a defensive four as any in the League. The midfield engine room was comprised of Tony Brown, Bryan Robson and the most underrated player in the team, Len Cantello. Then the three front men, Cyrille Regis, Ally Brown and Laurie Cunningham, each of them the very epitome of Atkinson's commitment to pace.

On a good day, such as when tearing into Bolton at full pelt, West Brom began to play with a panache and devil-may-care boldness that seemed better suited to Buenos Aires than the Black Country. In this respect, it was true of Cunningham most of all.

'For those of us who were then fortunate enough to see Laurie play, it was a privilege,' says Batson. 'He was a thing of beauty on the pitch, seemed to float across it. A feeling of calm came over the team whenever the ball went out to him, because you knew that invariably he wasn't going to lose it. I don't think sometimes you appreciate what you've got till it's gone. Laurie's time with us was short, but sweet and memorable too.

'Ron knew how to get the best out of his players as well and we respected him for how he did things. A lot of managers don't want to get close to the team, since it can be used against them. But Ron wasn't afraid to be part of the group, because both he and we knew that he couldn't be taken advantage of.'

'Every now and again, you get a team where the mix is just right and it's a pleasure to be part of it, on and off the pitch,' furthers Regis. 'Being in that West Brom side was a joy. Between us, we had chemistry, confidence and a winning mentality. It was like the perfect storm.'

Cunningham's family were regular visitors to the Hawthorns for West Brom's home games. Either his mother and father would come together, or Mavis would bring along his brother, Keith. Atkinson always made sure to make a fuss of them in the players' lounge after the match, presenting Mavis with flowers and plying each of them with champagne. The two brothers had by then long gone off in separate directions. As Laurie was rising through his sport, Keith had fallen into petty crime and been in and out of jail.

'I was a bit of a terror, put it that way,' says Keith. 'The first recollection I have of my brother as a professional footballer is being banged up and hearing from the other cons that he was on TV. I used to collect pictures of him. When the newspapers came in, I'd cut out anything that was about him and stick it in an album I kept in my cell. I don't think he ever came to visit me. Mom and Dad did, but not him. But then, I didn't want him to turn up in that situation.

'He seemed to enjoy playing for West Brom, more than he'd later do for Real Madrid. It looked like he'd got quite a few mates up there and if he was getting any stick off anyone then he hid it from me.'

Something that hadn't changed from their childhood was that Laurie, then and now, remained accident prone. When he was meant to visit his family in London after one game, he instead ended up in hospital. He'd been waiting with Nicky Brown at Birmingham's New Street station to board an approaching train, when he stepped in front of an opening carriage door and was knocked out cold.

In the second week of September, West Brom began their UEFA Cup adventure against Galatasaray of Turkey. The first leg was originally scheduled to take place in front of the Turkish side's fervent home fans in Istanbul. However, as a result of persistent crowd trouble at the club's Ali Sami Yen stadium, UEFA moved the fixture 200 miles along the Aegean coast to Izmir.

'The hotel in Izmir was the biggest dump you've ever seen,' recalls Atkinson. 'It didn't even have a dining room. The night before the match, I wouldn't let the players go to bed. I took them all out and we had a meal at a pavement café. On the day of the game, we had a swimming gala amongst ourselves. The kind of things you shouldn't do, but we weren't able to relax in the hotel.'

The unorthodox preparation nonethless worked. Albion strolled to a 3-1 victory with Cunningham, Regis and Robson scoring. As they were doing in the League, the side played with a carefree abandon that was rooted in Atkinson's conviction that they would score more goals than the opposition.

'The traditional thing to do in European games was to sit back in the away leg and try to nick something on the break, whereas we just went at sides,' he says. 'On reflection, maybe it was a bit naive.'

Back in domestic competition, the first true test of the team's mettle came at the Hawthorns on 23 September when Liverpool were the visitors. Having had the title wrested from them the previous season by Nottingham Forest, Liverpool had by then returned to what they considered to be their rightful place on top of the League. West Brom were snapping at their heels, but had lost their first game of the campaign a week earlier at Derby.

Albion couldn't escape their own half for the first thirty minutes of the match. This Liverpool team was as formidable as any to have competed in British football. Taking the reins of the club from the great Bill Shankly in 1974, manager Bob Paisley had built his side on the bedrock of two outstanding Scottish footballers: tenacious midfielder Graeme Souness and Kenny Dalglish, a striker of true guile. Such as it was, the secret of their success was to keep hold of the ball. In doing so they didn't so much beat other teams as grind them down, both physically and mentally.

In their vivid all-red strips, each of the Liverpool players seemed possessed of an assurance that his side would prevail. Next to them, in their navy blue-and-white-striped shirts, their West Brom counterparts looked cowed and uncertain. As the unseasonably warm afternoon wore on, they chased longer shadows. Yet Liverpool couldn't score and as the first half drew to a close, the West Brom team found a precarious foothold in the game.

'We'd got an absolute battering and as we came in at half-time, Ron could have been negative and gone on about all the things we'd not done,' says John Wile. 'But when we sat down he said, "Tell you what, lads, there isn't a team in Europe that could've lived with that lot today. But you've survived the best they've got and been fantastic." It was a great piece of management skill.'

Thanks to Atkinson's ministering, the Albion team came out for the second half convinced that Liverpool had peaked. The game turned, the home side now driving forward and turning their opponents around. This was one of Cunningham's good-mood days, and he as much anyone grew in stature. He taunted and teased the Liverpool defence, and he struck the first goal of the game. Regis grabbed a second soon after, but was wrongly ruled offside and it was disallowed.

In these minutes, it could have appeared that not just one match, but the whole tide of the English game was turning. Liverpool, relentless in their efficiency, first quaked and then wilted in the face of an onslaught of fearless attacking football. And yet, at the death, West Brom gave their win away.

It happened in a split second. Godden and Wile became embroiled in an argument, the cause of which neither man can recall. The goalkeeper was standing in the middle of his penalty box, eyes blazing, bouncing the ball up and down. He didn't see Dalglish lurking behind him, and couldn't react quick enough when the Liverpool man nipped in between him and his captain and stole the ball into the net. It was the decisive blow and the game finished drawn, 1-1.

For Albion it was a cruel and senseless end to the encounter, but on such fine margins are titles won and lost. Yet Atkinson was now able to gather his men and fire them with the knowledge that they had stood toe to toe with the best team in the land and pushed them to the limit. He would next instil in them a belief that they could go better and further.

Between 1978 and today, there's been no great change in the rhythm of a professional footballer's life. It has remained a routine of training and playing that runs through a nine-month long season. Of course, these days the mechanics of that process are very different. At a top-flight club such as West Brom, the act of preparing players for each season and maintaining them through it is now a forensic science loaded with minutiae on such things as heart rates, refuelling and diet. This doesn't allow for members of the team to slope off for a cigarette and a fry-up at the end of each session.

As a result, the game itself has become faster and more technical. The rapid proliferation of media has also led to an exponential increase in the amount it is broadcast and reported on and in the attendant interest in it. Yet the most evident and substantive change to the game has been to its economics, and the degree to which at the highest level this has separated those who play football from those who watch it. As well, there has been a marked shift in the demographic of football's support. It is a general rule that the game in the English Premier League of today is played by very rich young men to an audience that is at least comfortably middle class.

In this respect, the football of the late-1970s is wholly unrecognisable. It wasn't then gentrified or brand managed. In some regards it was a simpler, purer game, and in others an uglier one too. Clubs such as West Brom retained a position at the hub of their communities. Often as not, these were the areas of the country most affected by Britain's economic woes. As at most other clubs, the great majority of those who stood on the terraces at West Brom worked in the factories and plants of the town and its surrounding areas. Right then, these were places and people that were commonly clinging on for survival.

Money was tight and the time had passed when people could afford to go to every game. This much was clear that season in the gates at the Hawthorns. More than 33,000 saw the match against Liverpool, whereas less than 22,000 had turned out for Norwich just two weeks earlier. On 29 November, the local derby with Aston Villa attracted a crowd of 35,166. A fortnight after that match, the fixture with Middlesbrough brought in 19,865. The players were better off, but not by an unimaginable distance. When Laurie Cunningham left West Brom in 1979, he was on little more than £100 a week. Supporters alternately envied, admired and even idolised him and his team-mates, but they nonetheless continued to inhabit much the same world as them.

For home matches, the Albion players parked their cars at a school across the road from the Hawthorns on Halfords Lane. It was a common sight to see one or other of them deep in conversation with a group of supporters on the walk from there to the ground. During the week, the players were just as likely to be spotted out together in a local pub such as the Four in Hand. It was even known for them to frequent the Marksman off Carters Green, one of the town's roughest boozers. Cyrille Regis was a regular at a quieter pub a mile up the road in Hill Top, the Star & Garter.

'Cyrille was an electrician. He's a man of the people,' says John Homer. 'That was the thing. As a supporter you knew where the players had come from and had an affinity with them. At that time, football still had humanity. The players were of a generation that appreciated how lucky they were to be in the game. Even though the rewards were not as great, they were still getting paid more than my old man was for working in a brickyard in Netherton.'

Atkinson nurtured this connection between the team and its supporters. He instituted a rota for having the players attend supporters' club meetings throughout the season, telling them it was part of the job of being a footballer. One of his most well-used mantras was that none of them should forget who paid their wages.

'Players were more respectful of supporters in those days, because we were on a level,' insists Godden. 'It was a pretty depressed area, but we'd all of us go along together to the pub opposite the ground on a Saturday night and listen to a bloke on the piano, or a live band. It was all part of joining in with West Bromwich Albion.

'Most of the time, we had Wednesdays off. You only had to go into the dressing room on a Tuesday morning and say it was your turn to go down the Dog and Duck to draw the raffle, and you'd have fifteen of the lads saying they'd come along. Nothing silly, but we'd have a few beers, us and the fans.'

Outside of this home environment, the same awful, yawning chasm still opened up that seperated Cunningham, Regis and Batson from the others. All of the players expected stick from opposition fans, but the vitriol being directed at the trio was laced with a particular poison. The sound of it was hostile, but also now as familiar to them as radio static.

This much was true of all of the black players in the English game at the time. Yet their total number was then just fifty or so. In that regard, the collective black presence in the West Brom team made it a magnet for the extremists. At the FA and in the media, the racist abuse continued to go either ignored or unacknowledged. However, it was now so obvious, so prevalent at Albion's games, that it could be nothing but a fact of life at the club. It even drew the side closer together and gave them a common enemy, albeit one they never did comprehend in the same way.

'How can I say, we talked about it but we also laughed about it,' says Ally Robertson. 'The three lads were our mates and we all used to stick together, so it was nothing to us. If they were being called anything, the rest of us would just tell them to try harder to win the game and shut the crowd up.

'I used to say to each of them, "If people call you a black so-and-so, then so what? How many times have I been told I'm a Scottish twat?" I didn't give two hoots. The thing was we never, ever allowed anyone to call them 'nigger'. That's derogative. Anyone that did, I'd be the first to punch them.'

'What shocked me when I joined West Brom was the volume,' says Batson. 'The noise and level of the abuse was incredible. At times, it was almost like surround sound in the grounds. But it was such a regular occurrence, you almost got used to it.

'We'd get off the coach at away matches and the National Front would be right there in your face. In those days, we didn't have security and we'd have to run the gauntlet. We'd get to the players' entrance and there'd be spit on my jacket or Cyrille's shirt. It was a sign of the times. I don't recall making a big hue and cry about it. We coped. It wasn't a new phenomenon to us. From when I came to England, I was familiar with people shouting at me from cars or on the Underground in London.

'With the other players in the side, it was none of their business. It didn't concern them and they weren't sensitive to it. I also remember speaking to the BBC and confronting them about when they were going to say something about it. They told me it wasn't possible to make out what was being shouted. What a load of bollocks that was. All of the excuses I got were a joke.'

The three players were also now accustomed to receiving hate mail at the club. Cunningham got the most, on account of his relationship with Nicky Brown, which was well-publicised. Yet Bryan Robson also recalls being sent vile letters asking him how an Englishman could tolerate having black team-mates. One of the more regular correspondents to the club was an Everton fan, who'd send in an abusive screed each time Albion were due to play on Merseyside. He directed this at Atkinson, urging him not to select his 'monkeys' for the game.

'It was otherwise very well written,' says Atkinson, smiling.

'We treated a lot of it with humour. Before each game with Everton, Cyrille would say to me, "Gaffer, has he written?" He'd read it out and burst out laughing. We'd even stick it up in the dressing room. But then, we always beat Everton and the big man usually weighed in with a wonder goal.'

'I never knew how sincere Ron was about the three black players,' says Pat Murphy. 'He was a pragmatist and he enjoyed players that excited him; it didn't matter what their colour was. Cunningham and Regis thrilled him. He also liked good, solid defenders that didn't piss around, and in that respect Brendon Batson was perfect for him.'

It was Cunningham again who attracted the most menacing heat away from the football stadia. Death threats were posted to the house he shared with Brown in Birmingham. On one occasion, a petrol bomb was thrown through their front door. Brown remembers him calmly stamping out the flames licking at the doormat, as if it were the sort of thing that happened every day. His only recourse remained on the pitch. That season, more than any other, he was able to keep striking back and winning victories.

At the end of September, West Brom went to play Chelsea at Stamford Bridge in the League. The west London club was another that had become notorious for the ferocity of its support. As at West Ham and Millwall, this was most apparent when there was a black player in the opposition team.

'I wasn't a Chelsea fan, but my brother-in-law had a season ticket and he took me along to see the game,' recalls Lord Herman Ouseley, now chairman of English football's anti-racism campaign group Kick It Out. 'Going to football as a black man was then a very uncomfortable experience. You had to keep your head down and your wits about you.

'At the beginning of the game, the three West Brom players got fruit thrown at them. Each time one of them touched the ball, the booing was horrendous. After about twenty minutes, Laurie weaved his way through the Chelsea defence and Cyrille banged the ball into the net. The guys sitting around me were enraged. They stood up and the abuse reached a cacophony.

'Not long after, Laurie went through again and set up another goal. They were even more livid. But then one of these gorillas sitting in front of me turned to another and said, "Mind you, the nigger is fucking good, isn't he?" This was a moment of inspiration for me and I sat there with a glow inside. It was saying, whatever the odds, you can win people over by your talent and perseverance.'

The game against Chelsea was won 3-1 and took West Brom into the top three in the League. By then they had also completed the formalities of getting through to the next round of the UEFA Cup, seeing off Galatasaray by the same score at the Hawthorns.

It was clear that the side had now taken shape. Batson had added an extra dimension to it. Both he and his opposite full-back, Derek Statham, were reliable defenders but also able to attack sides down the flanks. The young Robson was emerging as the complete midfielder. Alongside him, Tony Brown and Cantello were in the form of their lives. Up front, Regis was the team's totemic presence. In the middle of the month, he followed Cunningham into the England U21 squad and made a victorious international debut in Denmark.

And then there was Cunningham. He gave to West Brom an edge that was intangible and unpredictable. The season was two months old, and he was sparking like a fire about to come blazing to life. His moments of brilliance flashed across a darkening gloom in the West Midlands. The *Express & Star* was then reporting another round of strikes over pay at the Ford car plant in Birmingham, and on the almost 80,000 industrial jobs having gone from the region.

A still more terrible event occurred that month. On 19 September, a thirteen-year-old schoolboy named Carl Bridgewater was completing his evening paper round in Stourbridge, not ten miles from the Hawthorns. One of his last calls was to Yew Tree Farm. The elderly couple who owned the property were out that day, but Carl knew them well and let himself in through the back door. It was his dreadful luck to have arrived at the house as it was being robbed.

One or more of the burglars took the boy at gunpoint from the kitchen and into the sitting room. Police found him there on the sofa, where at some time after 4 p.m. he'd been shot through the head at point-blank range with a sawn-off shotgun. The cold brutality of his murder shocked people in the West Midlands and across the country. It also seemed to encapsulate a feeling of hopelessness and desolation rushing to the surface.

Chapter Nine: Tora! Tora! Tora!

O ctober began badly for West Bromwich Albion. In the first week of the month they were knocked out of the League Cup by Leeds and then beaten in the League at Tottenham, with each game ending 0-1. These were rare occasions when Atkinson's team failed to score, and neither Cunningham nor Regis was able to sparkle.

At Tottenham, the cut and thrust came instead from a player who seemed just as rare and exotic to the English game as them. Running Spurs' midfield that day was Osvaldo Ardiles, a slight but deft Argentinian who'd starred for his country in the summer World Cup. In the aftermath of the tournament, the north London club had signed him and also his compatriot, Ricardo Villa. Their doing so marked a further step along the road towards British football arriving at a cosmopolitan perspective.

Extending this ideal to one of Britain itself becoming truly multicultural was still then liable to provoke fear and foreboding. A bleak vision of this was again being articulated by Enoch Powell, more than a decade after he'd foreseen the country drowning in a river of blood. The Wolverhampton MP skulked back to attack at this, his *bête noire*, like a beaten but ravenous dog.

Speaking to the *Express & Star* newspaper, Powell claimed England's 'coloured' population would double in the next twenty years. In this, he detected a threat to the nation as great as that of the Norman invasion of 1066. Raged Powell: 'I am thinking of the people of this country who no longer dare to step out of their front doors after dark, because thugs will steal their wallets.'

This was an opportune moment for the movie musical *Grease* to open in the UK, which it did to great fanfare on 19 October. Through its lens, beleaguered Brits escaped in their droves to an idealised America of the 1950s where life was lived to the beat of fast cars and young love. It was perhaps symbolic that the world being pictured in it was as pretty and white as Olivia Newton-John's central character, Sandy.

West Brom had been momentarily stalled, but they were soon enough moving through the gears again. Indeed, the loss at Tottenham seemed to spur them to renewed efforts. Straight after it they embarked upon a run of seventeen games unbeaten. This would take them surging past the might of Liverpool to the top of the League. However, it was the manner of their doing so that resonated rather than the fact of it. For in this glorious period of three months, they played with a style that took the breath away.

Their football had a dash and flair to it that cast off the chains binding the sport in England. It aspired to something greater and more utopian than winning games through the functionality that was then the norm. In that sense and at that time, it was as wondrous as the world of make-believe conjured up in *Grease*. At its core were also two lead characters that might have leapt from the pages of fiction, the unyielding Regis and the mercurial Cunningham.

'We were just frightening at that point and far and away the best side in the country,' insists John Wile. 'The younger players who came in, Laurie, Cyrille, Bryan Robson and Derek Statham, had got better from the year before. But everybody was at the top of their game. Regardless of where we went, if we didn't get a minimum of a draw we were disappointed. We thought we could win every game. This wasn't arrogance, but confidence.'

The charge began on 14 October in a League match against Leeds, before one of the most volatile crowds in the country at Elland Road. For much of it, they were second best to a strong Leeds side, and it was left to Wile, Robertson and Godden to stem the flow of their attacks. Leeds surged in front, but Tony Brown grabbed an equaliser against the run of play.

'We were getting a right good chasing, but hanging in there,' says Ron Atkinson, taking up the story. 'I was sitting on the bench thinking of bringing Regis off. It might have been the only time I ever thought of it. But then Statham got injured and I had to bring Willie Johnston on at left-back. In the last five minutes of the game, the big man went and got two goals.

'He'd taken a bit of stick off the Leeds crowd that day, but then we took stick as a team. And at the end of the game, he got a standing ovation off the park.'

Brendon Batson recalls the culmination of this match rather differently. 'I remember walking off after we'd beaten them and almost inevitably Laurie, Cyrille and I were together,' he says. 'The malevolence coming down from the terraces was almost unbelievable. In those days, I was always very glad that there were fences in front of the crowd. On that occasion it allowed us to bravely indicate the score to them.'

Their next game was a West Midlands derby against Coventry City at the Hawthorns. As these things go, it was a fixture lacking in the intensity that characterised Albion's clashes with Aston Villa or Wolverhampton. The city of Coventry was just too far up the M5 motorway to generate that kind of heat. But this contest was billed as being a battle for supremacy in the region, since Coventry began the game one place ahead of West Brom in the table.

On the day, Coventry wore an away strip that no one who attended the match is likely to forget. It was milk-chocolate brown in colour and entirely awful. Yet the trace memories of West Brom's performance that afternoon have lingered stronger. They tore into their helpless opponents from the kick-off, making a mockery of the closeness between the two sides in the League.

Flashing the ball about the pitch, Tony Brown, Robson and Cantello were an exercise in perpetual motion. Regis was destructive, Cunningham dazzling, both of them ruthless in establishing their dominance over their opponents. In total, it was scintillating, captivating and magical. Between them, Regis and Cunningham shared four goals. The final score was outrageous – West Brom 7 – 1 Coventry. A breathless report in the *Express & Star* the next Monday described it as: 'The most one-sided show since Custer took on the Indians . . . Never have I seen a team's defence cut to ribbons so decisively.'

'It was easy to play in that side, a doddle,' says Statham. 'All of us went through the games with massive smiles on our faces. We didn't have a care in the world. We just wanted to get out on the pitch two, three times a week.'

'Tactics went out of the window,' insists Atkinson. 'We were good defensively, because we had good defenders, but there was no point in telling that team to stick men behind the ball. We were better freewheeling. In that respect, I'd say the side we were most like was the Arsenal one of Thierry Henry, Dennis Bergkamp and Patrick Vieira.

'As regards motivating them, I'd seen a war movie called *Tora! Tora! Tora!* and I can remember bringing that up. It was about the Japanese at Pearl Harbor. I told the lads that it meant "Attack, attack, attack". So that's what I used to go in and say to them before a game – "Today lads, *Tora! Tora! Tora!*"'

As his side picked up momentum, Atkinson let slip to his favoured newspaper reporters that he'd had an offer from the United States to go and coach the Philadelphia Furies in the nascent North American Soccer League. He stressed that this was set to make him the highest-paid manager in the US. This served its intended purpose. The day after it was reported, he and his trusted number two, Colin Addison, agreed new and improved three-and-a-half-year contracts with West Brom.

Atkinson might also then have made a mental note of a pop record that was released in the UK that month. Titled *New Dimensions*, it was the new album from an American soul and R&B vocal trio called the Three Degrees.

Into November West Brom went, reeling off victories against Birmingham, Ipswich and Bolton. Their passage through to the next round of the UEFA Cup was made to seem just as perfunctory as they brushed aside the Portuguese team Sporting Braga 3-0 on aggregate. However, this win set them up for a far more challenging encounter. This was against the Spanish side Valencia, the hot favourites to win the competition.

Valencia boasted two of the stars of the 1978 World Cup in their glittering line-up. Both of their names were also familiar on the West Brom training ground as a result of Ron Atkinson's method acting. The Argentinian striker Mario Kempes had been the top goal scorer at the summer tournament and was also the most lethal marksman in La Liga in each of the two previous seasons. Tall, cavalier and with flowing black hair, there was something of the pirate about him.

Behind Kempes, the team's strings were pulled by the West German Rainer Bonhof. A bullish midfielder, Bonhof had won the World Cup with his country in 1974 and was most feared for his stinging free kicks. Alongside these two, the Valencia team was dotted with top-class players. The club itself had a rich history. Since its formation in 1919, Valencia had been the most consistent challenger to the two giants of Spanish football, Real Madrid and Barcelona. The Valencia trophy room boasted four La Liga titles and the same number of triumphs in the national cup, the Copa del Rey ('the King's Cup').

The first leg of the tie was to be played in Spain on 22 November. Valencia's home ground was the imposing Mestalla stadium, famed for its steep, banking terraces and intimidating atmosphere. It was an ominous place to have to go; the sense of dread it engendered was re-enforced by the fact that it had served as a concentration camp during the Spanish Civil War.

Arriving in the Mediterranean city, the Albion players were buoyed by their impressive form in the League but their nerves were nonetheless jangling. There was a very different temperature to the European matches and to this one most of all. Valencia had lost the away leg in each of their two previous matches in the competition that season, but had looked invincible at home. Four goals were plundered against CSKA Sofia of Bulgaria, and the Romanian side FC Arges Pitesti had been hit for five.

'We were supposed to be resting on the afternoon of the

game, but I couldn't sleep,' says Len Cantello. 'So I went down to the hotel lounge and found Big Ron. I asked him for a ball. I wanted to go and have a kick about on the tennis courts. He said, "Sit down instead and have a beer with me."

'At first, I thought he was trying to tell me I wasn't going to be playing. I had one bottle of beer and then he told me I could have another. When I'd finished it he said, "Right, now you can go and sleep that lot off."'

The noise inside the Mestalla that night was intense and overpowering, and it seemed for a time that it might choke the West Brom side. They fell behind within sixteen minutes of kick-off. Godden misjudged the flight of a corner kick, flapping at the ball and allowing Kempes's fellow Argentine, Dario Luis Felman, to rush in and bundle it into the net. Valencia's 50,000 supporters ratcheted up the volume still further, expectant of another goal deluge.

However, this early set-back didn't deter West Brom, but rather it jolted them to action. They started to keep the ball better than Valencia and move it quicker, tightening a grip on the contest and slowly, slowly subduing the crowd. Key to this was Cunningham, who came of age on the night. He began demanding the ball off his team-mates, and when it was at his feet he unleashed his full repertoire on the game.

He was imperious, sublime, and in the magical moment where the promise of great talent explodes into full bloom. The man tasked with trying to subdue him, Valencia's Angel Castellanos, was given a torrid evening. Cunningham toyed with him like a cat with a mouse, turning and twisting him like a corkscrew.

The home crowd hurled oranges at their menace as if this might knock him out of his stride. It did nothing of the sort. He left them gasping instead at his audacity in taking a corner with the outside of his foot, the ball whipping through the air. Three minutes into the second half, he silenced them. Sprinting onto a pull-back from Ally Brown, he steered the ball into the net for Albion's equalising goal. He and his team threatened to score more, but Valencia hung grimly on.

'The whole team played well, but Laurie was absolutely sensational that night,' says Atkinson. 'George Best would have been a comparison at the time, but now I think a better one would be Thierry Henry in his prime at Arsenal. He was as brilliant as that. Spanish TV was at the game and that was when Real Madrid first took an interest in him.'

Cunningham's showing in Valencia brought him gushing press notices. It also began to ferment in his mind the notion that he was meant for higher things and a grander stage to parade on. However, within just a week another black footballer at a Midlands club had written a much bigger story.

On 29 November 1978, Viv Anderson of Nottingham Forest became the first black player to be capped by England at senior level. Cunningham had been racing him to smash through this particular glass ceiling, but it was Anderson's name that went into the record books. He made his full international debut in an otherwise insignificant friendly international against Czechoslovakia at Wembley. The great rock that he, Cunningham and the other black players in the English game had been shouldering uphill was now set for its long tumble towards breaking open the floodgates.

'There wasn't any rivalry between Laurie and me about it,' says Anderson of the record. 'If there had been, you'd have never got him riled anyway. In fact, I don't think the matter of who got there first was ever mentioned between us.

'Of course, it was a big deal. Before the game, I got good luck telegrams from the Queen and Elton John. My mom and dad were on the telly. But as a young footballer, it was all about trying to play well. The one thing I had in mind was that I didn't want to let either myself or my family down.'

Winter was biting when Valencia landed in the West Midlands. To the Baggies fans used to the more mundane ebb and flow of League football, their doing so seemed fantastical. These were the days before European cup matches and continental league games had become a fixture of English television schedules. One might catch a glimpse of a spellbinding footballer such as Kempes through the wider coverage that was afforded a World Cup, but otherwise not at all.

The evening before the game, the Valencia team trained under the Hawthorns floodlights. Their being there was so out of the ordinary that small packs of Albion supporters turned up outside the ground on a frigid night to try and catch a glimpse of them. 'Me and my mate stood freezing on Halford's Lane and I got Kempes's autograph,' recalls Dave Bowler. 'I mean, the idea that Mario Kempes should come to the Hawthorns. Jesus!'

Ron Atkinson was also as an observer that night, but he took a less prosaic view. 'It was icy cold and Kempes was out there in a hat and gloves,' he says. 'I thought to myself, "This lot really won't fancy it tomorrow."'

If anything, it was colder the next night. Breath froze in the air and a rapier wind cut to the bone. Yet it was packed inside the Hawthorns and just as loud and partisan as it had been at the Mestalla. Indeed, those that were there claim the old ground never knew a better atmosphere.

Valencia made their intention clear from the outset, which

was to stop Cunningham by any means necessary. The hapless Castellanos had been replaced in their side by a more streetwise defender, Juan Daniel Cordero. The first time Cunningham skipped past, Cordero hacked his legs from under him. As the game progressed, one brutish lunge at Cunningham followed another.

However, this time it was West Brom who made the flying start. The game was just five minutes old when Statham tossed a hopeful ball into the Valencia box. It was allowed to bounce, rearing up and striking a defender on the hand: penalty. Tony Brown stepped up and sent goalkeeper Jose Luis Manzanedo the wrong way. 1-0. Unlike West Brom in Spain, Valencia recoiled. Albion began to dominate them, zipping the ball about on a pitch made slick with damp. Wile and Roberson smothered Kempes; Cantello suffocated Bonhoff.

In obsessing over Cunningham, Valencia neglected Regis. The big man pulverised them for it. This was one of those nights when he seemed able to run through brick walls. The more he outmuscled their defence, the more the will seemed to seep out of the Spanish side. Before half-time, Regis thundered into their penalty area and forced the ball through to Brown to score. The referee disallowed it for offside. West Brom netted again not long after the interval and once more had it chalked off for an infringement. Regis then hit the post with a soaring header. Valencia clung on by their fingertips.

Even then, there was almost a sting in their tail. Midway through the second half they were awarded a free kick twenty-five yards from goal. Kempes, who had up to then been inert, came to life to take it. He struck it hard and true, like an arrow, but Godden flung himself to his right and parried it out. After that, Valencia had the look of beaten men.

In the final minutes, Cunningham at last wriggled out of Cordero's clutches and cut an arcing ball back from the touch-line for the unmarked Tony Brown to volley in the winning goal. The result put West Brom into the quarter-finals of the competition. It spoke louder that they had got there by toppling one of the glamour names of European football.

'Valencia had expected to win the competition and quite easily,' says John Wile. 'They probably hadn't even heard of West Bromwich Albion, but we'd beaten them and well. It meant that people in the game now knew that we were a team to be reckoned with.'

For Cunningham, Regis, Batson and that entire West Brom side, this seemed the point of their arrival. It held the promise of being the gateway to further glories and bigger prizes. Yet if they had studied the other results in the competition that night a note of caution might have been struck. The team set to be their opposition in the next round, Red Star Belgrade, had seen off another of England's UEFA Cup representatives, Arsenal.

The facts of the matter were these: the Yugoslav side had edged their home leg by the odd goal and then battled to a 1-1 draw at Highbury, soaking up pressure and stealing the tie in its final minutes. However, these were lessons lost to Ron Atkinson and his team.

Chapter Ten: Footsteps in the Snow

The win over Valencia set the triumphal tone that endured at West Bromwich Albion through Christmas and into the New Year. This would amount to the defining crescendo of Cunningham, Regis and Batson's time together at the club, and as well to the highest peak of Ron Atkinson's managerial reign. Yet at the same point the country as a whole was sinking deeper into economic chaos and also facing up to the onset of a ruinous winter. The latter of these two events would end up having the decisive impact on Albion's season.

At the start of December, a pall of arctic weather settled over Britain. This helped to account for one of the lowest gates of the season turning out at the Hawthorns to see West Brom breeze past Middlesbrough 2-0. A week later, they rolled over local rivals Wolverhampton Wanderers 3-0 on their own patch and in conditions that were just as raw. A heavy snowfall forced the postponement of their next scheduled home match, against Southampton. Soon, this would become a familiar and destructive pattern.

For now, hope and expectation still surged at the club – even though they had all but vanished on Britain's streets and in its homes. Unemployment in the country had reached a post-war peak of 1.5 million and the cost of living continued to be driven up. Strong and purposeful government was required to stand firm in the face of these stresses, but this was lacking. The incumbent Labour regime was instead operating as a minority administration and clasping on to power thanks to a precarious pact it had agreed with the Liberals.

Attempting to stem inflation, Prime Minister Jim Callaghan imposed a 5 per cent limit on pay rises in the public sector. He was undermined almost at once in this by a series of booming settlements in the private arena. First among these was a whopping 17 per cent offer that the management at car giant Ford gave up to its workforce, caving in to union pressure and bringing to an end a bitter two-month long strike. The fall-out left Callaghan facing a vote of no-confidence in Parliament in the week between West Brom beating Middlesbrough and Wolves. He won this, but narrowly.

Emboldened by the outcome at Ford, tanker drivers were next to walk out for more pay on 18 December. A significant number of the strikers worked for major oil companies such as BP and Esso, and fuel supplies were seriously disrupted. The embattled government teetered on the edge of declaring a national state of emergency. This began the so-called Winter of Discontent in Britain. Still more corrosive and drawn-out industrial disputes followed in the weeks to come, and these all but brought the country to its knees.

One of the areas to suffer most acutely through this was the industrialised West Midlands. As a result of the fuel shortages, factory production lines in the region ground to a halt. Even though these recovered in the short term, this point marked the beginning of the end for the Black Country as a manufacturing power base. A strike by local bakers also incited people to panic buy bread in shops and supermarkets. This hurried along the mood of despair growing out of the housing estates and in the working men's pubs and clubs surrounding the Hawthorns and other football grounds like it.

Even the news was disrupted. As Christmas neared, the National Union of Journalists called its members out. In the Midlands, the proprietors of the *Express & Star* and *Evening Mail* newspapers were forced to publish skeleton editions. In being so diminished and with their assets stripped by circumstance, these now seemed like a portent of things to come. Since he was so attuned to the currents of the local media, given the sounding board it allowed him, this brought the encroaching gloom into Ron Atkinson's orbit.

'Bob Downing at the *Express & Star* and I hadn't been in to see him for a bit, so Ron rang both of us to find out what we were doing,' explains Dave Harrison. 'Normally, we used to have to troop along to the club every day to get a story off him for the papers. If there was nothing going on, he'd tell us we could write up that he was looking at signing such-and-such a player. It wasn't true, but it gave us copy.

'We told him we were out on strike and he invited us down to the ground for a cup of tea. Bob was first into his office. When I went in after him, Ron said to me, "You're not married are you, Scoop?" Then he handed me £30 and told me to buy a Christmas present with it for my mom. He also said that if I mentioned anything about it in the paper, he'd never speak to me again. That was Ron. He was a very generous bloke.'

At this time, Atkinson also engineered a story intended to

introduce some festive cheer to the papers. To bring this about, Cunningham, Regis and Batson were persuaded to be photographed in Santa Claus outfits. The subsequent picture was published beneath the headline: 'Guess who's dreaming of a white Christmas?' Cunningham suffered the indignities of this in silence and Regis accepted it as a fact of life. For his part, Batson felt as though he'd been railroaded into something beyond his control. It wasn't the last time that season that this would be the case.

On Boxing Day, the West Brom manager took his team to the capital to face Arsenal. Highbury was traditionally a difficult place to go to and win, and Arsenal had run into a rich vein of form. Just three days earlier they had crushed their north London rivals Spurs 5-0 at White Hart Lane, a result that brought them level on points with West Brom in the League.

The visitors began the game at a frenetic pace, rushing into a 2-0 lead within the first twenty minutes through goals from Bryan Robson and Ally Brown. In the second half, Arsenal turned the tide, prompted by their most influential player, a young Irishman named Liam Brady. They struck back from the penalty spot and thereafter pressed hard to take control of the match. Yet the Baggies withstood the onslaught to secure a hard-fought victory. They were now within three points of Liverpool at the top of the League, having played two fewer games than their closest rivals for the title.

In the *Express & Star* the next day, Atkinson declared the win at Highbury to have been his most satisfying of the season so far. In this respect, the upbeat note he struck chimed against the storm clouds billowing in the world outside. Further up front, the paper reported on two youths being hospitalised with machete wounds following a Boxing Day clash in Wolverhampton town centre between white and Asian youths. This was the sort of flashpoint that exposed the racial tensions simmering barely below the surface in towns and cities around the country.

Both the local and national press fixated on a different story two days later. Under increasing pressure to get a result of their own, the West Midlands police announced that they had remanded a 50-year-old man in custody in connection with the Carl Bridgewater murder. He was Patrick Molloy, described as 'unemployed and of no fixed abode'. In due course, Molloy confessed to robbing Yew Tree Farm on the afternoon Carl was killed and in the company of three other local men, James Robinson and a pair of cousins, Vincent and Michael Hickey.

The apparent ending of the hunt for the killers of the schoolboy was met with widespread relief, an almost collective exhaling of breath. In this one isolated case, there was the promise of a good and appropriate outcome. This was of justice being seen to be done and then swift and proper retribution resulting.

If it had to be boiled down to a single game for the three West Brom footballers and their manager of that time, it would be this one: 30 December, Manchester United at Old Trafford. At this point, Ron Atkinson couldn't wait for the next match to come around, and he savoured his team as much as did their most avid supporter. Here, they attained his ideal. Cunningham rose to another level. Regis summoned one of his most striking acts of strength and power. Batson was at his coolest and most assured.

Fortune was also at hand. Football then occupied a late-night niche on British television. Edited highlights of just two or three games from the Football League were broadcast each week of the season on the BBC's *Match of the Day* or on such commercial rivals as *The Big Match* in London or the Midlands-focused *Star Soccer*. As such, the great majority of the most gripping contests of the era have faded to memory. Not this one. It was filmed for *Star Soccer* and lives on, as vivid and enthralling now as it was then. Preserved in this state, it remains a true game for the ages.

Going into it, the two teams were in contrasting shape. West Brom arrived in Manchester chasing a fourth straight victory in the League. In their two most recent matches, against Liverpool and Bolton, United had shipped six goals without scoring. West Brom sat third in the table, United five places below them and as many points adrift (at this time two points were awarded for a win). Yet history was on United's side; Albion hadn't managed a win in their previous seventeen visits to Old Trafford.

It was a bitter day and the temperature barely nudged above freezing all afternoon. Flurries of snow swirled around the ground. Manchester was also in the middle of a public transport strike. Neither this nor the adverse weather deterred a crowd of 45,000 from attending the game. Atkinson fielded a line-up that had become familiar and unchanging. United's team didn't have the same settled look to it, but it retained a surfeit of skill and solidity. Going forward, England's Steve Coppell and the Northern Ireland international Sammy McIlroy provided craft and creativity. Two redoubtable Scottish centre-halves guarded the back, Gordon McQueen and United captain Martin Buchan.

The game took a little time to spring to life. Both sides initially seemed to be shaking off the ache of a hectic Christmas schedule, and the ball passed between them like a hot potato. But it settled to a bracing rhythm, the action swinging from one end of the pitch to the other. For West Brom, Tony Brown and Ally Brown tested United's goalkeeper Gary Bailey with long-range shots and Batson planted a diving header just wide of the post. At the other end, Godden was forced into a point-blank save from McIlroy.

It was all hustle and bustle, sweat and endeavour. Except, that is, for when the ball arrived at Cunningham's feet. For the briefest moment, this brought an oasis of calm to the game, with time seeming to stand still. Then he set off, gliding forward. His acceleration to full speed appeared effortless. As one, then two players rushed to close him down, he shifted his point of his balance one way or the other. Then he was gone in a flash, defenders trailing in his wake – like a will o' the wisp. It was then that one was able to hear clearest the chorus of boos reverberating around the ground in a low rumble.

On twenty-one minutes, United took the lead. Albion's defence cleared the ball from a corner, but only to the edge of their own box. United's right-back Brian Greenhoff was waiting there and he returned it on the volley, his shot looping over the despairing Godden.

Albion hit straight back. Cunningham collected the ball on the left-side touchline and cut infield. As he was doing so, the *Star Soccer* commentator, Gerald Sinstadt, attempted to make a point that until then had not been voiced on British television. 'The booing of the black players,' Sinstadt began, but this was as far as he got. Cunningham was too quick for him, slipping the ball into the penalty area for Tony Brown to swivel onto and score.

Cunningham now had wings. Within minutes he was flying once more and this time from the centre circle. He skipped past two lunging challenges and then released the ball to Regis. In the blink of an eye, Regis had back-heeled it into the path of the onrushing Len Cantello, who speared it into the top corner of the net from the right-hand side of United's penalty area. Five months later, ITV's viewers voted it their 'Goal of the Season'.

At 2-1 the contest seemed to be there for the taking for the visiting side. But no, United dug deep and West Brom capitulated. First, McQueen rose unmarked to head a corner home. Then McIlroy capitalised on another lapse in the Albion defence to give his side the lead, 3-2.

Again, momentum shifted. Tony Brown released a charging Robson through the middle. Bailey came to meet him and palmed his goal-bound shot to safety. Then with the referee's half-time whistle beckoning, Statham hoofed the ball into United's penalty area and Brown swept it up and into the net for 3-3. Atkinson had missed this last twist, having gone to the dressing room where he was running over in his mind how best to rally his team.

'We all came in and sat down and Ron said to us, "You're playing great. Keep going and you'll get the equaliser, no worries,"' says Tony Brown. 'Ally Robertson had to tell him I'd just scored. Ron didn't miss a beat. He said, "Well, keep going and you'll get the winner, no worries." It took all the nervousness out of the situation. We were still laughing when we went back on the pitch.'

From the start, the make-up of the second half was different. West Brom wrestled the initiative and restricted United to intermittent attacks. These floundered on the rocks of a stout defence marshalled by Wile and Robertson. Cunningham propelled his side forward, slicing through United's ranks at will. The booing was heard more often now and it was louder in volume. At one point it was being directed at Regis and the ball ran out of play. Sinstadt seized his chance. 'Once again there's some unsavoury booing of the black players,' he noted in his commentary, adding, 'which says nothing for their sportsmanship at all.'

His words seem mild now, but it was then a taboo to report the racist abuse that was being regularly meted out to black footballers in the British game, and Sinstadt broke it. His was a lone voice. In the subsequent press coverage of the game, there was no mention made of the barracking that Cunningham, Regis and Batson were subjected to at Old Trafford. In that regard, it was business as usual.

'It's the one thing that sticks out most in my mind,' Sinstadt says now. 'There was this almost *laissez-faire* attitude to the abuse of black players. It was sort of accepted, which worried me greatly. I determined that I was going to have a go about it at some point.

'You have to bear in mind that other than the FA Cup final and England–Scotland games, there were no live matches on television. It was all edited highlights. Even with a great game like that one, you were lucky to get thirty minutes of it on air. So if you intended to have a go about something, you had to judge when there was the most reasonable chance of it making the edit.

'That was in my mind during the game. I recall the perfect situation arising when the move began that led up to West Brom's first goal. I was aware of the sound coming from the terraces and I started to speak, but the priority was to go with the goal. I never had the same opportunity again when I was absolutely sure that what I said would be broadcast. In a way, it still disappoints me that I wasn't able to make a stronger point. But I got no comeback from what I said, either from ITV or the viewers.'

West Brom pressed on. Robertson had a header cleared off

the line by Greenhoff. Cunningham kept coming. On one mesmeric run he covered half the pitch and left three defenders behind. He was only stopped by a desperate challenge on the cusp of United's goal, the ball breaking to Regis. From twenty yards out, the centre-forward struck it first time and brought a spectacular diving save from Bailey.

The pitch had begun to cut up and it was almost impossible to predict which way the ball would bounce off the uprooted turf. This made it increasingly difficult for the players to bring it under control. But for Cunningham, that is. When he took it, and caressed it, the ball seemed fastened to his dancing feet. With thirteen minutes to go, he broke free again and made for goal. There was no stopping him this time. As Bailey advanced, he drilled the ball beyond the flailing keeper and into the far corner of the net to give his side the lead.

In the final minutes, Cunningham yet again stripped United's bedraggled defence. Sinstadt was moved to a second indelible reflection. 'And he's away again,' the commentator purred. 'To show that pace and grace and control.'

Considering this now, he says: 'I was thinking about Cunningham and Gareth Bale the other day. Because both of them went on to Real Madrid, but two more different wingers you couldn't imagine. Bale is all power, whereas Cunningham appeared to drift past people because his balance and footwork was so good. But then, he needed to be like that with the defenders that were around in his day. Otherwise he'd have ended up in the front row of the stand.'

This last dash of Cunningham's led to Albion's clinching goal. Off he went, down the touchline, leaving his attending full-back Stewart Houston for dust. The ever-willing Ally Brown accepted the ball from him and then rolled it into the box for Regis to come onto and hammer into the roof of the net. That was the final score: Manchester United 3–5 West Bromwich Albion.

'At that moment in time, we were playing above the ground,' says Atkinson. 'United's best player was their keeper, and by a mile. If it weren't for Gary Bailey, I honestly believe we'd have had ten goals or more that day.'

Regis celebrated his decisive blow with his arms spread wide and a huge grin across his face. He was rejoicing in the win, but then also perhaps hailing another, deeper victory. This had been won against the faction of United's support that had scorned him, and also Cunningham and Batson. This crowd and others like it. Never one to make a fuss about the abuse, Regis sucked it up outside of the game. But once on the pitch, he was able to look the mob in the eye. Look them in the eye and then beat them down.

There is one final moment from that afternoon that remains frozen in time. Atkinson and his Manchester United counterpart Dave Sexton were interviewed on the pitch after the game for the TV. Sinstadt asks Atkinson to nominate his man of the match. Atkinson replies: 'It would be a toss-up between one of the coloured front people and today, I think, Cyrille Regis.'

'Ah yes, we were still then referring to them as "coloured" players,' notes Sinstadt. 'In that period this was not offensive to many people. It was the black players themselves who made it known that they found it offensive.'

The result meant that West Brom ended the year just two points off Liverpool and breathing down their neck. This was shaping up to be a gripping battle for supremacy and between two contrasting ideologies: the ruthless perfectionism of Liverpool against the free spirits of West Brom. For the neutral, there was only one side to be on.

'I'm not even an Albion fan, but I couldn't wait to get home that night and watch the game against Manchester United,' says journalist Martin Swain. 'The sheer bravura of that side, the sweep of it, was just stunning. They also had that vulnerability that we Brits love to see in our teams.

'With regard to that particular contest with Liverpool, I'm reminded of the West Indies cricket team of the same era. It was a fairly joyless experience going to see them win Test matches in those days, because there were no cracks in their make-up. They had this kind of brutish efficiency. There was something of that about that Liverpool side too.'

'There is a common perception that the team was built by Johnny Giles, improved by Ronnie Allen and finished off by Ron Atkinson,' considers Bob Downing. 'I think that does Ron a great disservice, because he galvanised it. He got them playing football the way he wanted it played and everybody else longed to see it. Basically, it was the idea of, "If you score one, we'll get two."

'However, with that team it always comes back to the three lads – to Laurie, Cyrille and Brendon, because they broke the mould. I don't believe for a second it ever mattered to Ron what colour they were. All he cared about was that he'd got three very good players.'

It wouldn't be possible to follow the drama of Old Trafford, but there was nothing anti-climactic about West Brom's next game. This took place just two days later against Bristol City. The weather worsened the night before the match, and New Year's Day dawned chill and with a thick blanket of snow covering the Hawthorns pitch. This led to most other games in the country being postponed, Liverpool's among them. Atkinson saw an opportunity to reel the League leaders in and resolved that come what may, his side would play.

The Hawthorns ground staff and a band of willing supporters were rounded up to sweep snow from the pitch and terraces. Even then, the turf had been rendered bone-hard and treacherous by a sharp frost. It appeared a pointless task, but this didn't deter Atkinson. Just before Christmas he'd visited the Adidas factory in Strasbourg, France, and been shown a new brand of football boot specifically designed to be worn on Astroturf. Atkinson had ordered a consignment and he sent his team out to warm up for the game in them.

'The day before, I'd worn a pair of them for training,' he says. 'I'd said to Cyrille, "Look, I'm even better than usual." He was falling about all over the place, although to be fair he wasn't the best five-a-side player. The boys were out there in their new boots when the referee and the Bristol manager, Alan Dicks, came out to inspect the pitch.

'You'd never even entertain playing the game today and neither of them wanted it to go ahead. But there were 25,000 people in the ground by then. Bomber Brown went flying past us and shouted over to me, "Gaffer, this is brilliant!" I turned to the ref and said, "He's played 700 games – if he wants to go ahead, I'm happy with that."'

Atkinson had ensured the dice were loaded from the start. Bristol City was a dogged mid-table side, but one West Brom would have been expected to beat in regular conditions. With their players struggling to stand up, the Bristol cause was hopeless. The only surprise was that they kept the score to 3-1.

'Joe Royle, who's a big pal of mine, was the Bristol centre-forward,' relates Atkinson. 'Before kick-off, he came walking past the referee's room, outside of which was all this paving. I could hear his metal studs clattering on the concrete. He told me there was no way the game should be played under these conditions. I said to him, "Joe, if you think it's dangerous and don't want to get hurt, stand still." The first time he ran was in the seventy-fifth minute when Alan Dicks pulled him off.

'I actually think that was our best performance of the season. I'd told the lads it was going to be tricky and we'd have to help the ball on a lot. But I couldn't believe the quality of our play. Cantello was playing push-and-runs as if he were on the best surface at Wembley.'

It was a match meant for Laurie Cunningham above all others, and on that afternoon he was unplayable. He glided across the rutted pitch with the poise of a ballet dancer and showed off a conjuror's mastery of the ball. Admiring him in that moment, Atkinson was convinced that there was no greater talent to be seen in the English game right then.

'I had this one saying about Laurie,' he remembers. 'That he was so good he could run on snow without leaving footprints.'

Out in the country, 1979 began just as wretchedly as the old year had ended. Troops were put on standby to deliver petrol supplies as a result of the ongoing tanker drivers' dispute. Motorists and shoppers were launched on a fresh wave of panic buying. On 6 January, MPs demanded the emergency recall of Parliament to address a rising sense of hysteria. Escaping to football in the midst of this, and most especially the kind of thrilling football being dished up by West Bromwich Albion, was like finding a light in the darkness.

'That's a significant point,' says Pat Murphy. 'I can speak with authority on what a grim time it was, because I was working on the local TV news show *Midlands Today* and doing football reports for radio in Birmingham. Life was bloody hard for people and football was very, very important to a lot of them.

'What was it Marx said? The opium of the masses and all that. It's all there in terms of what football can do to unite people and give them a sense of purpose. That was definitely the case with that West Brom side. They were such a shot in the arm and made people feel good about themselves.'

'Those were really tough times in this area,' says author and Albion supporter Dave Bowler. 'The redundancy notices were starting to come out in 1979. It was miserable, but you could go to the Hawthorns and know that it was going to be exciting and you'd be entertained. I'd paid £10 for a season ticket to stand in the Smethwick End. That still is the best value I've ever had.'

The tremors set off by Atkinson's team and the presence of Cunningham, Regis and Batson were also now being felt in the wider culture. The makers of the popular table football game Subbuteo produced a West Brom team set that included three black figurines. Such was the attention to detail that one of these was given a moustache like Batson's. The club even registered in the annual appraisal of the cultural landscape outlined in the music paper *New Musical Express*.

'That was when I knew we'd cracked it,' says supporter John Homer. 'You opened up the *NME* and their "in" thing was West Bromwich Albion. That's your two loves right there, music and football. It was the ultimate show of respect and it'll stick with me to my dying day.'

Yet there was also a down side to the increased attention and acclaim. It fostered in Atkinson a craving for more, and he was impetuous about pursuing it. He was compelled to break the British transfer record, spending £516,000 of the club's money to sign David Mills from Middlesbrough. Mills was a decent footballer but no star, and he would never justify Atkinson's extravagant outlay. His arrival tipped the balance of the team, and in the shattering of his confidence one could also detect the breaking up of its foundations.

Not that this was on anyone's mind on 13 January. On that day the Baggies travelled to Norwich for a match that would send them to the top of the League. There was perhaps too much football in their legs and it was a scrappy performance, but a Regis goal earned a 1-1 draw to lift them a point clear of Liverpool. This was a peak for the team, but it also brought its three most striking components into the sharpest focus.

'It's very hard to tell people now what Britain was like then,' suggests Martin Swain. 'The country was undoubtedly far more racist. Look at the culture of the time with things like *Love Thy Neighbour* on TV. You didn't have black guys watching games. Or but for the occasional player, being in teams. Then this West Brom side appeared. To begin with they were almost like oddities, curiosities in a huge white landscape. That was one element. But the other thing was that they were exciting, swashbuckling and just bloody great.

'For me, it was all encapsulated by Regis. Cunningham was possibly a bit more erratic, but Regis was off the scale. For a huge number of white kids in Britain, he'd have been our first black hero. He was the first one that a twelve-year-old white kid would go out on the playing field and want to be. That's a massive thing. From a social point of view, this country hasn't produced a more important sporting team than that one. We've now got a multicultural country and I love it, and they're part of the reason why. That is their triumph.'

'There is a lot of truth in that,' concurs civil rights activist Derrick Campbell. 'Their skill on the football pitch was their currency, and it gave them a key to access people from different backgrounds and walks of life. I think a prevailing view was, "Can you believe that they're black?" They were so good and they were black. It was almost the "I can't believe it's not butter" moment. That alone created discussion and mystique.'

Chapter Eleven: The Three Degrees

From their perch on top of the Football League, West Brom's players and their manager must surely have allowed their thoughts to drift to the possible glories to come. It had been more than half a century since the club had won its solitary League Championship and there was now the promise of another, and in its centenary season too. This being the case, such wanderings were soon stilled as winter closed in and stopped them dead in their tracks.

The team was able to negotiate its passage into the Fourth Round of the FA Cup, doling out another thrashing to Coventry after a replay and with Brendon Batson scoring one of his very few goals. But then their season ground to a halt. Blizzards swept the UK during the last week of January, with drifts as much as ten-feet high closing a fifty-mile stretch of the M6 motorway in the Midlands. There were further heavy snowfalls and then temperatures plunged below freezing. Streets and parks and pitches were turned white and the air to ice.

Football fixtures around the country were wiped out. In the

seven weeks between the draw at Norwich that sent them to the summit of the table and the start of March when the weather at last broke, Albion were able to play just two League games. Even more damning than this enforced state of inertia was the frustration of knowing that their rivals Liverpool were untroubled by it. With the ambition and foresight of champions, the Merseyside club had installed undersoil heating at its Anfield ground. Unlike the Hawthorns, their pitch wasn't ravaged by frost, and the Liverpool machine was kept ticking over.

The Reds had reclaimed their lead in the League and charged six points clear of their challengers by the time West Brom got back into action. This landed them a damaging psychological blow. In due course, the resulting fixture backlog would exert an ever-greater physical toll on the Baggies. All they could do in the meantime was turn up for training: five-a-side games in the snow if the team was able to clear the pitches at Spring Road. Then off to the pub. Round and round this same routine went, momentum dying on the vine.

'We'd just come through that period where we'd beaten Arsenal, Manchester United and Bristol City and had five wins on the bounce,' says Atkinson. 'In that spell, I think we could've overcome any team in Europe. If it weren't for the weather, I still believe we'd have gone on to win the League that year. In fact, I think we'd have been out of sight by the end of February. But there you go.'

The bleakest picture of all was forming across the country. At the start of January, Prime Minister Callaghan rushed back from a conference in the Caribbean in an effort to calm the mounting unrest. Landing at Heathrow Airport, he tried to put on a jocular front when confronted by reporters. This gave rise to the defining newspaper headline of the time, on the front page of the *Sun* on 10 January. It spoke of a government fatally disconnected from the mood of its people and of events spiralling out of control, and it ran to just three words: 'Crisis? What crisis?'

On 22 January, Britain was hit by its biggest day of strike action since the General Strike of 1926. This mass walk-out was led by public sector workers who were protesting their proposed wage increases and thousands of whom stayed out indefinitely. Public transport was stopped. Ambulance drivers were reported to be refusing to take 999 calls and the army was drafted in to provide a skeleton service. Almost half of the hospitals in the country were restricted to treating emergencies.

As this stand-off progressed, two particular disputes encapsulated all the fear and loathing of the time. A strike by refuse collectors led to local authorities running out of space to store waste and being forced to use local parks instead. Litter piled up on the streets. In London, Westminster Council co-opted Leicester Square as a default rubbish dump. The *Evening Standard* newspaper was soon reporting a plague of rats being attracted to the area. A separate action by the nation's gravediggers carried with it the threat of still more gruesome consequences. The media cranked this up by running a spate of stories about the looming prospect of Britain's dead going unburied.

At West Brom, Ron Atkinson resolved to lighten the air by hosting a party for his team and their wives and girlfriends at his new house on the outskirts of Birmingham. This was a break with established tradition. None of the players could recall ever being invited to the home of a manager. On arriving, they were impressed by the grandeur of Atkinson's pile relative to their own more modest dwellings. Each of them took in the expansive driveway and the big Jag parked out front, and the heated swimming pool round back, concluding that Atkinson had gone 'posh'.

The party was in full swing and running to the next morning when Laurie Cunningham, Cyrille Regis and Tony Godden determined to have a race in the pool. Before going in, they had to break the ice that had encased it for weeks.

'We asked Ron if he minded and he shot back, "I don't give a shit; you're the ones who are going to freeze,"' recalls Godden. 'The girls were waiting at the end of the pool with glasses of brandy to warm us up.'

'I remember Laurie and Cyrille diving into the pool and I always said Tony Godden dived over it,' says Atkinson. 'It was frozen over again the next morning. I stood there thinking to myself that four hours ago I'd had three of my best players in it. Later the same night, I'd got a phone call from the police. Someone else who was at the party had been arrested for drunk driving.'

Nicky Brown went to the party with Cunningham. Like him, she'd grown used to the social whirl that carried on at a football club, but she was also able to stand outside of it. From this perspective, there was more to be taken in than high jinks and the sometimes bawdy celebration of men in their prime of life. On that particular night she was able to behold all that Ron Atkinson had become, just as on others like it she faced up to starker realities.

'Champagne Charlie with his gold bracelets, he was having a power rush,' she says of Atkinson. 'The club had bought him a big new house and his wife was wearing furs. He was in the newspapers all the time. Money and women are best friends, so all of a sudden he was surrounded with all this stuff. It takes a big person not to get carried away with it. You can't blame the man for it.'

'Bert Millichip also threw a garden party for the team each summer. We all went into the pool at one of those as well. That was to prove that blacks don't sink. That was said somewhere along the way. There was another party we were at around that time that I remember vividly. I was sat in a group with the chairman of another club and he hadn't realised who I was. He told us that niggers would soon be taking over football and that he'd never allow one of them in his team.'

There was just one game that West Brom could then be certain of going ahead and this was their return fixture with Liverpool. Set for 3 February at Anfield, it was drummed up as a straight shoot-out for the title, and for Atkinson and his men the timing of it could scarcely have been more inopportune. It had been three weeks since their last competitive match, and in the interim the club had been hit by a bout of cold and flu, which further debilitated them.

At the best of times, going to Anfield represented a formidable challenge. In more recent seasons it had been made to seem impregnable. Like a well-fortified citadel, the sight of its walls rendered raiders impotent and powerless. Most visiting teams were overcome before a ball had even been kicked. Liverpool had gone fifteen home games without defeat so far that season, conceding just three goals. Spurs had left fortress Anfield on the wrong end of a 7-0 pummelling and Derby went down 5-0. Even in their pomp, it would have been a tough task for West Brom to grab a result there. In their current state of ill-preparedness, it seemed to be asking the impossible of them.

Atkinson's team had carried all before them for months, but the weeks of inactivity had blunted their edges. Recognising this, and being ruthless in pressing home an advantage, Liverpool went for the jugular. In the opening exchanges, they harried and pressured their visitors and were soon dominating them. With red shirts swarming around his team and shots raining in on their goal, Albion captain John Wile tried to rally his troops. 'Come on lads,' he roared, 'circle the wagons!'

West Brom held out for twenty-one frantic minutes before being breached. Once again, it was the devilish Kenny Dalglish who put them to the sword. David Fairclough, the Liverpool 'super-sub', added a second not long after half-time. Game over, it seemed.

On the end of a beating, West Brom appeared toothless. Cunningham was subdued and out of sorts. Regis cut an even more frustrated figure. More than anyone, he needed to have built up a head of steam. Forced into a standing start, he was misfiring badly. Had he faced a straight battle of strength against a brutish defender, as was the case most weeks, he might even then have prevailed. Instead, he ran into the exception to the rule. A majestic-looking Scot with the glare of a hawk, Alan Hansen relied on speed, skill and his football brain to best opponents. This he did almost as a matter of course. He had Regis in shackles from the start to the end of the game, cutting off West Brom's most direct route to goal.

'There are two types of defender, the hard men and the more intelligent footballers,' says Regis. 'I could handle the ones who wanted to kick me. The horrible ones were the guys who could read the game and knew when and how to step in front of you. And Alan Hansen was the very best of these.'

Shorn of the fulcrum of their attack, West Brom reeled like a boxer trapped on the ropes. But with the clock running down, Ally Brown poached them a goal back and hope sprang again.

Scrapping to the bitter end, almost unbelievably they carved out a second chance right on the verge of the final whistle. It fell to Cunningham. It was the sort of climactic moment that brought him to life: the ball at his feet and salvation in his gift. Before and after, this was when he could be relied upon to pull off an act of magic. A feat that would lift voices, make hearts soar and suck the air out of a stadium. But not now, not when he was required to do so most of all.

Now Cunningham's nerve failed him and the chance went begging, and for Albion, with it the game. There would be darker days and nights ahead for Cunningham. In the longest and loneliest of these, did his thoughts race back to the crucial point in this one game and keep picking at it like a scab? In those few fateful seconds at Anfield was he able to determine the cold, hard truth that would haunt him to his ruin? That he had got as far as the line marking out true greatness, but been unable to cross over it.

The game was well enough summed up in contemporary newspaper reports. Writing in the *Daily Mail*, Ray Matts concluded: 'This clash between English football's royal family and the exciting new aristocrats took on a cup atmosphere with a 52,000 full house and thousands locked outside . . . But some [of the West Brom] players, notably Cyrille Regis, appeared to be over-awed by the occasion.' However, a bigger picture revealed itself in the immediate aftermath of the contest. Slumped on the blood-red coloured benches of the 'away' dressing room, the West Brom players sat together in dead silence. Deflated, it was as if all belief had seeped out of them.

In this single but most shattering loss they had felt their dream of ruling English football being crushed. For all the miles, mud and matches they had battled through, it had taken just ninety

171

minutes for that hope to be extinguished. That these were ninety minutes that ill-luck had deprived them of proper preparation for made the fact all the harder to bear. Normally, the next week would have brought another game and with it the chance to work a defeat out of their system. However, the 'big freeze' was unrelenting, and instead the bitter aftertaste of disappointment hung around like a bed smell. Like an open wound, it became infected with a sense of fatalism and self-doubt.

There were other setbacks, minor in comparison, but these might also have suggested to them that their wondrous moment had gone. Cunningham had been called up to the full England squad for the first time, for a European Championship qualifier against Northern Ireland on 7 February. The last West Brom player to represent the national team had been Tony Brown, who won his first and last cap against Wales in 1971. To have one of their own crowned at the highest level would also bestow recognition on the achievements of the club as a whole. But for the time being at least, this was still not forthcoming. In the event, Cunningham never made it onto the Wembley pitch. For this game and too many others in the future, Peter Barnes from Manchester City was preferred in his place. Barnes was a skilful if fleeting winger, but he hadn't an ounce of Cunningham's inspirational ability.

The very same week, Brian Clough made Trevor Francis Britain's first million-pound footballer when signing him for Nottingham Forest from Birmingham City. This dwarfed the sum Atkinson had shelled out for David Mills just a month earlier to set the previous transfer record, and Clough had got his hands on a much more influential player. For the Albion manager, it was as though he'd been betting on a poker hand of Kings and then discovered his rivals were holding Aces.

After their reversal at Liverpool, another three weeks drifted by before Atkinson's team were again called into action. This was for a home game against Leeds. They controlled it for long periods, but lost. The result dropped them to fifth in the League, with Liverpool now growing distant on the horizon and the title slipping through their fingers like melting snow.

February passed into March, snow and ice turning to rain. Atkinson continued to scheme for ways of keeping his club in the public gaze and it was then that he alighted upon the Three Degrees. An all-girl singing group from Philadelphia, they had formed in 1963 and been signed to the Steel City's foremost soul and R&B label, Philadelphia International Records. A couple of prodigious black music impresarios presided over International, Kenny Gamble and Leon Huff. They had meant for the Three Degrees to be their version of the Supremes, Berry Gordy's flagship act at Motown.

The Three Degrees line-up had revolved through the years, but in 1976 it settled on its most familiar incarnation. This was of Helen Scott, Valerie Holiday and their statuesque focal point, Sheila Ferguson. The group was now working with famed disco producer Giorgio Moroder, and enjoying a string of UK hits. The previous year, Prince Charles had declared them his favourite pop act and they had performed at the heir to the British throne's thirtieth birthday party in a blaze of publicity. At the point of Atkinson's interest in them peaking, the Three Degrees were touring the UK and due in Birmingham for a date at a club called the Big Night Out. Using Cunningham, Regis and Batson as bait, he invited them to the Hawthorns and arranged a photocall to record the occasion.

'I just remember hearing through our press agent that there were three black guys playing for West Bromwich Albion,' recalls

Valerie Holiday. 'I was in love with soccer at the time, so I knew of them as a team. We were going to be in the immediate area opening a shopping mall, so it seemed like a fun thing to go and do. And of course, we were very flattered to be asked.'

Warming up the local press for the visit, Atkinson told them he'd got his own version of the Three Degrees. The real thing arrived at the Hawthorns on a damp, overcast afternoon during the first week of March. They were shown around the dressing rooms and introduced to the three footballers who'd now become their namesakes. The six of them were made to look as if they had swapped white fur coats and striped West Brom shirts and then led onto the pitch to face a phalanx of reporters and photographers.

'For us, it was a case of trying to get to know the guys while the pictures were being taken,' says Helen Scott. 'I thought the three of them seemed a little shy. But it was awkward for all of us, because we didn't know what all these press guys wanted from us.'

The resulting photographs were splashed over the pages of the *Evening Mail* and the *Express & Star* on 10 March. In these, the players and pop stars are draped over each other and smiling for the cameras. Caught out of their natural environment, Regis and Batson both seem stilted and uncomfortable in striking a pose. Cunningham on the other hand wears a look of insouciant cool, as if this was how he composed himself every day of the week. 'West Bromwich Albion's Three Degrees meet the three sizzling singers,' gushed the accompanying copy. In total, the story now has the tone of an ancient relic dug up from an altogether different and less enlightened era.

'If you think about it now that seems such a racist thing to have done,' concurs Martin Swain of the *Express & Star*. 'Look at the photograph: they've got the three of them dressed up like New York pimps. But it was of its time. There's a harmless, non-malevolent air to it too.'

'I suppose there was a perverse sense that the "Three Degrees" was used as a term of endearment,' notes Derrick Campbell. 'But in the black community, we saw it as an act of ridicule.'

Still, the association endured. The following month the pop group were the club's guests at the Hawthorns for a League match against Everton. That night, Regis, Cunningham and other Albion players accompanied them to Holy City Zoo, the popular Birmingham club that was owned by the Aston Villa striker Andy Gray. Regis turned up in his second-hand car, his newest friends in a chauffeur-driven limousine. Batson declined to join them.

'I'd got embarrassed by it to be honest,' he says now. 'It was just so contrived. It was a form of affection and it wasn't done in a derisory way, but it got too much. I was a married man as well. It also went on too long and there was resentment in the dressing room at the focus on us. That wasn't the case with everybody, but with certain of the more senior players.'

At Holy City Zoo, the partying ran deep into the night and moved on from there to Cunningham's place. En route, Regis was tailing the Three Degrees' black Daimler when he lost control of his car on a deserted side street and pranged it. This kind of mishap had become a regular occurrence. By Regis's own estimation, around this period he was stopped and breathalysed on at least thirteen occasions. 'The police would let me off when they recognised who I was,' he wrote in his autobiography.

He wasn't unduly troubled by this latest scrape. Just as he did on the football pitch, he picked himself up and got on with it.

He'd also shrugged off whatever discomfort he'd felt at the earlier photocall. That night, he sensed a kindred spirit in Sheila Ferguson and the two of them zeroed in on each other.

'I know the two of them dated a couple of times after that,' says Helen Scott. 'I'm not sure anything came of it, but they remained friends. There was a club in London that we knew of and which was a bit more private. Later on Cyrille came by there to see us whenever we were in town, but not so much Laurie.'

The rock guitarist Eric Clapton was another to be found hanging around the West Brom team at this time. He'd begun turning up in the players' lounges at their London games and even took out a full-page advert in the club's centenary brochure to proclaim himself their 'Number One Fan'. Less than three years before, Clapton had made his infamous drunken tirade against immigration in Birmingham. Extolling the virtues of a team with three black footballers in it was perhaps a convenient way for him to repair his damaged reputation.

'Clapton gave us all gold-plated discs of one his albums,' recalls Regis. '*Slow Down*, was it? No, *Slowhand*. I've still got it around somewhere, or at least my ex-wife has.'

The team was presented with the chance to bounce back in the League via an away match against the side they found easiest to suppress, Coventry. They did so 3-1, with David Mills making an encouraging full debut – one of his few noteworthy games in a Baggies shirt – and scoring the decisive goal. However, Ron Atkinson was pragmatic enough to know that Liverpool's lead over them was in all likelihood unassailable and that the FA and UEFA Cups now offered him the best odds of getting a tangible reward from that season.

West Brom flew out to Belgrade, then the capital of communist Yugoslavia, on 6 March for the first leg of their UEFA Cup quarter-final. Established in 1945 by a group of Serbian resistance fighters, Red Star Belgrade was the country's most successful club and had won their national title twelve times. They had first competed in continental competition in the 1957–58 season, reaching the quarter-finals of the European Cup where they were pitched against Manchester United. On 6 February 1958, the plane carrying United back from their away leg of the tie crashed on the runway at Munich airport, killing eight of Matt Busby's 'Babes'.

An uproarious crowd of 95,300 filled Red Star's vast concrete bowl of a stadium for the game with West Brom. For once, Atkinson set his team up not to concede a goal, and for more than eighty minutes they frustrated their hosts in a match characterised by niggling fouls and stoppages. But four minutes from time they gave away a cheap free kick on the edge of their own box and Red Star's prolific blond striker Dusan Savic, converted it. It meant that the Albion squad returned home frustrated, but with a by no means insurmountable deficit to overcome.

Next up was an FA Cup Fourth Round clash with Southampton at the Hawthorns, and again the margins were slender. In a tight, tense game, the visitors escaped with a 1-1 draw. The replay went ahead at Southampton's compact Dell ground just two nights later and finished with the teams sharing two goals again. But extra time caught up with weary West Brom legs and a late strike saw them off 2-1. It was now all or nothing in Europe.

Before then, it was back to the grind of the League. Less than forty-eight hours after being run ragged at Southampton, West Brom had to face bottom-of-the-table Chelsea at the Hawthorns.

The Midlands had endured a further heavy snowfall and a combination of meltwater and rain reduced the Albion pitch to a mud bath that night. Both sides laboured on it, the game becoming a war of attrition that the home side sneaked 1–0.

Two more close-fought victories followed against QPR and Derby. There was next to no free-flowing football to be seen at either of these games, each of them descending into a pitiless slog. It was Cunningham who dragged West Brom over the line in both, scoring two sublime goals.

'Against Derby, Laurie got the ball on the left-hand side of their box and bent it round the 'keeper with his right foot,' describes Atkinson. 'It's the sort of skill that's been cultivated now, but you didn't see it then.

'Big Jack Charlton was manager of Sheffield Wednesday at the time and he was at the game. He and I were talking after the match and he told me that Laurie would never score another goal like it. I took him into my office. We recorded the games on spools of film in those days. I dug the one out with the QPR match on it and said to Jack, "Here, watch this." Just two days earlier Laurie had scored an identical goal from virtually the exact same spot.'

Red Star came to town on 21 March. The Hawthorns was expectant, packed to its rafters. Under the glare of the floodlights, West Brom tore out of the gates and laid siege to the Belgrade goal. On forty-one minutes, a Regis header brought them back on level terms in the tie. The pulsating atmosphere turned feverish, nostrils filled with the scent of blood and glory.

Half-time came and went and still the flow of the game was all one way. Red Star's players tried to break up its rhythm with a series of fouls and time-wasting tactics. It worked to the extent that it frustrated the home team and the crowd, but it seemed

(left) 'Laurie was very much aware of the significance of playing for England. He loved his bacon sandwiches and roast dinner on a Sunday.'

(below) 'At that moment in time, we were playing above the ground …': Regis puts Manchester United to the sword during Albion's famous 5–3 victory at Old Trafford.

'Aye, he was a flash bugger ...': Ron Atkinson on the Great Wall of China, 1978.

Cunningham, Batson and team-mates on the ground-breaking but ill-starred 'Friendship Tour' of China. 'Big Ron described those three weeks as the longest three years of his life.'

Cunningham and West Brom
director John Gordon en route
to negotiating his transfer to
Real Madrid, summer 1979.

'That's all he ever wanted – the
world …': Real Madrid's star signing
is paraded at the Bernabeu.

(above) 'It was like living in a goldfish bowl …': Cunningham and girlfriend Nicky Brown's relationship didn't survive Madrid.

(left) With ex-West Brom team-mate Bryan Robson at Manchester United in 1983 and at the beginning of his wanderings. 'He'd changed. He wasn't as flamboyant,' says Robson.

Regis in the twilight of his career at Wolverhampton Wanderers, 1994: 'I have no regrets. Some decisions I made were right, some were wrong, but that's the way life is.'

(left) Forced out of the game by injury, Batson went on to become Deputy Chief Executive of the PFA and one of the game's most respected administrators.

(below) Regis, Batson and comedian Frank Skinner launch the 'Three Degrees' Celebration Statue, July 2013. 'The three of us in one team, it was iconic, it was radical. We changed the face of football.'

'He realised your dreams for you …': Regis in his pomp at West Brom.

'Pace and grace and control …': Laurie Cunningham as he is forever freeze-framed.

their armoury was otherwise empty. Yet still they hung on and still Albion strived in vain to land a knockout punch.

In the final minutes, Red Star fell back again into their own half. West Brom came after them, throwing men forward. There was no thought given to regrouping and coming again in extra time. Of course, it was a trap, and in their naivety and blinded by their desperation to claim a prize, West Brom walked right into it.

Red Star hurled the ball back up field. Three of their forwards gave chase. Hopelessly exposed, Ally Robertson was left to stop them. He tried, but in vain. Savic popped the ball past him and fired it into the net, clinical as an assassin. The goal was recorded at eighty-eight minutes. The Hawthorns fell silent as a tomb. It was another agonising defeat to absorb, another step too far.

'How many chances did we make that night?' asks Robertson, still hurting twenty-five years later. 'But that was also us not learning. Because we were battering them we kept on charging up field, going for goal and never thinking that they could score one as well. One thing is for sure, that would never have happened to Liverpool. They were used to being in that situation. They'd have settled for extra time and gone on and won the game from there.'

Time also ran out for Jim Callaghan at the end of that month. In the House of Commons, the Conservative leader Margaret Thatcher tabled a motion of no-confidence in his government. On a night of high drama on 28 March, Callaghan lost this by a single vote. The Prime Minister had declined to save himself by turning down a last-minute deal with the Ulster Unionists, the party to which Enoch Powell had defected.

A General Election was called for 3 May. This would soon enough lead to radical changes to the political and social landscape of the country. It remains a moot point as to whether or not these benefited the British people as a whole. Likewise, change would also be forced upon West Bromwich Albion at the end of that season. However, it is inarguable that this wasn't for the better of the club. In fact, it left it broken.

Chapter Twelve: Gone to Dust

The arrival of spring is a time of renewal and of new life coming to bloom. That year, it was also the ending of things at West Bromwich Albion. Their title challenge, their spirit, the team itself, all came undone. The events occurring on the football pitch were inevitable and unavoidable. The result of damage inflicted during the long, hard winter just past. What happened off it was more to do with the frailties and failings of men. These were of a lack of foresight and fortitude, and a commensurate surfeit of arrogance and hubris.

Even the recent past is a distant country and the structural framework of football in the late-seventies was very different to the game we now comprehend. Back then there were two more teams in the top division of the Football League and forty-two games to a season rather than thirty-eight. There was no such thing as squad rotation. Like the rest, the top clubs maintained a small playing staff to compete in the League and also domestic and European cup competitions. The game itself was slower, but also the pitches it was played on were heavier, more gruelling and energy sapping.

These were the circumstances that brought about Albion's doom at the climactic point of the 1978–79 season. Ron Atkinson was able to call on just fifteen players in all but two of their fifty-nine games during the campaign. He fielded the exact same side in more than half of these. The spate of cancellations through the winter left them with a fixture pile-up to plough through, when their meagre resources were drained and running on empty.

'We were playing two, three times a week,' says Derek Statham. 'We were all of us out on our feet, tired and jaded.'

Their breaking point was in April. Eight games in twenty-four days. Two of these were on consecutive days at Easter. Deep down there was a collective belief in the dressing room that Liverpool were now beyond catching, but still they summoned the will for one last push. It ran to sixteen games; none of these free-flowing and all of them ground out. For all the plaudits won for their attacking football, Atkinson insisted that this team of his could also win ugly. That it had guts as well as great craft. Here was the proof. They lost just once. However, that defeat came in the game they could most ill-afford to lose.

Easter was begun with a battling 1-1 draw at Southampton, Regis scoring. The next day, Good Friday, brought about the same result against Arsenal at the Hawthorns. Then there was hope and something to grasp at. Liverpool travelled to the West Midlands on Easter Sunday to face Aston Villa and got beaten 3-1. On the following Monday, West Brom went to Bristol City knowing a win would bring them to within four points of the League leaders and with a game in hand on them: striking distance.

The scene was set for a triumph. Ten-thousand supporters followed the team down the M5 motorway and poured into

Bristol's Ashton Gate ground in a sea of blue and white. At the turn of the year, at the zenith of their season, West Brom had run rings around these same opponents, waltzing in the snow at the Hawthorns. However, this side was now the ghost of that one. Their legs had turned to lead and their will was exhausted. In the stands and on the terraces, the massed ranks tried to bring them back to life, as if the noise of their voices might be a magical elixir. Their fervent support and the hard slog of games, the sweat and strained sinew, all of it was in vain. Bristol ran out 1-0 winners with Cunningham and Regis passing through the game like shadows. And that was that, their race run, the flickering embers of their season gone to dust.

The formalities of it still had to be completed. Six more games running to the middle of May. Nothing left to play for but the consolation prize of finishing closest to Liverpool. The dramas now being played out happened off the pitch and in the background, and these were just as ruinous. At this time clubs held players to short-term contracts and negotiated these at the end of each season. It was a widely held belief that the Albion board of directors were parsimonious in such matters. Or, to be more accurate, it was said that the club was run as if it were a corner shop.

True or not, the fabric of the team began to be unpicked. Len Cantello, who'd joined West Brom from school in 1967, handed in a transfer request. Atkinson accepted it. Undervalued to the last, Cantello was lined up for a move to struggling Bolton. One or two of his team-mates suggest Cantello's wife was homesick for her native Lancashire and he was acting to save his marriage. Cantello disputes this.

'Bluntly, it was over money,' he insists. 'I was tired of seeing other players being brought into the team and getting paid double what I was on. I wasn't envious, but I wanted the club to be fair. To be honest, it was the worst decision I've ever made. But you make your bed and lie in it.'

'A lot mistakes were made at that time,' says John Wile. 'Len was a very, very good player and critical to our team. He wanted something like £10, £20 a week extra, and the club wouldn't give it to him.'

The second contract rebel was Cunningham. He had grown frustrated with the club's lack of haste in offering him a new deal. Moreover, he was on just £120 a week and like Cantello was aware of a significant disparity in what he was being paid compared to others in the team, Regis among them. According to Nicky Brown, he took counsel from Albion director John Gordon. In Brown's telling, Gordon advised him to seek a move and with his help 'we kind of cleverly put it out there that Laurie was looking to leave.' Gordon seems to have concluded that this did not represent a conflict of interest on his part.

Cunningham's potential availability peaked Real Madrid's interest most of all. The Spanish giants were on the point of winning their nineteenth La Liga title and wanted to sign a star player from overseas to propel their tilt at the following season's European Cup. Real had held a virtual monopoly over Europe's premier competition in the fifties and early sixties, but it had been thirteen years since they had last lifted the trophy. Fresh in the minds of the club's powerbrokers were the memories of how Cunningham had torn Valencia to shreds.

Bands of scouts were dispatched from Madrid to watch West Brom's remaining games. They were conspicuous at the Hawthorns in their dark overcoats and darker glasses, looking like Mafioso. A move to Spain's most extravagant club promised to make Cunningham rich beyond his wildest dreams. This was at a time when the average cost of a house in Britain was £13,650. Inflation had risen to 17 per cent, hiking the price of a pint of milk to 25p and a gallon of petrol to 79p. The gap between the incomes of the highest and lowest earners in the country had narrowed to its closest-ever point.

'Of course, there was the money,' says Brown. 'Laurie was always thinking about the bigger picture. He'd come from a family of real hard workers who'd fought to make their way in the world. He thought of what he would be able to do for them.

'But it didn't matter that much to him. Because he knew by then that it was just a means to access stuff, that it didn't buy happiness. He would be fine so long as there was still the funk, the soul and the reggae and we had our six dogs. He was also a curious man. The prospect of going to Spain was like getting a new job, or having a promotion. Plus, how about living in the sunshine and learning to dance the flamenco?'

Keith Cunningham puts it more simply than that: 'My brother always said that he'd have gone to Real Madrid for nothing.'

Britain was riven with agitations, tensions and troubles as the decade drew to a close. On 23 April, St George's Day, the National Front staged a rally in Southall, west London. The district was targeted on account of its vibrant Asian community and potential to be a flash point. Events came to a head at a meeting the NF held at the town hall. As this was going ahead, the building was surrounded by 3,000 protestors drawn from the local community and also such activist groups as the Anti-Nazi League and the Socialist Workers' Party. This crowd was met by another almost as large comprised of police officers.

At a certain point, members of the Metropolitan Police's

Special Patrol Group moved to break the gathering up. Officially, they were armed with batons. However, it was later claimed that coshes, crowbars and sledgehammers were found in the lockers of some of the officers involved. In the resulting melee, Blair Peach, a 33-year-old who taught special needs children at a school in the East End, was pursued down a sidestreet and beaten to death. No one was ever charged with his killing. A second protestor, Clarence Baker, singer with the reggae band Misty in Roots, was also struck on the head and remained in a coma for five months.

Margaret Thatcher and her Conservative Party swept to power in the General Election less than two weeks later. Thatcher had adopted a hard-line stance on immigration and this succeeded in gutting the National Front of all but its most extreme support. The NF won less than 200,000 votes in the election, a mere 0.6 per cent of the national total. This rolled back the gains the party had made in previous polls and marked the end of it as a force in mainstream politics.

However, it didn't follow that the cancer the NF had spread had been cut from the national debate. Voters in the Portsmouth North constituency returned the Tory candidate, Peter Griffiths, as their new MP – a position he retained for the next eighteen years. This was the same Peter Griffiths who'd fought and won the Smethwick seat in such contentious circumstances in the 1964 poll. The same Peter Griffiths who'd later written of his time in the West Midlands: 'I myself have watched West Indians in large cars arriving at the office of the Ministry of Labour in Handsworth to draw their weekly allowances of unemployment pay . . . It is a galling sight to hard-working people.'

Along the south coast from Portsmouth, Jeremy Thorpe was turfed out of the North Devon seat he'd held for twenty years.

Thorpe had run a hopeless campaign. Just five days on from the election, the former Liberal leader went on trial with three other men for the attempted murder of his alleged gay lover. All the moral squalor of the period seemed to find a place to reside in Court One at the Old Bailey. Billed as the 'Trial of the Century', it ran for three weeks, at the end of which Thorpe and his fellow defendants were acquitted on all charges. Thorpe hadn't given evidence, so a jury never got to hear his side of the story, or him be cross-examined on it.

'But the key man was Thorpe's fellow defendant, David Holmes,' says former *Sunday Times* reporter David May. 'He was also gay and had been best man at Thorpe's wedding to his first wife. Holmes didn't give evidence either, but later told his story to the *News of the World* saying that he had acted at Thorpe's incitement, but only to frighten and not kill Scott.'

The final week of West Bromwich Albion's season began with a lacklustre defeat at Spurs. This had been preceded by four straight victories that had kept Liverpool in sight, but still tantalisingly out of reach. Their remaining League game against Nottingham Forest would determine which team finished second best to the champions. It was scheduled for a Friday evening, 18 May. Two nights beforehand, Len Cantello had his testimonial game at the Hawthorns.

These fixtures were regular dates on the football calendar. The vast majority of players were still making no more than modest earnings out of their short careers in the game. In granting their most loyal servants the gift of a testimonial, clubs allowed some of them to fortify themselves against a long and looming retirement. There was a standard format to the games and in the normal course of things they passed without incident or making a ripple. The host club invited a guest team to participate in a friendly match in honour of the player being recognised, and this went ahead in a convivial atmosphere.

In contrast, the very idea of Cantello's testimonial stirred up waves. The conception of it pitched an all-white West Brom team against an 'all-blacks' side made up of Regis, Cunningham, Batson and other black footballers then playing in the English game. It prompted an outcry from various anti-racism groups. Their fear was that the separatist nature of the two teams would bring an equally divided crowd to the match and encourage widespread abuse to be directed at its black participants.

'The lads on the organising committee had just wanted to do something completely different,' says Cantello. 'Don't forget, our five-a-side games in training were always the English lads versus the rest, or old 'uns against young 'uns. So we got together with Cyrille and asked him if he thought he could pick a team to beat us. He said that he could and without a shadow of doubt.

'There was never a thought that it would be a problem or an issue. We were all on the same side. We didn't look at each other as black, Irish or whatever; that didn't come into it in that particular dressing room.'

In the event, the match was a success. It took place on a shirt-sleeves evening and before a good-natured crowd of 7,000. Speaking to the *Daily Mail* in 2012, Batson recalled looking around the Hawthorns terraces before kick-off and seeing 'more black and Asian faces than we would normally get for a League game. It was anything but divisive. None of us had felt uneasy about the idea or hesitated for a second.'

Batson and his team took to the field in brilliant all-white strips. Among the others in the side were two central defenders from Wolves, Bob Hazell and George Berry, Stoke City's upcoming striker Garth Crooks, Ian Benjamin from Sheffield

United and a couple of lads from Hereford United, Winston White and Valmore Thomas. There were also two youngsters drawn from Albion's youth ranks, Remi Moses and Vernon Hodgson. The eighteen-year-old Moses was the most highly rated of the club's new batch of recruits. Short but stocky, and with a crown of afro hair, he was a Manchester lad and a nippy, tough-tackling midfielder. He hurried and harried, snapped and bit. Cantello's game was his official coming out and after it he was soon enough saddled with a sobriquet as predictable as it was unwelcome: 'The Fourth Degree.'

The stories this group could tell, then and thereafter. Bob Hazell might have reflected on the abject poverty he'd hauled himself out of in Handsworth. No one from his home patch ever told Hazell he was the best footballer in the area, but he was doubtless the most committed. Within weeks of the next season starting, Garth Crooks would be able to recount how he'd scored a hat-trick for the England U21 team at Leicester City's Filbert Street ground and still got booed by a vociferous section of the home support.

These were the things that each of them shared and which ran to their core. The battles fought and the vicious slights that had been absorbed and that they were still expected to endure. Perhaps it was this that put steel behind their smiles in the team line-up photograph taken that night. One thing is for certain, they went out determined to win the game. And win it they did, 3-2.

'Oh, we were up for it, big time,' says Regis. 'Not just because it was black versus white. All of us just had that winning mentality. And looking back at that team now, those were the guys that were at the vanguard of black football.'

No one knew it just then, but this was also the last time Laurie

Cunningham would grace the Hawthorns. He picked up a knock during the game, which ruled him out of the Forest match. There were better, more memorable and dramatic games that season, but none that summed it up quite so well as this last one. Brian Clough's title holders had sneaked up on the rails in recent weeks to get within a point of West Brom. A win would push them into second place, whereas Albion needed only to avoid defeat to secure runners-up spot.

Like Cunningham, Bryan Robson was also injured and missing from the West Brom line-up. Forest meanwhile had one eye on the European Cup final that they would be contesting less than two weeks hence. Nonetheless, there was a crackle and fizz to the game. Albion had recovered their attacking bearings and Forest came on neat, tidy and purposeful. The two most cavalier teams in English football putting on a show, even it was for one of its least gilded honours. West Brom had the better of it, but spurned their chances. Forest took the best of theirs, Trevor Francis scoring late on, and to them went the spoils.

Forest went on to Munich and there beat the Swedish side Malmo to win the biggest honour in European football. There was nothing for the vanquished West Brom players but a dull, gnawing ache in the pit of their stomachs. This was the bitter realisation that they had taken so little from a season to which they had given so much. Reporting on the Forest match, the *Express & Star*, stuck a knife into raw wounds: 'Albion came to the end of their road last night and found they had taken a long trip to nowhere.'

'They were probably the best team never to win the Championship,' says reporter Bob Downing. 'A lot of them were convinced they were going to do it that season. To end up finishing third was an absolute choker. It knocked them for six.'

In such close proximity to the moment, this is what the Albion side appeared to be: glorious failures, but failures just the same. Of course, no one at the time could possibly have foreseen that the ultimate measure of them would not be made in games won or lost, or in the trophies that might have been but never were. It would not have been countenanced that this team, that season, changed British football more than any other before it or since. And as well, changed British sport in general and perhaps the whole damn country.

The sight of Laurie Cunningham, Cyrille Regis and Brendon Batson together in West Brom's stripes was the tipping point for a generation of British kids. It broke down for them the real and imagined barriers that had held them back. It spurred them into the game and brought to it zest, colour and a public face that more accurately reflected the make-up of modern Britain as a whole. Liverpool's title, Forest's European Cup, distant echoes now, all part of the normal hum and drum of sport. The clarion call that was begun at the Hawthorns continues to ring out far beyond that – loud and clear and indelible.

'At the time, those of us who just looked at the three of them as footballers thought, "God, they're good and aren't West Brom good now as well,"' says the broadcaster Pat Murphy. 'But as one looks back in retrospect, it all begins to fall into place. You remember the appalling racism at places like West Ham, Millwall and Chelsea. Obviously, there was great dignity shown there. And on that basis, they were pioneers and trailblazers, role models and examples. Call it what you will.

'That isn't to say that the three players would've thought that of themselves. Cyrille was humble because of where he'd come from. Brendon was intelligent and well grounded. He'd done his apprenticeship at Arsenal and been around the block. One might say Laurie was the exception. He was the kind of player that you didn't see much of at the time. But I perceived him as a quiet lad who just wanted to play football.'

'It's a cultural thing, not just a football matter,' adds journalist Chris Lepkowski, who now reports on the club for the *Evening Mail*. 'And speaking as an Albion supporter, I feel a tremendous sense of pride in that fact.

'One of the first matches I covered for the paper was at Portsmouth in 2002. At half-time, I was walking up to the press box at Fratton Park and chatting to a colleague. There was an old Jamaican guy coming up behind me. He must have picked up my accent and he tapped me on the shoulder. He told me that he wasn't a fan, but that he was there to see Albion. When he'd first arrived in England from Jamaica, he'd heard about this club with three fantastic black players. He said that he'd come along to pay his respects.'

At the end of the season, Regis and Cunningham did at least win recognition for their football. Regis was acclaimed 'Young Player of the Year' by his fellow professionals. It perhaps goes without saying that he was the first winner of the award to be black. He expressed a measure of embarrassment upon picking it up. He had scored seventeen goals during the campaign, but suggested that more than half of them had been created for him by Cunningham.

At the end of May, Cunningham made his belated debut for the full England team when Ron Greenwood selected him for a Home International against Wales at Wembley. The game itself was a turgid 0-0 stalemate that spoke volumes about the parlous state of the national team. It was not an environment that encouraged instinctive acts of daring or untamed mavericks such as Cunningham. He did show off tantalising flashes of his club form, but he was on a leash and a victim of Greenwood's rigid conformity.

He was cheered on by a small band of supporters in the stadium that night. Atkinson and Regis had driven down together from Birmingham for the game, and Cunningham had invited along his brother Keith and their childhood pal, Eustace 'Huggy' Isaie. These two parties collided in the Wembley players' lounge after the game and to the evident bemusement of Atkinson.

'It was kind of a strange experience,' remembers Isaie. 'We were all of us dressed up in suits, but I was wearing a West Brom Albion club tie that Laurie had given me. Cyrille came over to say hello to Keith and brought Ron with him. Ron kept staring at me with a puzzled expression on his face. He thought I was one of his fringe players, but he had no idea which one.'

Atkinson might not have been aware of it at this point, but Real Madrid had stepped up their pursuit of Cunningham. In Brown's account, the Spanish club flew Cunningham and her out to Ibiza straight after the Forest match.

'Real came and got us and hid us out on the island,' she claims. 'We needed some time to think things over. Cyrille joined us. We were staying in San Antonio and these were still kind of the hippy days of the town. There were lots of people wearing cheese-cloth and attempting to find themselves.'

This elaborate subterfuge continued on the night of the England-Wales fixture. A contingent from Real Madrid met with Cunningham, Brown and John Gordon in an underground car park opposite Wembley Stadium to begin discussing personal terms. These were concluded the following weekend when the couple and Gordon were flown out to Madrid to meet with senior officials from the club. This last trip gave rise to an enduring myth that Cunningham had gone to the Spanish capital of his own volition and knocked on Real's door, offering his services. This is no more credible than Brown's assertion that he was invited to play football with Bob Marley while they were on Ibiza. Marley did make a summer visit to the island, but in 1978.

Nonetheless, Cunningham left Madrid having determined his immediate future. He confided as much to Regis and Tony Godden at West Brom, and also to his England team-mate Viv Anderson before a World Cup qualifier in Bulgaria on 6 June.

'Laurie and I roomed together and normally I did all the talking,' says Anderson. 'He would keep to himself, even if it was just the two of us. But on this occasion, he was flicking through a car brochure and pointing out all the new Mercedes models. I thought I was doing well having a Mini.'

Formal talks between West Brom and Real Madrid were begun during the last week of June. Atkinson hosted these at his home and in the company of chairman Bert Millichip, the club's secretary, Alan Everiss and John Gordon. The Madrid delegation was led by Real's long-serving Managing Director, Antonio Calderon, who arrived determined to play hard-ball over the size of Cunningham's transfer fee.

'I'd asked Bert Millichip to let me be our lorry driver,' says Atkinson. 'I told Calderon that we wanted £1.5 million for Laurie. He offered £250,000. I had a little Yorkshire terrier at the time, never barked at anyone. But it started growling. I said, "See, even he knows how ridiculous that is."'

The two clubs eventually settled on a £950,000 fee. On 28 June, Cunningham was announced as the first Englishman to sign for Real Madrid. In the *Express & Star* that evening he was pictured alongside a beaming Atkinson and a more taciturn

Calderon. The latter is draped in one of the scarves that hawkers had done a brisk trade selling outside of the Hawthorns for the past two years. Stitched into it were four words: 'Laurie Cunningham is magic'.

'Laurie phoned me and told me to turn the TV on that night because he was going to be on the news,' recalls Bobby Fisher. 'He was always a bit over the top with regard to that sort of thing, so I just sort of humoured him. But he said, "No, no, I'm an overnight millionaire."'

Atkinson concurs with Brown and Keith Cunningham, maintaining that it wasn't possible for Albion to hold on to Cunningham once Real came calling. Perhaps, but then also the club believed he was replaceable and were eager to take the money on offer. Certainly, Atkinson's side was no one-man team, and Cunningham was a flashing comet. He played 114 games for West Brom and scored thirty goals. These were drops in the ocean next to the statistical contributions stacked up by such stalwarts as Jeff Astle, Tony Brown and, in due course, Cyrille Regis. Yet he brought something different to West Brom, a unique element without which the formula of the team could not be the same. At his best, he was devastating, explosive and without equal.

If the *Express & Star* is to be believed, the transfer moved him to make one of his most expansive public utterances. It quoted him as saying: 'It's a sad day for me. I have enjoyed my three years with Albion, but they messed me around so much when I attempted to get another deal that I felt my future lay at another club. With the World Cup finals taking place in Spain in 1982, I am hoping to get acclimatised and really make a bid for a place in the England squad.'

'It just needed for there to have been a little bit of dynamism and vision in the West Brom boardroom,' Regis says. 'They should have realised that they had a great side, players who were twenty-one and twenty-two years old and playing the kind of football that we did. Kept the nucleus of that team together and then added to it. Why muck it up?'

Regis contends that the Baggies could have kept hold of Cunningham had they acted earlier and made him a better offer. He was still just twenty-three and with time and his best years ahead of him. Had he remained, things would likely have turned out different for him and perhaps also for the club. But if not then, he would still have gone at some point. For all his apparent reticence, he had a grander vision for himself than slogging through the English mud.

From the time he first began kicking a ball about on the backstreets of north London, Cunningham looked to a distant horizon and a more wondrous idyll. He was withdrawn off the pitch, but on it he sought acceptance, attention and acclaim. All this and more than that, more even than mastering the game, through football he craved meaning and a reason for being. He believed he was never going to find that higher purpose by remaining in the West Midlands or in England, if at all.

'In all honesty, I don't recall Laurie ever standing up and saying he was going because of this or that,' says Brown. 'As much as anything, I think for him it was a case of, "Okay, there are more black players coming through in England now. This is happening. Let's go to the four corners and try something new." And certainly, I don't believe West Brom as a body, as a club, realised what they had until he'd moved on.

'I once told his mom, Mavis, that all I'd talked about as a child was of one day going off and travelling. She said to me, "That's all our Paul ever wanted too – the world."'

Chapter Thirteen: Too Much Too Young

The pre-season of 1979 was the last time West Bromwich Albion could be considered a big-spending club. Flush with Real Madrid's money, Ron Atkinson was allowed to plough it back into the rebuilding of his team. Ironically, his former running mate Malcolm Allison was just then embarking on a disastrous tenure as manager of Manchester City and had set about dismantling a promising young side. It was Atkinson's opinion that he was the major beneficiary of Allison's folly.

His first signing from Maine Road was Gary Owen for £465,000. The 21-year-old was a popular player with City's fans and also captain of the England U21 team. A bustling, ball-playing midfielder, Owen stood out on the pitch on account of his hunched posture and apparent lack of a neck. In acquiring him, Atkinson congratulated himself on a good bit of business. He believed he'd got a ready-made, but younger replacement for the departed Len Cantello.

'I'd got to know Cyrille, Bryan Robson, Derek Statham and also Laurie through the U21s,' says Owen. 'So I was aware of the potential that West Brom had and of the fact they had an exciting manager who let them play with flair and abandon. The attraction of going there at that time was the calibre of players like Regis, Robson and Brendon Batson.

'There's no two ways about it, Big Ron also has a silver tongue. He made it very clear to me how he thought my going there would enhance the team and help it to push on even further.'

Within weeks, Owen's City team-mate Peter Barnes had followed him to the Hawthorns for a fee of £750,000. Barnes was twenty-two at the time, a year younger than Cunningham, and Ron Greenwood's first-choice winger in the England side. Atkinson again felt able to trumpet that he'd improved the team. His third signing was John Deehan from neighbours Aston Villa. A strapping striker, Deehan had scored forty goals in 110 appearances for Villa and was also an England U21 international. He was expected to complement Regis and add greater firepower to the Albion attack.

There would be no arduous trip to the unknown before this season began. In the stead of China, Atkinson took his new-look team out to the Spanish Costa del Sol on a bonding exercise and to soak up the sun. He returned flush with optimism and to face a return match against the Chinese national team at the Hawthorns as a curtain-raiser to the forthcoming campaign.

'I remember Ron being very positive from the beginning, never showing any negativity,' says Barnes. 'Gary and I were both living in the Europa Hotel in West Bromwich at the time and Ron was also there on match day. After a pre-match meal, all the players went back to Ron's room and he stood there before us dressed up in his gold jewellery, an expensive watch and a nice suit. His team-talk was never complicated. He just told us to go out and attack.'

On a glorious summer's day, West Brom took up Atkinson's challenge and dismembered the hapless Chinese with a series of rapier thrusts. Owen and Barnes sparkled. David Mills came into the side for the veteran Tony Brown and for the briefest moment promised to be a commanding presence. The team as a whole prowled and purred. There seemed no reason to believe they wouldn't be a force to be reckoned with once again.

Yet for all Atkinson's bombast, doubts had begun to creep in among some of the more established players. These were as black and foreboding as the shadows extending across the Hawthorns pitch in the late-afternoon sun during that first match. Skipping past a lightweight Chinese team was all well and good, but they had the more revealing evidence of training and the close combat of the daily five-a-side games to go on. These told a different story. It suggested that Atkinson hadn't bought quite as well as he thought.

'We'd lost Len who was a grafter and Gary Owen never quite did that,' John Wile told writer Dave Bowler. 'He was like a dog with a bone for an hour, all over the show, but he faded late on in games. Peter Barnes was very erratic. Good players both of them, no question. But they weren't as consistent as the guys they'd replaced.

'John Deehan came in on a lot of money, more than the rest of us. He was twenty-two and living in a big house outside of Birmingham. People like Ally Brown, Alistair Robertson and me were ten years older, had smaller houses and were getting paid less. That upsets the dressing room. As a player, you don't mind so much if someone comes in and will give you thirty goals a season. But when they don't make a huge difference it eats away at the spirit of the team.'

'Why would you let Laurie go and buy Peter Barnes?' asks

Regis now. 'Why sell Len Cantello and get Gary Owen? It was bizarre. But it was out of our hands.'

There was a further ill omen to come out of the China game. During the course of it, Regis picked up a knock on his knee and had to be withdrawn. It soon became apparent that he'd damaged cartilage and would require surgery. This kept him sidelined for more than three months and in that time West Brom's season went from bad to worse. They won just once in their opening nine games in the League and crashed out in the First Round of the UEFA Cup 4-1 on aggregate to the unfancied East German side, Carl Zeiss Jena.

Liverpool brushed them aside 3-1 at Anfield, and Nottingham Forest recorded a crushing 5-1 victory at the Hawthorns. Deehan was proving to be a less than adequate stand-in for Regis and would go on to score just three goals all season. On 6 October, a 2-1 reversal at Middlesbrough sank them into the relegation places and on the same number of points as the bottom club, Bolton. The doubts that had been bubbling under in the dressing room burst to the surface.

'I fell out with Peter Barnes after one game,' says Tony Godden. 'He had all the skill in the world, but he was a lazy sod and not in Laurie's class. Ron will always say, "Well, I sold the reserve England winger and bought the man keeping him out of the side." But there was no comparison between the two of them. Barnesy said something to me in the dressing room after the game and I had a go back. Ron stepped in and the tea went everywhere. I ended up having a row with Ron. I told him he always defended the likes of Barnes and never his grafters.

'After a home match, the team and the press guys used to go for a drink in the Europa. Ron was sat at the end of the bar when I walked in that evening and the room went quiet. Everybody knew we'd had a bust-up. He shouted over to me, "TG, what do you want to drink?" I said, "A bottle of champagne, please." And that was it, finished. One thing about Ron, he never held a grudge.'

When Regis returned to the side results improved for a spell, but then went into free-fall again. Derek Statham wrecked his cartilage in the same game as Regis made his comeback and barely played again that season. David Mills vanished on the field and then from the team. A crestfallen Atkinson took to referring to him as his 'albatross'. Even the normally metronomic Batson struggled for consistency. Yet having each come into the team feeling like outsiders and as if they had everything to prove, he and Regis both now took a leading role in binding it together as it threatened to break apart.

'Both of them are terrific characters,' says Barnes. 'Brendon was a great talker in the dressing room. He was very serious about his game when he went out on the pitch, but a joker off it. He was always taking the mickey out of people and smiling and laughing. Cyrille was more of the silent type. Yet he was one of the lads who liked to go out on the town and have a few beers. He dressed in snappy suits. He was a nice guy, very charming and mild-mannered. But put him on the field and if someone upset him, he'd be like a man-mountain.'

'A lot of problems were sorted out in a social environment,' says Owen. 'That was more so with Cyrille than Brendon, because Brendon was a family man. You were able to say things over a beer or two in more relaxed surroundings that couldn't be said in the workplace.

'Cyrille was a joy to play with. He was so strong that you could knock the ball into him and know that he'd protect it and hold it up. Brendon was a great team player. He had pace and was a fine athlete. I can't remember a winger ever getting the better of him. He didn't get the international recognition he was due, because he was as good as any right-back in the country during that era. But next to the bigger clubs, West Brom was seen as being unfashionable. Phil Neal played for Liverpool and so he was the England full-back at that time. I remember the *Evening Mail* organising a petition to get Ron Greenwood to notice Bryan Robson's performances, but he had to leave the club in the end to make that breakthrough.'

The West Midlands birthed a blazing movement in youth culture that right then exploded out across the UK and marked the beginnings of a profound shift in the social make-up of the country. This was 2 Tone, and it was founded on a conglomeration of bands that rose up on the local club scene, and had its musical roots in the ska and rocksteady sounds originating from Jamaica in the fifties and sixties. At the forefront of this were the Specials, from Coventry, and principally their keyboardist, musical mastermind and all-round driving force, Jerry Dammers.

The son of a prominent clergyman, Dammers was born in India in 1955 and attended the well-heeled King Henry VIII School in Coventry. As a teenager he passed through phases as a mod and a hippy, before fixating on Jamaican music. He met bassist Horace Panter while studying art at the city polytechnic. Panter had also been seduced by ska's clipped beat, and the pair of them formed the Specials in 1977.

From the outset, Dammers determined that both the band and their audience should be multi-racial. The Specials' line up solidified over the next two years. Beanpole singer Terry Hall was a local lad who'd left school at fifteen to sing in a punk band called Squad, and he had the demeanour of a hangman. Guitarist Roddy Radiation (nee Byers) was plucked from the regional rockabilly scene and drummer John Bradbury had a background in soul and reggae. Each of them was white. Singer Neville Staple and guitarist Lynval Golding were both native Jamaicans whose families had brought them to the English heartlands on the cusp of the sixties. Staple's 'toasting' style, chanting over the band's effervescent rhythmic attack, gave the Specials their distinctive flavour.

In 1979, Dammers founded a record label to release the Specials' first single, 'Gangsters', a reworking of Jamaican ska man Prince Buster's 1967 hit, 'Al Capone'. Articulating Dammers's multicultural intentions, the label was christened 2 Tone Records and was characterised by the striking black and white colour scheme it used for its artwork and graphics. 2 Tone's soon-to-be iconic logo was based on a photograph of the Wailers' guitarist Peter Tosh: an attention-grabbing print of a man in a black suit, tie, loafers and pork-pie hat, with white shirt and socks.

'Gangsters' hit the UK Top 10 in the summer of 1979. It was swiftly followed by a string of landmark singles on 2 Tone. Birmingham band the Beat had a hit with their ska-themed take on Smokey Robinson and the Miracles' soul standard 'Tears of a Clown'. The Selecter also burst out of Coventry on the back of two rallying tracks, 'On My Radio' and 'Three Minute Hero'. They were fronted by the bewitching Pauline Black, who best of all symbolised 2 Tone's rich melting pot and the divides it set out to breach. Born to a Nigerian father and English mother, Black was adopted into a white family and brought up being unaware of her heritage. A seven-piece band from London, Madness, also joined the 2 Tone gold rush via their own tribute to Prince Buster, 'The Prince'.

2 Tone reached its climactic point in the autumn of '79. In October of that year, the Specials' self-titled debut album crashed into the UK charts. Produced by Elvis Costello, *The Specials* merged the ebullient sound of ska with the urgency and lyrical fire of punk. Bottled up in its songs were the frustrations and dissatisfactions of a British underclass growing up out of sight and mind on bleak and soulless inner-city council estates – the 'concrete jungle' of one of the album's defining tracks. Such an environment was home to the teenage girl in another of the record's standout songs, 'Too Much Too Young', and of whom Hall sang: 'You're married with a kid when you should be having fun with me.'

The next month, the Specials, the Selecter and Madness all performed on a single edition of the BBC's *Top of the Pops*. This sealed 2 Tone's crossover into the mainstream. The visual message being transmitted by a band such as the Specials was as potent as the one sent out by Cunningham, Regis and Batson at West Brom. Hordes of white school kids around the UK rushed to take up their look, wearing the uniform of Jamaican rude boys like a badge of honour.

'It was a special time, a sort of golden age of tolerance and togetherness,' says Ali Campbell, then recording UB40's debut album, *Signing Off*, which would make stars of him and his band the next summer. 'Yes, we had our problems with the National Front and the British Movement, but that was just the obvious politics of depression and the kids rebelled against it.

'What I saw developing then was a multiracial and multicultural society that looked as if it would go on to be even better. We were anticipating a rainbow nation, but that's all gone now. In the thirty years or so since then, very sadly I think we've taken on an American style of politics and got a generation now that is self-segregated. You've got white gangs, black gangs and Slavic gangs. In Balsall Heath, the Indian kids will chase you down the street with baseball bats or hockey sticks if you're white.'

However, and as Campbell freely admits, it wasn't the case that all of 2 Tone's audience embraced its utopian vision. 'UB40 actually shirt-tailed the movement,' he says. 'We were a reggae band, but we kept our heads down and got on ska-themed bills at places like the Electric Ballroom in Camden. The skinheads in the crowd used to '*Sieg Heil*' us and generally we'd come off stage covered in spit. But the thing that they hated us for was playing too slow. It was because of the make-up of the band that we had constant death threats.'

A further seismic event emanating from the Midlands during this same period got even more widespread attention. The trial of the four alleged killers of schoolboy Carl Bridgewater unfolded at Stafford Crown Court and in the full glare of the media. It took place in an alternate reality to the one in which Jeremy Thorpe had been judged earlier in the year. Patrick Molloy, James Robinson, Vincent Hickey and seventeen-year-old Michael Hickey had fallen through the cracks of British society and out to the margins. They were unemployed, petty criminals and odd-job men living from hand to mouth. On 9 November, the Stafford jury convicted Robinson and the Hickeys of murder and Molloy of manslaughter. Robinson and the two cousins were handed down life sentences and Molloy got twelve years. They left to serve them as the most vilified men in the country.

Yet the case against them was unravelled through the slow and painful passage of time. It was made clear how scant the evidence had been linking the four men to the scene of the crime. It was proven that the investigating police coerced Molloy into making his confession and implicating the others. The Hickeys' stated alibi gained credence as more witnesses were found to come forward. Two moves to appeal were rejected and one dismissed before Robinson and the Hickeys were at last set free on 21 February 1997. Molloy had died in prison sixteen years earlier.

The identity of Carl Bridgewater's killer or killers is still unknown, and the case remains unopened. During the long and wretched course of it, nothing was proven but for the fact that British justice of the time could be just as prejudicial against class as race.

West Bromwich Albion tumbled into the new decade in a mess. Twice beaten in the League, 4-0 at Ipswich on New Year's Day and 3-1 at Nottingham Forest, and turfed out of the FA Cup by Second Division West Ham. The Forest defeat left them hovering precariously above the relegation zone and facing a difficult-looking trip to Crystal Palace.

Atkinson wasn't one for chopping and changing his team. He had kept faith with his players to this point, trusting them to dig themselves out of the rut they were in. But he sensed the Palace game was a pivotal point of their season and took action, handing young Remi Moses his first-team debut. His reasoning was that the combative Moses would 'snap and snarl and keep everyone on their toes. The Palace game was a big one for us. If we lost it, I thought we might keep on falling.'

Going into the last fifteen minutes at Selhurst Park, West Brom trailed Palace 2-0. The home side had been bright and dynamic, full of zip and intent. For all Moses's additional energy, the visitors appeared bereft of confidence and were flailing like drowning men. They looked directionless and their cause hopeless, but somehow they found redemption. As the clock wound down, out of nothing, Ally Robertson got up for a corner and grabbed a goal back, his first in almost two years. Then Regis snatched an equaliser, wildly celebrated. These two quick strikes turned around not just this one game, but their whole season.

They suffered just two more defeats in their next seventeen games and had climbed to tenth in the League by the end of the campaign. Nevertheless, it still felt as though the flame that had burned so bright through the previous season had been dimmed. Liverpool had romped to the title again, and this West Brom team made no impression as timeless as that of the previous one had when led to victories at Old Trafford and against Valencia by a swaggering Cunningham. Remi Moses had at least emerged as a player for the here and now. He was a regular in the side after the Palace game and brought to it propulsion and a look of solidity.

The fact that Moses was black led people to stretch for comparisons between him and Cunningham, but there were none to be made on the pitch. Where Cunningham was smooth and fluid, Moses buzzed and darted, one legato and the other staccato. Cunningham struck like a cobra; Moses had the persistence of a ferret. One was a mercurial attacker and the other a grafting midfielder. It just so happened that both were guarded and introverted off the pitch and neither was destined to fulfil his great potential.

'When I first joined the club and was playing in the reserves, Big Ron asked me if there was anyone coming through that he should keep an eye on,' says Batson. 'I told him to put his money on Remi. He was extraordinary. His debut against Palace was the best I've seen from a lad that age. He wasn't the greatest socially and never said boo to a goose. But he was a tremendous footballer and like a quiet assassin on the pitch.'

Regis was also restored. He was again an immovable slab of muscle and menace, and with Cunningham gone he was now the centrifugal force of the team. There was a snapshot of him at his most imposing towards the end of the season: 8 March, versus Coventry City at Highfield Road. West Brom launched an attack along Coventry's right flank. The ball was sent spearing down the touchline and Regis gave chase at full throttle. Rushing across to meet him was Coventry's full-back Brian Roberts, looking like a Viking with his helmet of blonde hair and luxuriant moustache. Roberts came in low, side on and also at pace. At the point of impact, it seemed inevitable that he was going take both the ball and Regis into touch. But he didn't. Rather, he hit Regis and bounced off him, sprawling to the turf as if he'd just run headlong into a rock-solid barrier. Regis powered on, passed to Barnes and Albion scored.

'Brian told me he recalled making a clean contact with the ball and that was the last thing he remembered,' says Martin Swain, reporting on the game for the *Coventry Evening Telegraph*. 'He said he'd never felt anything like that in his life.'

There was also now a trickle of young black footballers coming into the game and making inroads at the top level. That season, Garth Crooks at Stoke City scored fourteen goals in a relegation battle and broke into the England U21 team. Vince Hilaire, a deft midfielder at Crystal Palace, was another to win U21 recognition. A South Londoner, Hilaire joined his local team from school and made his first-team debut for them in March 1977. Under manager Terry Venables, Palace had assembled a young, attractive side that won promotion to the First Division two years later and was hailed 'the team of the eighties'. Venables's abrupt departure to QPR the next season put paid to that fanciful notion, but Palace's best moments often as not came with Hilaire at the centre of things, and he was the supporters' 'Player of the Year' in 1980.

Born in Falmouth, Jamaica, in 1958, Luther Blissett was the third up-and-coming black player to ascend to the England U21 ranks in the 1979–80 season. A robust striker, Blissett was plying his trade at Graham Taylor's Watford in the Second Division. His goals had shot the Hornets to two successive promotions and he was top scorer again when Watford reached the top flight for the first time in 1982. By then, Blissett was a full England international and in 1983 he followed Laurie Cunningham out to the continent, joining AC Milan in Italy for £1 million. However, Blissett's direct style wasn't cut out for the Italian game and he returned to Watford after just one season.

Other, even younger players had made their debuts in the First Division. A cultured midfielder, nineteen-year-old Paul Davis had come through the ranks at Arsenal and took his first team bow in a North London derby against Spurs on 7 April 1980. Davis progressed to making 447 appearances for the Gunners up to 1995. Later on, he was joined at the club by two more skilful black footballers, David Rocastle and Michael Thomas. The three of them helped Arsenal to the title in 1989. Down the road at White Hart Lane, Chris Hughton, a Londoner of mixed race origin, began a long and successful career at full-back for Spurs. At Coventry, teenage defender Danny Thomas was introduced to the first team and became a regular in the side the next season. He went on to link up with Hughton at Spurs, from where he also won two full England caps.

Nonetheless, such breakthroughs were still few enough in number to seem out of the ordinary, and there remained a dearth of black faces at some of the biggest clubs in the country. Tony Whelan, a local lad from Salford, had been on Manchester

United's books in the late sixties but didn't appear for the first team in a competitive game. Two more seasons would pass before a black footballer broke that bar at Old Trafford – when United signed Remi Moses from West Brom. At Liverpool, a Toxteth lad, Howard Gayle, flitted into the team in October 1980, but it wasn't until John Barnes arrived at the club in 1987 that significant progress was made in that regard. It took even longer for that to be the case at Everton. Two black players, Mike Trebilcock and Cliff Marshall, each made a handful of appearances for the club in the sixties and seventies respectively. But it took the signing of the Nigerian international Daniel Amokachi in 1994 for an unspoken apartheid at Goodison Park to be smashed.

In stark contrast, the experiences black players had of being subjected to racist abuse through the game weren't isolated. This remained rife in football. At Wolves, George Berry enjoyed an otherwise fulfilling season. His performances for his club caught the attention of his adopted country, Wales, and he was selected for a European Championship qualifier against West Germany. He might even have begun to feel part of the furniture at Wolves, having been a fixture in their team for two years. He was to stand corrected. In February, Wolves were dumped out of the FA Cup by Watford at Molineux. Towards the end of the game, Berry was targeted for retribution by one of his own supposed supporters.

'Some bloke started shouting abuse at me and I just lost it,' he told writer Simon Lowe. 'I jumped into the crowd and started to beat him up. We went to the police station and I got a bollocking from the Chief Inspector, but it all got hushed up.'

West Ham had been relegated to the Second Division at the end of the 1977–78 season. This spared Cunningham, Regis and Batson a visit to the Upton Park bear-pit in the League, but the Baggies had to go there for an FA Cup Third Round replay in

January 1980. As the teams trooped out onto the pitch, Regis and Batson were again showered with bananas by the East End crowd. Batson recalls 'looking at the contorted faces in the stands' at Upton Park that night, on which 'you could see all the rage and hate'.

'There were lots of instances where we went to grounds and bananas were thrown onto the pitch,' says Gary Owen. 'On one occasion, Cyrille picked one up, peeled it and ate it.

'I remember being with him one time in South Africa. A company took a group of black and white players out there on a promotional trip. It was only then that I appreciated what black players in England had to face. The country was still under apartheid and we went into the black townships. At times, I felt uncomfortable being white. The roles being reversed, it hit home how difficult it was for the likes of Cyrille, Brendon and Laurie just to go about doing their everyday job, and the psychological pressures they must have been under.'

Regis turned twenty-two the month after the cup match at West Ham; still so young, but having travelled so far. A professional footballer for more than three years now, he'd borne the weight of all of that rage and hate like a Stoic and through it arrived at his own point of enlightenment.

'I wasn't daft enough to think it was 5,000 racists shouting abuse at me,' he says. 'A very small minority of them were racist, but it was a mob mentality. That thought of, "My mate's singing it, so I'm singing it too." Also, there was the idea that it might put a black player off his game. No, no. That wasn't going to happen. We turned it around and internalised the anger.'

Chapter Fourteen: Black Pearl

Laurie Cunningham and Nicky Brown landed in Madrid in July 1979. The start of summer was so hot in the Spanish capital that for them it was like stepping into a furnace, and in more ways than one. They were installed in one of the oldest and plushest hotels in the city by the Real Madrid hierarchy and paraded at a series of glittering social events. These were attended by the cream of Madrid society. Among those turning out to greet Cunningham were Spain's reigning monarch, King Juan Carlos, and the singer Julio Iglesias, once a goalkeeper for Real's youth team. It was a relentless round of handshakes and small talk and Cunningham kept a smile fixed on his face, as good as ever at keeping guard of whatever tumult was going on behind his facade.

There were otherwise inauspicious beginnings to the couple's new adventure. Brown's fair skin made her particularly susceptible to the baking sun and both of them were stricken with upset stomachs. The lobby of their hotel crawled with paparrazi. People stared at them in restaurants and out on the street. In all their excitement at Real's whirlwind courtship, nothing had prepared either of them for what it would actually mean for Cunningham to be the intended star player of the world's most exposed football club. How wild and terrifying all the anticipation and expectation of him would be. How invasive and exhausting they would find the relentless attention and scrutiny. Or how jarring it would be to realise that their lives were now no longer their own. It soon became apparent to them that it wasn't so much a case of his joining Real Madrid as belonging to them.

It wouldn't be entirely accurate to say that Real Madrid considered itself to be more deserving of exaltation than other football clubs from the very start, but it would be close. Founded as plain old Madrid Football Club on 6 March 1902, to begin with the newcomers were just one of a handful of challengers to the first powerhouse of the Spanish game, Athletic Bilbao. The upstarts of Madrid claimed their first honour defeating the Basque club in the final of the Copa del Rey in 1905. 'Real', the Spanish word for royal, wasn't added as a prefix to Madrid FC's name until 1920, when King Alfonso XIII bestowed his patronage on the club.

In 1929, Real Madrid was one of the ten founding members of the Spanish football league. This was christened La Liga, as if the organisers were assured of its pre-eminence from the outset. The club was made to wait for success in this competition as well, their future great rivals Barcelona winning the inaugural race for the championship. Madrid secured its first title in 1931 and won La Liga again the following year, establishing the duopoly that has largely presided over Spanish football ever since. These formative years prefigured the greatest period in the club's history and also the most controversial. This was forged in the hothouse atmosphere of the Spanish Civil War of

1936–39, which wrenched apart an essentially loose confederation of nations and brought the Fascist dictator General Francisco Franco to power.

Franco held Spain in an iron grip until his death in 1975, and during this time Real Madrid came to dominate the game at home and in Europe. In the course of Franco's reign, the club won fourteen La Liga titles and the European Cup on six occasions. In the 1950s, world-class players such as the Argentinian Alfredo Di Stefano, a scorer and maker of goals who struck like a flash of lightning, and the masterful Hungarian, Ferenc Puskas, were brought to Madrid. The two of them became the nucleus of one of the all-time great teams. It reached its apogee in the 1960 European Cup final at Scotland's Hampden Park, with a sensational 7–3 victory over the bewildered Germans of Eintracht Frankfurt before a crowd of 127,000. Radiant in their pure white strips, Madrid put on an exhibition through that game that was audacious, magisterial and altogether breathtaking. It was a brand of football that appeared not to have originated in that era, but to have arrived from a point in the future where the game had come to attain the level of high art.

Yet Madrid's glorious rise was inextricably linked to that of Franco's, and the club was perceived to be both favoured by and sympathetic to the dictator. This ignored the fact that the capital had suffered terrible deprivations at the hands of Franco's forces during the civil war and also that the club's republican President of the time, Rafael Sanchez Guerra, was imprisoned at the end of the conflict. However, it was true that the man who was subsequently seen to have done most to elevate Real had fought on the Fascist side. A former Real player and manager, Santiago Bernabeu was elected President of the club in 1943. Upon his ascension, he telegrammed one of Franco's most notorious enforcers, General Moscardo, and invited him to patronise the club.

The stain of Real's association with the regime was made indelible by a single game. This was the deciding fixture of a two-legged semi-final of the Copa del Rey – renamed the Copa del Generalisimo under Franco – in 1943. Real's opponents were Barcelona and they were trailing the Catalan side 3-1 from the first match. Before kick-off in the return leg in Madrid, Barcelona's players were visited in their dressing room by one of Franco's officials and reminded that they were only being allowed to participate in the competition through the good graces of the regime. The contest itself unfolded as a farce and Madrid ran out 11-1 winners.

Thereafter, a view has prevailed across Spain and also outside of it that Madrid is the pampered club of the establishment and Barcelona the embodiment of bold resistance. A simplistic aspect, which fails to take account of the many grey areas between two poles of black and white. Nonetheless, it is undeniable that an acute sense of superiority and entitlement was encouraged and has thrived at the club. This dictates that there is no good or glory in coming second best. At Real Madrid, winning is all.

In 1944, Santiago Bernabeu began building the club a stadium to match the lofty image it had of itself at one of the city's most upmarket addresses, on the Paseo de la Castellana. Opened three years later on 14 December 1947, and eventually given his name, the Bernabeu was to become a football cathedral. Inside this vast concrete and steel coliseum, such gods of the game as Di Stefano, Puskas, Gento and Kopa revelled in the benediction of an adoring congregation that swelled to 125,000 in number during the next decade. To star at the Bernabeu was to stand on the shoulders of giants.

The Real Madrid team that Cunningham was being added to had won La Liga in three of the past four seasons. It was a dogged, obdurate side largely made up of home-grown players, such as the studious-looking midfielder Vicente del Bosque, who'd later manage Spain to triumph in the 2010 World Cup, and Jose Camacho, a thick-set defender who approached each game as if it were to the death. Their coach was a dour but shrewd Serbian, Vujadin Boskov, who'd cast the team in his own image. One might admire their work ethic, but there was nothing about Boskov's Madrid to capture the imagination or make hearts race. They had also failed to replicate their domestic success in the cauldron of continental competition, and had crashed out of the previous season's European Cup to the Swiss side Grasshopper Zurich, which was tantamount to a humiliation.

'They were known as the Madrid of the Garcias, which is the equivalent of being called the Manchester United Smiths,' says *Guardian* newspaper journalist Sid Lowe, an experienced commentator on Spanish football. 'There was a keen sense that this was a team that had been built on old-fashioned values and that it was a little bit rudimentary and not particularly glamorous. Although to a certain extent some of the players in it were pushing boundaries – Del Bosque's father had been in a Franco prison camp and he was very left-wing in his outlook. That was very different to the general perspective in Spain at the time.

'But overall they were a grey-seeming team. Laurie Cunningham was bought to add to it that spark of excitement and flair. He was very definitely meant to be the glamour figure.'

At its core, Real Madrid was a deeply conservative institution – just as Spain itself was at that juncture. The beginnings of a cultural revolution were being felt at the fringes, but the country as a whole was still coming out of the shadows and blinking into the light after Franco's death. The old general might have gone, but the residue of his far-right politics continued to hold sway in many areas and at all levels of Spanish life. The influence of the Catholic Church was also powerful and persuasive. Spaniards were compelled to uphold the values of unquestioning faith, hard work and marriage. Real Madrid expected its players to be dutiful and preferred them to be married.

It was never likely that Laurie Cunningham and Nicky Brown were not going to feel like interlopers in such an environment. They were a mixed-race couple when such a thing was almost unheard of in Spain. He was fast seduced by the city of Madri, by its flamboyant architecture and its vibrant nightlife, the clubs where one could dance till dawn as if in defiance of all other strictures. However, he was no more given to timely and obedient servitude than he had been at Orient or West Brom, and she had just as little intention of falling meekly into line. Inevitably, trouble lay ahead for both of them.

'I was expected to dress in a certain way by the people at Real Madrid,' says Brown. 'All of the other wives got done up to the nines. They wore A-line skirts and strings of pearls. I was told to wear a bra. As a woman, you were supposed to be seen and not heard. If you did speak up and say something that might be construed as socially or politically strong or opinionated, it was translated as "I love kittens." You were meant to associate with the other players and people who were as well-off as you were. It was all about maintaining appearances and we were seen as being renegades just by being ourselves.

'There wasn't a black face at the club and all of a sudden there was Laurie, his family and our friends running around the players' lounge. They didn't have soul brothers in Madrid, and Laurie's brother couldn't help but appear menacing. Keith dressed the way he did in Tottenham: a long black leather coat and dark glasses. He was like Samuel L. Jackson at his most dangerous-looking. They didn't get the concept of us being a mixed-race couple, because Spanish married Spanish. So there was a lot of curiosity going on and presumption. But also they didn't know what it was like to have a good party and so we were invited everywhere and asked to bring along all of our friends. To make the hosts look interesting.'

'The new constitution was only established the previous year and it was a transformation that was founded on collectively forgetting about everything,' says Lowe. 'Not talking about what had happened under Franco-ism and moving on.

'Reading the Spanish press cuttings of the time, there was an obsession with the fact that Laurie was black. It doesn't seem as if this was rooted in dislike, but more the idea that he was impossibly exotic. His being there was very exciting for some people in Spain, but then again, a challenge for others. This was seen to be something different and there wasn't necessarily a rejection of that, but if things went badly for him then it could easily be turned into one.'

Cunningham and Brown were separated within a week of their arrival in Madrid. The team left for a training camp in Holland and were gone for two weeks. He didn't speak a word of Spanish and barely ever would. At this early stage, he felt himself isolated and out on a limb. This was nothing new for someone who was as self-contained as he was, but the circumstances of it were different. In the past, he had always made a conscious decision to be sealed off. Even then, he'd managed to find common ground and a shared sense of experience with the likes of Bobby Fisher and Cyrille Regis.

The rest of the Madrid team regarded Cunningham with cold suspicion. After all, he had come to them as the so-called star. He was young and better paid than them. They were dismissed as labourers and he was being hailed as an artist. The fears and resentments that coursed through a dressing room were the same in Real Madrid as at West Brom. During that long and testing fortnight, he answered their doubts on the training pitch. He showed off his full repertoire: the outrageous jinks and flicks; a swivel, a feint and a burst of pace that left even a killer like Camacho looking benign. As he had always done, he found a state of grace with a ball at his command.

Years later, the astute Del Bosque said he saw in Cunningham all the qualities for which the Madrid faithful have now deified the Portuguese superstar Cristiano Ronaldo. To that extent, Cunningham returned to Spain from Holland having put his marker down. He had even impressed Real's other overseas player, Uli Stielike, and this was no small achievement. Signed from Borussia Monchengladbach in 1977, Stieleke was an established West German international and a formidable presence at the back or in the centre of midfield. He had a military bearing and was nicknamed 'The Stopper', which accurately conveyed his approach to football and life in general. Renowned for his sense of order and self-discipline, Stieleke set himself exacting standards and expected others to submit to the same rigours as he did. In that respect, he kept his distance from Cunningham and waited to see what kind of professional he would turn out to be.

In time, Cunningham grew closer to other players at Real Madrid. Of the first teamers, his two most regular acquaintances were Gregorio 'Goyo' Benito and Juanito. The 33-year-old

Benito had been a junior national champion at the javelin and was now a reliable centre-back for Real and for Spain. The younger Juanito was a lively striker noted for being a selfless team player. Upon joining the club from their city neighbours Atletico in 1977, he announced that playing for Real Madrid was like 'touching the sky'. In effect, he was the sort of cog in the machine that Cunningham was brought to Real to enhance or else replace. There was a terrible symmetry to the fact that Juanito also died in a road accident in 1992, aged thirty-seven. Cunningham also drew one of the fringe players at Madrid into his typically compressed inner circle, Miguel Angel Portugal.

Real's fans gave the club's new signing an effusive welcome. At an open training session back in Madrid, Cunningham's feats of conjuring brought cheers and a standing ovation from supporters massed in the public stand. As ever, the acclaim buoyed him and sent him into the new season with a spring in his step. He made his competitive debut for Real in front of 100,000 fans at the Bernabeu and scored twice in a 3-1 win over the side he'd first tormented the season before, Valencia.

The next game at the Bernabeu, he scored an even more significant goal, in the first El Clasico of the season against Barcelona. Inflamed to boiling point through the Franco era, the rivalry between the two great clubs was as intense as any in sport. Their mutual antipathy ran deep and was rooted in much more than just football. There was an ideological chasm separating the two clubs and their supporters. Real saw themselves as Spain's club, Barcelona as the shining beacon of an independent-minded Catalonia. Real believed itself to be a bastion of solid, traditional values, while Barcelona propagated the idea that it was a centre for progressive thinking. In the most basic terms, Real Madrid ran to the political right and Barcelona to the left.

In his book *Morbo: the Story of Spanish Football*, writer Phil Ball characterised El Clasico games as 'a re-enactment of the Spanish Civil War'. Inflicting defeat on their despised enemy was the victory most desired and held up above all others at Real. Cunningham's strike helped propel them to a 3-2 win in the opening skirmish of that campaign and accelerated his growing stature at the club. The Madrid supporters began referring to him as one of their own and christened him their 'Black Pearl'.

These were amongst Cunningham's happiest days at Real. Yet Nicky Brown claims even then that she detected a storm brewing on the horizon. He may have won over those on the terraces of the Bernabeu, but this, she says, fuelled petty jealousies among his team-mates. She'd also seen the manner in which he was regarded within the upper echelons of the club and how football at this rarefied level looked when its glossy veneer was peeled back.

'One of us had to learn Spanish and there's nothing like love to get you to do something with dedication,' she says. 'I was also a watcher of people. I picked up a lot through listening and observing, all of it disappointing. There was no love there. That had been lost at Orient. He was like a racehorse to them and could be replaced just like that.

'The crowd loved him, but envy appeared in the team. It was like a pride of lions where the males are always scrapping for their place in the pecking order. Not a happy environment. Laurie was like the young lion that comes along to challenge an old leader. But at Real Madrid no one was going to be sent off into the wilderness without putting up a fight.

'Most of these guys had grown up poor. Benito was a lad from a small village. His mom still came round to his house once a week to cook him a traditional peasant soup for dinner. They found themselves at Real and earning that kind of money. No one was going to take that off them.'

Sid Lowe makes a less prosaic appraisal of Cunningham's situation. It is one that would perhaps chime more with ex-colleagues of his at Orient and West Brom. 'I've spoken to a few of his former team-mates at Real and the overwhelming perception of Laurie was that he didn't have a bad bone in his body, but he was a bit dizzy,' he says.

'In terms of the way they viewed football, he possibly wasn't seen as being as committed as the rest of them were. That was a very tough, aggressive Real Madrid side and he was theoretically the fantasy player. He had the talent, but as time went on, I think it was felt that he could and should have been better than he ended up being. The players that were closest to him would argue that this was ultimately as a result of injury. But in particular, the relationship he had with Stielike was a very cold one.'

Away from the internal politics at Real, Cunningham settled down to life in Madrid. At first, the club moved him and Brown out of their hotel and into a luxury apartment within walking distance of the Bernabeu. The couple soon exchanged this for an even more ostentatious four-bedroom house in Las Matas, an exclusive enclave popular with Madrid's moneyed rich some sixteen miles from the city centre. Their new home was located on a well-to-do estate that was patrolled by security guards and walled off from prying eyes. Goyo Benito lived on the same complex.

Cunningham gave off every indication of being a man at peace with the world. He and Brown lived with their four sheepdogs and a Great Dane a neighbour had asked them to adopt. He spent his time at home enjoying their swimming pool or idling away the hours doing structural drawings or sketching out ideas for clothing designs. His favourite spot for dinner was a local sports club that was owned by an Englisman, John Fitzgibbon. He paid for his brother Keith to come over from England and stay with them for three months at a time. He acted as referee in the regular games of football that Fitzgibbon organised for the community of British expats and in which Keith often turned out.

'He seemed contented and very relaxed,' says Keith Cunningham. 'He knew how to adapt to things. He liked to go out and have a dance too, but he didn't go over the top. He might have a glass of wine, but nothing more.

'The only guy from the team that he used to have round to the house was Benito. The pair of them would go out to dinner together too. He didn't mix with a lot of the other players. It seemed to me that the manager and other people at the club always wanted him to associate with them more, but my brother was his own man. He did what he wanted to do.'

'You got everything for free,' says Brown. 'We got the house. We were given a new BMW because that's what all the Real Madrid players drove. You didn't have a Mini. That didn't suggest wealth. If we walked into a stereo shop, we'd get given a new Bose system because we might have rich friends coming round to the house who'd see it and want to buy one. We had a complete new Japanese kitchen put in. You had to be careful. You start to take the value of stuff for granted and that wasn't how we were.'

On the football pitch, Cunningham and Real Madrid continued to flourish in tandem. He bloomed in the unique atmosphere of Spanish football: the huge crowds and the carnival of noise; the pockets of supporters who'd share a bottle of wine during a game and leap to their feet to celebrate a moment of great skill. Cunningham gave them plenty to cheer. He was like a matador and the defenders his bulls. He'd tease them forward, the ball as bait. He'd show it to them, make them charge for it and then at the point of contact, whip it away, leaving them to hack and bore at thin air. The more he did it, the more enraged they got, until he'd bled all the fight out of them.

'I'm not saying it because he was my brother, but he was brilliant for Real Madrid,' says Keith Cunningham. 'He was beautiful in every game that he played in during that season. To see him get the ball and go swivelling around people . . . It was so overwhelming that I'd jump up from my seat and tip my beer over the people in front of me.'

Cunningham was able to date his greatest ninety minutes in Real Madrid's white, and perhaps his best of all: 10 February 1980. This was the reverse fixture with Barcelona at their Nou Camp stadium, when he kissed at perfection. He was like a conductor leading a symphony, seeming able to set the tempo of the whole game and to determine the exact moments to bring it to a crescendo.

In bleached-out footage of the match, at a certain point one sees him collect the ball wide on the left, near the halfway line. He pushes it ahead of him, ambling after it so that it might seem as if he were unsure of what to do next, but in reality he was coiled like a spring. Barcelona's full-back, an Argentinian named Rafael Zuviria, is tempted in and then ruthlessly punished for his presumption. Cunningham shifts from inert to explosive in one fluid, effortless movement, past Zuviria before he can blink or think, and off and running to the edge of the Barcelona penalty box. Without breaking stride, and at full pace, he curls the ball with the outside of his right foot across the face of Barcelona's goal and directly into the path of an oncoming team-mate, who scores. It is an exquisite and audacious pass, the measurement and angle of it as precise as a mathematical formula. Madrid ran out 2-0 winners and effectively ended Barcelona's interest in the title.

To perform as a Real player at the Nou Camp is to face the wrath and scorn of more than 100,000 rabid Barca supporters. It came rolling down from the high, vast terraces in an unchecked torrent, deafening and menacing – a declaration of war. Yet at the final whistle of this game, the Nou Camp rose as one to applaud Cunningham from the field. It was – and still is – an act so unprecedented that Madrid's sports newspaper *AS* ran a piece commemorating it on the twenty-fifth anniversary of its happening under the headline, 'The man who ran riot in the Nou Camp.' *AS* quoted a Barca fan comparing Cunningham to his own club's maestro, the Dutchman Johan Cruyff, who starred for Barcelona for five years from 1973 and once guided them to a 5-0 win in the Bernabeu. 'It was like seeing Cruyff but with black skin,' the supporter concluded. 'That kid could do anything with a football.'

'The idea of Cunningham getting a standing ovation at the Nou Camp sounds as if it should be apocryphal, but it's not,' says Sid Lowe. 'What is nonsense is the suggestion posited later that Barca's fans were on his side because he was a black guy and they were showing they were different. It was an extraordinary performance from him and he put them to the sword. That in a way was a problem for him, in the sense that people kept on harking back to it.'

He had other great games that season. Boskov often referred to his brilliance in a 4-1 crushing of Malaga. However, the master class that Cunningham gave in the Nou Camp left him with a conundrum he couldn't hope to solve: how could one ever be better than perfect? This was difficult enough for him to comprehend in his prime. After injuries had taken their toll, it broke him.

The chase for La Liga boiled down to a two-horse race between Real Madrid and Real Sociedad from the Basque country. The sides ran neck-and-neck until the end of it, with Sociedad having the edge in their games against each other, drawing 2-2 at the Bernabeu and humbling Real 4-0 in front of Sociedad's own fans. Crucially, Real Madrid were otherwise invincible in their own back yard and won each of their remaining sixteen games at the Bernabeu. They hit four without reply past Atletico Madrid, five against Hercules and eviscerated Rayo Vallecano 7-0. It was their home form that was decisive and Madrid edged Sociedad to the title by just a single point.

Real also completed a domestic double that season, beating the minnows of Castilla 6-1 in a Copa del Rey final staged at the Bernabeu. Yet the prize they most coveted eluded them. They negotiated a perilous route through to the semi-finals of the European Cup. Their opening tie against the Bulgarian side Levski-Sofia was won comfortably enough 3-0, but they only sneaked past Porto of Portugal on goal difference in the Second Round, with Cunningham registering the crucial strike in the away leg.

This set them up for a quarter-final tie with the Scottish champions, Glasgow Celtic. They slumped to a 2-0 defeat at Celtic's Parkhead Stadium and in an atmosphere as fevered as any generated by the Madridistas at the Bernabeu. Celtic clung on to their lead until the forty-fifth minute of the return leg, but then Cunningham intervened. His first significant influence on the game was a moment of impudence and supreme self-confidence. On the verge of half-time, Real Madrid won a corner. Cunningham took it with the outside of his right foot, a skill as rare as it was fiendishly difficult to execute. The ball arced into the Celtic box and then plunged as if falling from a cliff top, coming down under the crossbar and right on to the head of the leaping Santillana. Ten minutes after the re-start, Stielike was the beneficiary of Cunningham's munificence. He played a quick one-two on the edge of the Celtic box, skipped past two defenders and looped the ball onto the penalty spot for the German to fire into the net. Four minutes from time, Juanito won the contest, finishing off a move that was started by Cunningham.

Their semi-final opponents were Hamburg, who in Kevin Keegan had a high-profile Englishman of their own. Keegan was crowned 'European Footballer of the Year' in 1978, but wasn't able to affect the first match at the Bernabeu, which Madrid won 2-0. Cunningham scored in Germany, but it was a catastrophic second leg for his team as Hamburg rolled them over 5-1. Spain might be theirs for the ruling, but not the rest of Europe.

At the end of the season, Cunningham was given pause to reflect on another, more ominous development. He'd become a marked man in La Liga, a target for whatever thuggish treatment opposition defenders saw fit to dish out. It wasn't as though he hadn't been subjected to bruising tackling in England, but there seemed to him an even more malicious intent to the challenges in Spain.

'He couldn't quite believe how much the defenders in Spain were allowed to hurt him,' says Sid Lowe. 'But that was the nature of the game in La Liga at the time. If it were still the case now, the matches would finish with both teams having just six players left on the pitch.'

'When Laurie came off after a game you could see stud marks all over his legs from where he'd been kicked,' says Brown. 'He'd thought that with the Spaniards being Latin, they'd play the game like Brazil and he loved Brazilian football. That's when he began to have enough and his attitude to the game changed. I believe that he knew his career was in danger through injury. The referees didn't handle it and nor did the club. He was just left to bear it and that was a heartbreaking thing to have to watch.'

Cunningham began the next season in good form. He was rested, having had a holiday in Ibiza that he and Brown took with Cyrille Regis and his girlfriend, and as dashing on the pitch for Madrid as ever. Real had prevented him from joining up with the England squads for most of the past year, but he'd also resolved this dispute.

Ron Greenwood selected him for a World Cup qualifier in Romania on 15 October 1980. England laboured to a 2-1 defeat in Bucharest, lacking in both flair and invention. Cunningham sat on the bench until the game was as good as lost and he was only thrown on for its last gasping. It was his sixth and last appearance for his country. The glorious international career that seemed inevitable when he'd scored on his groundbreaking debut for the U21 team just two years earlier was over before it had ever got started.

'Whenever I saw him playing for England, he'd get the ball and just roll it down the side of the opposing full-back for Ray Wilkins or one of the other midfielders to run onto,' says Ron Atkinson. 'I challenged him about it after one match, asked him why he wasn't taking his defender on. He told me that's what Ron Greenwood had instructed him to do. Are you serious? Having bloody Ray Wilkins running on ahead wouldn't bother any team. Laurie's game was all about getting at people. It was such a waste of him.'

The next month Cunningham's wings were clipped in Spain and he came crashing to earth. He was playing for Madrid in a hotly contested La Liga game at Real Betis on 16 November. Betis' chief henchman, Francisco Bizcocho, felled him with a stamping challenge, breaking the first toe on his left foot. It sounds now like a relatively trivial injury, but it proved to be the ruin of him. In the first instance, the injury had left the toe rigid and unyielding. Cunningham had gained a crucial advantage by being feather-light on his feet, able to run on the tips of his toes like a ballet dancer. He was now robbed of that ability and it left him fatally handicapped.

Cunningham's relationship with the all-powerful board of directors at Real Madrid was also soured in the wake of the injury, and this was just as damaging to him. He'd run into trouble before for missing the occasional training session, but then he was scoring goals and winning games for the club. It was a different matter when he was sitting on the sidelines. Days after his operation, he was spotted in a nightclub with a plaster cast still on his foot. The club took a righteous stance against this latest indiscretion. Playing to the gallery, Real's President, Luis de Carlos, fulminated that Cunningham had flouted the moral guidelines laid down by the club's patriarch, Santiago Bernabeu. He was given a two-month suspension and a one million pesetas fine.

'It was a massively overblown reaction on behalf of the club,' says Lowe. 'They came down on him not just because they thought he deserved it, but also because they felt a very keen need to be seen to be doing so and to be upholding values. Camacho said to me later that Laurie didn't do anything wrong, but that he failed to realise where he was and what club he was at.'

From then to the end of the season, Cunningham played just forty-five minutes of first-team football for Real Madrid in La Liga. Without him, the club came second to Real Sociedad, in a reversal of the previous campaign's shoot-out. On this occasion, the two sides were only separated by goal difference. Real were also dumped out of the Copa del Rey by Sporting Gijon, but made it to the final of the European Cup, where they faced Liverpool in Paris on 27 May.

Despite his evident lack of match fitness, Boskov recalled Cunningham for the European final at the Parc des Princes. His manager doubtless hoped that he might be the key to unlocking Liverpool's miserly defence, but he did so in vain. Cunningham's performance was fitful and erratic. It contained no more than trace elements of the player he'd been the season before, like echoes in a well. The game itself was an ugly, unedifying contest, with brutality trumping skill. Madrid won the battles for midfield and defensive superiority, but Liverpool claimed the war. Their solitary goal came from an unlikely source, full-back Alan Kennedy scoring in the eighty-second minute to give them victory.

The next season was even more desperate for both Real and for Cunningham. The team slipped to third in La Liga behind a surging Sociedad side and the hated Barcelona. He suffered a string of injuries to his left knee that required three surgeries and left his leg laced with ugly scars. Later, he'd recount how defenders would use these scars as points of reference to aim kicks at. He was most embittered by one incident in particular that he said occurred in training. Cunningham claimed he was put out of action for months by a team-mate making a deliberate lunge at his shattered knee, tearing a ligament.

'He felt as if he was being kicked out of football and again because of the racist element,' says Bobby Fisher. 'He believed people were jealous of the money he was getting, but also there was the fact of him being black. He was just coming back from rehabilitation when he was taken out in training. He was most sad about that and that was the finishing of him at Madrid.'

Others are less certain of the veracity of this account. The writer Phil Ball likens it to an urban myth. He adds: 'If it did happen it was probably Camacho that took him out, but Camacho took everyone out because that was his game. If there was no one else around he'd foul himself.'

'I've never been able to stand that story up,' continues Sid Lowe. 'I'm not saying it didn't happen, but I haven't managed to confirm it and I do have some doubts. I know Laurie's brother and Bobby Fisher have hinted that there was something much darker going on. I think they perceive a level of rejection of Laurie that his team-mates deny. But then, of course they'd deny it.

'Camacho spoke to me in a way that suggested he was genuinely fond of Laurie. Del Bosque wasn't a great mate of his, but he didn't have a problem with him. There is a hint from one or two of them that they saw Nicky as the problem rather than Laurie, but I'm just as cautious about accepting that view.'

The statistics for that season show that Cunningham was able to make only three appearances in La Liga for the team. He flickered in the home leg of a UEFA Cup quarter-final against the German side Kaiserslautern. However, in the reverse fixture he was sent off for retaliation before half-time and Madrid slumped to one of their worst ever European defeats, 5-0. He was also in the side that exacted revenge on Sporting Gijon in the final of the Copa del Rey in Valladolid on 13 April. These were the last times he was seen in a Real Madrid shirt.

Cunningham knuckled down through increasingly long

periods of recovery and rehabilitation, determined and uncomplaining. Yet no matter how much he strived to regain fitness, he couldn't escape the plain fact that he would never, and could never again, be the same footballer. The best of him was lost.

'It was the ultimate frustration for him,' says Fisher. 'He'd always been able to express himself on the football pitch, but he was no longer anywhere near having the elegance, fluidity and beauty that he'd had in his prime.'

'Was I surprised that it didn't work out for Laurie at Real Madrid? No, I wasn't,' concludes John Wile, Cunningham's captain at West Brom. 'It was disappointing to see him get injured. But I thought that the inconsistencies I saw in his game at Albion went with him right through his career.

'I also think back to incidents like the one where he took himself off to the shower at half-time in that game we had at Middlesbrough. He was a fantastic footballer when he hit the heights, but there was a flaw in his character.'

Chapter Fifteen: Ghost Town

Just like the soaring heights that Laurie Cunningham navigated at the beginning of his time with Real Madrid, there was something deceptive and illusory about West Bromwich Albion's successful 1980–81 season. Through it the club was able to mount its second credible challenge for the League title in three years, with Ron Atkinson's reconfigured team acquiring a look of permanence and consistency. This gave the impression of foundations laid on solid ground, whereas in truth they were pitched on shifting sand.

Perhaps the most withering blow of all to be inflicted on the club came on 24 September 1980. On that date, Albion's vice-chairman, Tom Silk, and his wife, Catherine, were killed when their private plane crashed over France. A successful businessman, Silk believed that a football club could be the conduit through which a man could realise his dreams. He had progressive ideas about developing Albion into the sort of institution that could have continued success, and he had been Atkinson's keenest advocate. In the sense that he dared to speculate, Silk was a man of the times. He was also a very necessary counterweight to the more cautious and pragmatic Bert Millichip. His passing meant that West Brom would never again break any transfer records or aspire to a place among the game's elite.

'There were a lot of boardroom hassles and a number of the players were coming to the end of the road too,' says Pat Murphy. 'As well, Ron was of a certain age and had aspirations. The club wasn't able to sustain what had been started, because they couldn't get enough bums on seats or investment from the board. If only. Those two words might sum up that time at the club.'

Following Silk's death, Atkinson grew frustrated at a lack of support from the West Brom board and at its intransigence. On the pitch, he still meant for his side to entertain first and foremost, and the football they played was attack-minded and pleasing on the eye. Yet this team didn't have a maverick spirit to call upon or a wild streak to it. Games were won, but none were left burnt into the minds of its supporters. There was instead a staple of odd-goal victories against such middling clubs as Southampton, Crystal Palace and Brighton & Hove Albion.

In defence, West Brom were tough and unyielding with Tony Godden, Brendon Batson, Derek Statham, John Wile and Ally Robertson still in tandem. The midfield was busy and effective. Remi Moses and Bryan Robson were the heartbeat of the side and paired together for all but three games during the campaign. However, the team's most reliable weapon was again Cyrille Regis. Still just twenty-two, he'd recovered fitness and was once more battering and bullying defenders, and scoring outlandish goals.

Albion sat sixth in the table at Christmas. By the start of March, they had climbed to third. Heading into the business end of the season, they beat a string of accomplished sides at the

Hawthorns: Liverpool, Nottingham Forest and the League leaders, Ipswich. This last win came on 4 April and brought them to within six points of Aston Villa, who'd leap-frogged Bobby Robson's team as a result of it, with five games left to play. Their next match was at Villa Park on the following Wednesday night. Win it and they would give themselves a fighting chance of taking the title.

In the event, it was a typical local derby, closely fought, fast and frenetic. Yet there was a familiar ending to it for West Brom. The psychological fault-line running through Atkinson's Albion again pulled them up at the decisive hurdle and the contest was settled by a late goal from Villa's Peter Withe. Villa went on to win the League. Albion finished up in fourth place, with the consolation of having qualified for another crack at the UEFA Cup.

A crowd of 48,000 watched the match at Villa Park, but in general attendances were down in the Football League. Gates slumped by as much as a third at West Brom that season and the Hawthorns didn't get close to being full. The deserted seats and terraces made for a flat, lifeless atmosphere at stadia across the country. Going to football, one got the impression of turning up at the fag-end of a party that had wound down, but was being kept going by the most hardened and desperate revellers. If there were curtains they would have been drawn to block out the light, and the mood was sour and stupefied. In part, this decline was attributable to the menace of hooliganism, which continued to taint the game, and also to the moribund nature of much of the football on offer. However, the most salient factor was that people simply couldn't afford to watch the games.

After two years in power, Margaret Thatcher's Conservative government had been able to do nothing to reverse the country's economic decline, and Britain had sunk into recession. For a great swathe of the population, the threat of unemployment and the pressures of high inflation remained a constant, inescapable fact of life. In the West Midlands and other regions, the landscape was dotted with the skeletons of closed factories and plants. Where it hit hardest, this bleak outlook and the harsh prospects of finding other work engendered a communal sense of ennui: a dull acceptance that British working folk would never again have it so good.

'With Thatcher, it became a community of self, didn't it?' suggests Albion supporter John Homer. 'People had to really think about how they spent their money. And if you lived in the Black Country it came down to whether you went to the football or ate. Two years before that you couldn't even move your feet at the Hawthorns and now you were sat next to rows of empty seats. You were left feeling bereft. Especially since that period of flair and sparkle had been so wonderful, but also so brief.'

Lagging behind in the opinion polls and with morale sagging, Thatcher and her embattled government caught an unlikely break in the week West Brom's title challenge rose up and then fell. On 2 April 1981, Argentina's ruling military junta launched an invasion of the British-owned Falklands Islands and claimed them for its own. An archipelago stranded in the freezing South Atlantic, the Falklands were a relic of the old Empire and an outpost few in Britain had heard of to that point. However, Thatcher's declaration of war on Argentina and her ordering of a British task force to recover the Falklands whipped up a kind of crazed national fervour. Thatcher tapped into this and extrapolated from it the idea that one could triumph through nothing more than an old-fashioned spirit of get-up-and-go.

She succeeded to the degree that millions of Britons were convinced that being prepared to work hard and speculate was enough for them to prosper. Yet as simplistic a credo as Thatcherism was, it was also divisive and destructive. It rewarded privilege and encouraged intolerance. It made social outcasts of those who were presumed to lack the smarts and gumption to pull themselves up by their bootstraps and better their lives. Nowhere was this scorn and subsequent neglect felt more keenly than in Britain's depressed inner-city areas.

Thatcher reaped a whirlwind during the spring and summer of 1981. Brixton in south London was the first district to flare up during the second weekend of April. The rate of unemployment in the area was highest among the black community – it ran to 50 per cent – and tensions had been simmering since the turn of the year. These were exacerbated by a Metropolitan Police initiative to reduce crime in Brixton. Codenamed Operation Swamp '81, it sent teams of plainclothes officers pouring onto the streets to stop and search anyone suspected of having committed a crime. That April, a thousand people in the district were pulled up by police within the first five days of it starting.

Brixton exploded on the afternoon of Saturday 11 April. The spark for this was an incident that occurred the previous day when police were called to the scene of the stabbing of a local black youth, Michael Bailey. A crowd of 200 or so black and white youths subsequently gathered and confronted the attending officers. In this febrile atmosphere, wild and inaccurate rumours that the police had left Bailey to bleed to death were spread through the community. At 4 p.m. the next day, a full-scale riot broke out. Police vehicles and buildings were set on fire, shops were looted and police and rioters fought pitched battles on the streets. This conflagration burnt deep into the night and accounted for 250 injuries to the police and public, and eighty-five arrests.

'Bloody Saturday' in Brixton set off a slow-burning chain

reaction across the country that erupted into effect in July. During the course of that month rioting broke out in Toxteth in Liverpool and in Moss Side in Manchester. In the West Midlands, tensions flared in deprived areas of Wolverhampton and Smethwick and in Handsworth in Birmingham. In each instance, the root cause was the same: urban decay fostering a sense of hopelessness and an exponential escalation in hostilities between police and the local communities. In the year preceding the riot in Handsworth, an estimated 40 per cent of black youths in the area had been stopped and searched. Speaking in its immediate aftermath, Sheila Wright, the local Labour MP, said: 'The feeling I get from listening to the kids here is that they have no future.'

The government's response was to commission an inquiry into the rioting from Lord Justice Scarman. Published in November 1981, the Scarman Report made clear that the out-breaks had been the result of extreme social and economic problems afflicting Britain's inner cities. Scarman stressed an urgent need for government action to prevent 'racial disadvantage' from becoming an 'endemic, ineradicable disease threatening the very survival of our society.' Reporting on the botched police inquiry into the murder of black teenager Stephen Lawrence in February 1999, a second Judge, Sir William Macpherson, con-cluded that Scarman's recommendations had been ignored.

'It was a terrible period,' says civil rights activist Derek Campbell. 'We had overt racism in the police force. In Handsworth, they were simply targeting the black community. There were policies and decisions made in this country that took no account at all of the ethnic minority communities. We were seen as being people that would cause insurrection and make problems and we had no rights. We were not valued in British society.

'In Handsworth, it was only because those disturbances

affected business that anything happened. Not because people felt sorry for us. We were seen to be damaging the reputation of the area and so for a time money was thrown at the situation to stop us from doing it again. However, it was a short-term measure and then everything went back to normal.'

This scorched backdrop prompted a more eloquent form of protest to come roaring out of the West Midlands, at the head of which were two of its leading multi-racial bands. The previous May, the Beat from Birmingham had released 'Stand Down Margaret', a howl of rage masquerading as a frothy ska track in which the the band's singers, Dave Wakeling and Ranking Roger, chanted how bleak and sorrowful the future looked.

Speaking about the song to Shirley Halperin of the *Hollywood Reporter* in 2013, Wakeling said: 'That time signalled a breaking of the English spirit. Thatcher turned neighbours into competitors. A generation saw their parents give up on life as they saw their own opportunities stunted. They saw the town where they'd grown up being dismantled. The scapegoats for this were everybody who seemed different.'

The soundtrack of the summer of 1981 was the Specials' 'Ghost Town', which spent three weeks at the top of the UK singles chart in June. Inspired by the creeping desolation and despair bandleader Jerry Dammers witnessed in his native Coventry, it arrived like a cold wind blowing through a graveyard. Dammers's nightmarish vision of urban collapse was set to a sparse, spooked beat and the haunting invocation that their hometown was becoming like a ghost town. Repeated over and again, it carried the weight of an impending apocalypse.

A separate musical movement had also sprung up out of Britain's inner cities. This was Oi!, the bastard offspring of punk rock and mouthpiece for a particular strain of white, working class rebellion. Oi! cast off punk's art-school affectations and was rooted instead in the yobbish sound of pub rock and football terrace chants. Its leadings proponents were bands like Sham 69, Angelic Upstarts, The 4-Skins and the Cockney Rejects. The last named group was a gang of rough and ready West Ham fans with affiliations to the club's notorious hooligan crew, the Inner City Firm.

The issues of unemployment, police harassment and urban violence were all covered in Oi!'s lyrical manifesto. However, it was damned by its association with far-right groups such as the National Front and the British Movement, since it harvested from the same fertile recruiting pool of disaffected skinheads and football fans. This was further stoked by the release of the agenda-setting *Strength Thru Oi!* album in May 1981. Compiled by the then music journalist Garry Bushell, its title appropriated the Nazi Party's 'Strength Through Joy' slogan and featured on its cover a sneering skinhead, Nicky Crane, who at the time was serving four years in prison for racist violence.

'Bushell didn't understand that Oi! was a Nazi expression of right-wing supremacy,' says Roger Huddle, founder of Rock Against Racism. 'He thought it was the true representation of Britain's working-class youth, not ours. The fact that you could have two expressions didn't enter his head.'

There was upheaval of a different sort at West Bromwich Albion that summer. At the end of the season, Manchester United had again finished among the also-rans, and manager Dave Sexton paid for the club's years of under-achievement with his job. In their search for Sexton's successor, the Old Trafford board soon alighted on Ron Atkinson. Memories of the manner in which

United had been dismantled by his West Brom side two years earlier were still sharp. This was accomplished with a swagger that had once been the exclusive preserve of the Red Devils in the halcyon days of Best, Law and Charlton, and when the sixties and United had both swung.

The prospect of restoring United to greatness and emulating the feats of such a giant of the game as Matt Busby was the glamour job Atkinson craved and he leapt at it. This was troubling enough for Albion, but Atkinson also added collateral damage. He made Bryan Robson his first signing at Old Trafford and then snapped up Remi Moses. In fairness to Atkinson, Moses pitched up at the Manchester hotel United's new manager was being lodged at and volunteered his services.

'It was the middle of the night and he knocked on my door and announced he'd come to sign for me,' says Atkinson. 'I was in the middle of doing a deal to bring Frank Stapleton from Arsenal and we had to find another room to stick Remi in. He was there till two in the morning. Smashing little player and just what United needed at that point. It was a tragedy what happened to him.'

Moses's 150 games for United were stretched out over an eight-year period and his Old Trafford career was blighted by injury. He was eventually forced to retire from the game at twenty-eight: a shooting star that burned out. He later found work as a property developer and as coach to the Manchester Warriors inline skating side, settling to a quieter life outside of football. Robson took a different, more elevated path at United. He went on to become the most decorated English footballer of his generation, captain and mainstay of both his club and national teams, winning ninety caps for England and in 1993 helping United to their first League title in twenty-six years.

Atkinson's Old Trafford reign was in many regards the mirror image of his time at West Brom. He again fashioned a youthful, exciting team, but one that was also flawed and vulnerable. They ran hard for the title in his first season at the club, but were beaten to it by Liverpool and came in third. Trophies were won – the FA Cup in 1983 and 1985 – and these made Atkinson United's most successful manager since Busby. However, Busby had brought to Old Trafford the League title and the European Cup, and these were the peaks the club continued to aspire to and which Atkinson was unable to reach.

He came closest in the 1985–86 season, which United began with a run of ten successive victories. They fast opened up a seemingly impregnable lead in the League, but then choked and trailed in a distant fourth behind Liverpool. Atkinson was sacked after United made a wretched start to the next campaign. His replacement was a younger up-and-coming manager, a flint-eyed Scot named Alex Ferguson. United recovered from his going, but Albion didn't. Atkinson's departure tore the heart and soul out of the club.

'The start of it was Laurie and Len Cantello being sold,' says Cyrille Regis. 'But it was still a decent side. And then Ron left. Bryan Robson was the most complete footballer in the team and it was a no-brainer for Ron to take him to United. He had a big fight to get him out of the club. He told me he'd come back for Derek Statham and me, but never did. Things started to change then.'

In Atkinson's stead the West Brom board re-appointed his predecessor, Ronnie Allen. It was a fatal mistake. During his spell in Saudi Arabia the already remote Allen had grown more sombre and inward-looking. Next to the warmth and well being Atkinson had emitted, he returned to the club like an ice storm. Allen froze out Tony Brown and moved on Peter Barnes. In their place he brought in workmanlike footballers such as Steve Mackenzie from Manchester City and Andy King from Everton, and also two misfiring Dutchmen, Martin Jol and Romeo Zondervan.

West Brom won just two of their opening twelve League games of the 1981–82 campaign. At a later point in the season, they lost ten of eleven matches. They were knocked out of the UEFA Cup 4-1 on aggregate by Grasshopper Zurich in the First Round of the competition. The radiant vision of Atkinson's marauding side faded to grey, and gates at the Hawthorns fell as low as 11,000. Two years earlier the club had lit up both the Black Country and English football, but now it was as ravaged-looking as the town and area it served.

'The players that had come into the side didn't have the same attitude or work ethic, or appreciation of the team being the most important thing,' says John Wile. 'It was hard. I was falling out with people in the dressing room on a regular basis and having to try to motivate them at half-time or through games. We'd gone from being a very well organised and disciplined team to one that had split into factions.'

Brendon Batson took the mess that Allen presided over on and off the pitch as a personal affront. Schooled at Bertie Mee's rigorous Arsenal academy, he was a man of strong convictions about how things should best be accomplished. He compiled a list of his grievances with the new regime, concluded that they were unlikely to be satisfactorily resolved and submitted a transfer request, which was promptly turned down.

'Big Ron had dominated the club and his going left a gaping hole,' he says. 'In his place you had a manager who just didn't seem to grasp what we'd done and had hoped to do.'

However, in the midst of this ruinous drama Cyrille Regis

was having his most productive season as a goal-scorer. He'd never been especially prolific, but now was scoring at a rate of a goal per two games in a struggling team. In the League, he struck a brace of hat-tricks, against Birmingham and Swansea City. Yet there was one goal of his in particular that stood out. Not on account of it being extraordinary, though it was, but because it could be viewed as a shining monument to a vanishing age.

It was the only goal of an FA Cup Fifth Round tie with Norwich at the Hawthorns on 13 February. Watching footage of it now, there's no sense of what's to come. It's an unseasonably bright day, but the ground is half full and the game ragged. No time or place for wonder. Ally Robertson wins the ball in the centre circle and loops it towards Regis. He's surrounded by defenders, has his back to goal and has forty yards to travel. You expect him to hold the ball up or lay it off, to conform to the nature of the contest. Instead, Regis takes it on his chest, spins and runs with it, shrugging off one, two challengers and leaving a third defender sprawling in his wake. He dashes ten yards and looks up just once, then fires. He hits the ball right-footed and with such force that he's bent double and off the ground when it begins its unstoppable trajectory. It proceeds in a perfect, vicious arc into the top left-hand corner of the Norwich goal, the net bulging.

Freeze-framed as he turns to celebrate, Regis has both arms raised and is beaming. The late-afternoon sun bathes him in an amber glow. He is a king in his kingdom, but also a picture of unconfined joy. Right there and then, he seems to epitomise all that had been won and also lost inside and outside of the club and the game.

'It was one of my best years,' he says. 'Ronnie Allen was a

factor for me, because he was the only manager I ever played for who'd been a forward, and he understood a striker's mentality. I'd never had a lot of stamina and he was used to training top-class players abroad. He told me that he didn't want me crossing the halfway line. Before that, I'd been expected to chase back and defend corners and free kicks because I was good in the air. So I had more explosive energy that season. That allowed me to zip past people in the last half-hour of a game.'

In the aftermath of the Norwich match, Regis was called up by Ron Greenwood to the full England squad for the first time. The occasion was a Home International against Northern Ireland at Wembley on 23 February. The week of the game an anonymous-looking envelope arrived at the Hawthorns marked for his attention.

'Inside it there was a bullet and a handwritten note,' says Regis. 'The letter said: "If you put a foot on Wembley turf you'll get one of these through your knees." In football, we laugh at everything. So we put it up on the dressing room wall and had a good laugh about it. I've still got the bullet somewhere.'

'Cyrille used to change near me and when he got that I told him I'd rather he didn't,' adds John Wile. 'We had to make light of it, because really there was no other way of dealing with something like that.'

Regis came on as a sixty-fifth-minute substitute for Trevor Francis at Wembley in a game won 4-0 by England. In doing so he became just the third black player to represent the country after Viv Anderson and Laurie Cunningham. The match otherwise passed without incident and Regis made two further appearances for England that year, against Wales and Iceland, but he was never given the benefit of an extended run in the team.

There was no improvement in West Brom's form in the League and they were in increasing peril of relegation. However, they managed to reach the semi-finals of both the League and FA Cups. Tottenham were their opponents in a two-legged League Cup tie. Both games were tight and fractious, but the north Londoners were the better and more potent side, and were expected to win. The teams drew 0-0 at the Hawthorns and Spurs duly ran out 1-0 winners at White Hart Lane the following week.

It was a different matter in the FA Cup semi-final that took place at Highbury on 3 April. Pitted against Second Division QPR, Albion were hot favourites to progress to Wembley. However, the Arsenal stadium had been the scene of Atkinson's undoing four years earlier at the same stage of the competition. Allen also now sent his side to their doom there. In advance of the game the Baggies' manager fixated on QPR's veteran midfielder Tony Currie. Currie was a class act and a former England international, but at thirty-two he was past his best and likely to struggle against the more mobile Gary Owen, who'd become a fixture in the West Brom side.

'At 12.30 p.m. on the day of the game, Ronnie Allen got us together at our hotel and read his team out,' recalls Ally Robertson. 'We'd trained all week with the regular team and lined up how we'd expected to play, but he'd changed it. He announced he was dropping Gary Owen and replacing him with Martyn Bennett, a centre-half. We were all looking at each other thinking, "Where the hell has that come from?" The game turned out to be a nightmare. We started off bad and got worse.'

Allen decided to set his side up to guard against the dormant threat posed by Currie. It made for a tortuous spectacle. The supposed superior team encamped in their own half, their opponents given licence to possess the ball but unable to do anything constructive with it. Even Regis succumbed to inertia. Marshalled by the strong but limited Bob Hazell, he hardly had a kick.

Scoreless at half-time, the West Brom players trooped off to the dressing room and into what John Wile describes as a 'hell of a row' with their manager. It did them no good. The second half was a horror show, deathless. In the end it was decided by a freak goal, Robertson attempting to make a clearance and the ball rebounding off QPR striker Clive Allen's knee and into the Albion net.

There was nothing left for them to play for now but survival in the League, and with the dressing room mutinous and rancorous. Six successive games were lost after the QPR debacle and West Brom slipped into the relegation places. Edgy, unconvincing wins against Wolves and Notts County dragged them back out of it, and it all came down to the penultimate fixture of the season against Leeds at the Hawthorns. A victory would be enough for Albion to retain their First Division status and relegate the Yorkshire side, whose empire had crumbled. Defeat would instead send them into the abyss.

Regis won the match with his twenty-fourth goal of the campaign, but there was no time to celebrate it. The loss sent Leeds' fans on a rampage. Fighting broke out on the terraces and outside of the ground, with uprooted seats and chunks of masonry being used as missiles. This was also a riot borne of frustration and anger, but at nothing more than a game. In that regard, it seemed to reflect the ugly, brutish and senseless tone of the period as a whole.

★

In the summer of 1982, Regis signed a new contract with Albion. He reflected later that this was a mistake and that he was 'about to enter my wilderness years'. The club went there with him. Allen resigned at the end of the season and was replaced by an unsung Scot, Ron Wylie. A grafting midfielder with Aston Villa and Birmingham in the fifties and sixties, Wylie's inglorious coaching career to that point had amounted to spells as an assistant at Villa and Coventry, and a couple of years in charge of a Cypriot side, Bulova. He was a decent man, but an uninspiring choice.

Shorn of Allen's pernicious influence, West Brom had a better time of it the next season and finished eleventh in the League. However, the rot continued below the waterline. The average gate at the Hawthorns fell again to 15,260, the lowest it had been since 1914 in the shadow of the Great War. John Wile and Ally Brown were sold off and on 30 October 1982, Brendon Batson's playing career came to a premature end. He was playing for West Brom at Ipswich that afternoon and the team was on its way to a 6-1 defeat. Going in for a challenge, Batson felt his leg twist and his knee buckle.

'It was the same one I'd injured as a sixteen-year-old at Arsenal and I knew that pain all too well second time around,' he says. 'It was what's called a bucket-handle tear to the cartilage. The Sunday morning after the game, I went to see my daughter riding in a show-jumping event in Birmingham. I was walking up a flight of steps to the viewing gallery and I felt my knee go. That was it, done.'

Batson was 29-years-old and never played again. He'd made 220 appearances for West Brom, but statistics didn't begin to tell the tale of his career. As a defender, he was outstanding, as a man, even more so. In both cases he was never less than resolute, strong-willed, determined and defiant, and he had needed to be at the time he came into football. He was gone from the hurly-burly of the game too soon, but left having made an immense imprint on it.

Without him, West Brom's story turned into a bad farce. Ron Wylie lasted less than two years as manager. The team was again cannon fodder in his second season and he was sacked halfway through it. Like Allen, Johnny Giles returned to the club and also failed at the second time of asking. Giles begot Ron Saunders, who'd led Aston Villa to their 1981 title but had then got Birmingham relegated. A taciturn and seemingly humourless character, Saunders was at the tiller when Albioin finally dropped into the Second Division, having won just four games during the whole of the 1985–86 campaign. Out went Saunders and back came Atkinson like the prodigal son, only to walk out on the club again within a year. Rudderless, West Brom drifted into the shadows of the lower leagues. They would be stuck there for sixteen years.

'It happened right in front of me and was terribly sad,' says Derek Statham, who remained at Albion until 1987. 'It was obvious what was going on at the club: they were getting rid of the higher earners, bringing in a lot of rubbish, and were prepared to face the consequences. All that had been built up was allowed to fall apart and it was inevitable how it was going to end.'

Regis was at the Hawthorns until 1984. Injuries had taken a toll on him by then. The constant pounding to his knees and ankles dimminished his pace and mobility. He had also been wrung out having to lead the line of an ailing team. However, the simplest truth was that he had increasingly missed Laurie Cunningham. He was his own man and a powerful presence, but Cunningham had been a lightning bolt for him to spark with and fire off. In his last two seasons at the club, Regis was teamed with a gangling young black lad named Garry Thompson who'd been signed from Coventry by Ron Wylie. Thompson was a good, honest player, but not a magical one. Not someone who could detonate Regis.

'I'd never had to handle a dip in my career up until that point,' says Regis. 'I didn't know how to deal with a loss of form over a long period. Or with constantly playing when you're not fully fit. That was happening to me a lot, especially under Ron Wylie. I was seen as the mainstay of the team. Not being boastful, but in a sense it was like if I was out there, then there was hope.

'I didn't understand that form is temporary and talent permanent. Being out there all the time without being quite right, it affects the whole way that you play. You get a bit stale. The team also wasn't doing well, so it was a constant battle. Johnny Giles came back and wanted to change things around. He felt that I'd got too complacent.'

Regis was put on the transfer list. Coventry City bid £250,000 for him. It was the first and last offer West Brom got. In the hierarchy of West Midlands football, Coventry ranked below West Brom, Aston Villa, Birmingham and Wolves, and above only Walsall. This was despite the fact that they had been in the top flight of the Football League since 1967, having risen from its basement under the stewardship of the club's most famous son, Jimmy Hill. They had also trailblazed to the extent of having the first all-seater stadium in England.

Yet Coventry was perceived to be a small-time club that was operating above its station. It had never won one of the game's major honours and began each season with the primary objective of survival in the First Division. In the two most recent campaigns,

Coventry had achieved that by the skin of their teeth. For Regis, going there would be at best a sideways move.

'Two years before I'd been on the verge of the England team and won 'Midlands Footballer of the Year',' he says. 'I was sure that once word got out that Coventry wanted me, other clubs would come in. But no one did and that hurt. Not the Villas or the Evertons, just a bottom-four club. Man, it affects your confidence and self-esteem. So I made an emotional decision rather than a career one. Looking back, it was a really, really bad one.'

Chapter Sixteen: Born Again

Cyrille Regis went to Coventry City at twenty-six fearing his best days had gone. The team he joined had a rag-tag look to it. It appeared to have been assembled more in hope than expectation. The manager was Bobby Gould, a bullish character who'd played for Coventry and nine other clubs during a meandering career as a jobbing striker. Gould's time in management would follow the same course, and among his recruits to Highfield Road were the ex-England centre-forward Bob Latchford and Regis's erstwhile Albion colleague Peter Barnes. Both of them were also using Coventry as the latest staging post in their long drifts through the game.

Next to these journeymen, Coventry had a sprinkling of fresher, rawer talent. Like Regis, 22-year-old full-back Stuart Pearce had trained as an electrician and been snapped up from a non-league club down south, Wealdstone. Pearce was so intense and committed on the pitch that he acquired the nickname 'Psycho'. He would go on to bigger and better things at Brian Clough's Nottingham Forest and become a fixture in the England team. Forward Terry Gibson stood five-foot-four in his socks and had failed to make the grade at Tottenham, but was nippy, skilful and pugnacious. A nineteen-year-old local boy, Lloyd McGrath was a diligent midfielder and among the wave of black youngsters who were now following Regis's path into the professional game. John Barnes at Watford had just then broken into the England squad and future internationals Ian Wright and Paul Ince would emerge in the next two years at Crystal Palace and West Ham respectively.

Such as it was, the soul of the club belonged to the two eccentric characters who marshalled the team's defence. Looming goalkeeper Steve Ogrizovic looked like a giant from a children's fairy-tale. He was twenty-five, but could pass for two decades older and had hands the size of buckets. Ogrizovic had been a policeman before becoming a footballer and was a prodigious smoker. Centre-half Brian Kilkline also appeared more ancient than his twenty-two years with his flowing hair and eruption of facial hair. He was built like an oak and had the bearing of a barbarian warrior about to go off and do battle with Roman legions. Kilkline was referred to as 'Killer' among his team-mates on account of his up-and-at-'em approach to both football and life in general.

In short, Coventry seemed to be a mess, and they played like it for two years. Regis's first season at the club looked like ending in relegation until the team strung together three successive victories to save themselves at the death. The last of these was a 4-1 win over champions Everton on the final Saturday of the campaign, with Regis bagging a brace of goals. Gould had been sacked at Christmas and replaced by his assistant, Don Mackay. A Glaswegian and a former goalkeeper, Mackay was an able deputy but not a leader of men. Under him, Coventry also scraped through the next campaign. Two points separated them from the drop on this occasion, which put added value on a 3-0 home win they recorded against Ron Saunders's sinking West Bromwich Albion.

These were desperate times for Regis. He was meant to be for Coventry all that he had been for West Brom, which is to say formidable and almost larger than life itself – not just a part of the team, but its strongest component. The trouble was that Regis felt as though his powers had waned, and he found himself going through the motions.

'I'd ended up being a big fish in a small pond,' he says. 'Everything was focused on me and I wasn't playing well, so there was double the pressure. We were a poor side and always having to win the last game of the season to stay up. Nothing against Coventry, but I was a better player than that.'

Regis had slipped his moorings off the pitch, too. In 1983, he married his long-term girlfriend Beverley and had fathered two children with her, a son, Robert, and daughter Michelle. However, Regis wasn't rooted by family life. In fact, he ran from it and also from the anguish of his own apparent decline. He'd always enjoyed a night out, but now these were more frequent and there was something more wilful and destructive about his drinking and carousing.

'I was causing Beverley a lot of pain,' he told the *Sunday Mercury* newspaper in 2010. 'It was a tough cycle to get out of. I was stuck in a vortex of work hard, play hard, partying and girls. Every so often I'd get a call from a newspaper to tell me they were going to run a story saying I was with this girl or that girl. That happened to me a couple of times during my early days at Coventry. Nothing ever came of it, but I would clutch the phone in terror and think of the embarrassment and shame if my wife, family and the public found out.'

Regis's saviour in football was the unremarkable-looking figure of John Sillett. A former defender for Coventry from 1962-66, Sillett was in his fifties, bald, overweight and known to one and all as 'Snozzer'. He also had an infectious enthusiasm for the game and a zest for life. In this respect at least, he was very much like Ron Atkinson. When Don Mackay was dismissed at the end of the 1985–86 season, Sillett and Coventry's more reserved Managing Director, George Curtis, were paired up to run the football side of the club. Sillett's infectious *joie de vivre* injected life into the place and fired up the team.

Coventry finished tenth in the League the next season. Freed from the shackles of a relegation battle and inflated by Sillett's promptings, Regis was rejuvenated. He found himself again the point around which a team coalesced, top scoring with sixteen goals and rolling back the years. One of Regis's strikes was the last in a 3-0 home win over Third Division Bolton Wanderers in a Third Round FA Cup tie. Played on 10 January 1987 in front of a sparse 10,000 crowd, it was a low-key beginning to the ultimate triumph of Coventry's season. They proceeded through the competition with more impressive away wins against Manchester United, Stoke and Sheffield Wednesday, and into a semi-final with Second Division Leeds at Wednesday's Hillsborough stadium.

For Regis, FA Cup semi-finals held recent and bitter memories. In this, his third, he got echoes to begin with of the two abject defeats he'd previously suffered with West Brom and of other, darker days. The underdogs Leeds started at a gallop and Coventry froze. Regis was stuck on the periphery of things and unable to get a foothold in the game. In so being he was at least spared the tribal chorus of boos that rose up from the Leeds supporters whenever Lloyd McGrath or winger Dave Bennett, Coventry's third black player, got the ball.

Leeds took the lead in the sixteenth minute and seemed rampant. Yet the game turned on one fleeting moment that involved Regis. It seemed insignificant at the time, but it had a profound effect. Reeling from Leeds' assault, the Coventry defence was reduced to punting long, hopeful balls upfield. Nearing half-time, Regis got on the end of one. He took it on his chest, felt Leeds' centre-half Brendon Ormsby coming up close behind him, spun and ran. In three, four strides he was clear of Ormsby and at the edge of the Leeds box. He shot, the ball screwing just wide of the goal.

'But that was a sight of the old Cyrille,' says reporter Martin Swain. 'The whole Coventry team took off from that instant. You could sense how it gave them all a lift. To watch an athlete be able to do that and on such a big stage, it's what us mere mortals gaze at in wonder.'

The game went into extra time, but a resurgent Coventry won it 3-2 and went on to their first Wembley final. It was still then true that the climactic point of the FA Cup was English football's grandest occasion. The nation stopped to watch the final, and Regis's last command performance took place before 100,000 spectators inside the stadium and a live TV audience of many millions.

Tottenham's artisans were in opposition on a sun-kissed afternoon in May and were odds-on favourites to lift the famous trophy. The Spurs side was blessed with an elegant but formidable midfield trio of Osvaldo Ardiles and the England internationals Glenn Hoddle and Chris Waddle. Each of them was blessed with prodigious abilities to manoeuvre a football and capable of seizing hold of a game and dictating its course. That season they had an especially lethal striker to finish off their orchestrations. Sharp as a needle point, Clive Allen was enjoying a golden campaign and had helped himself to forty-eight goals.

Allen duly notched his forty-ninth of the season just two minutes into the game. Waddle slipped his marker, Greg Downs, with almost arrogant ease and crossed for him to score. In that instant, the outcome of the match seemed certain. It was the last time it would appear so. Coventry's cup run had given them self-belief and reserves of inner strength, but also a sense of destiny, and they didn't capitulate. In this regard, Regis was especially significant to them. The final wasn't his greatest game, not even close. However, he had an influence on it simply by being. He was the team's anchor, a fixed point for them to send the ball to and immovable once in possession of it. The devastating burst of speed had gone from his legs, but he retained the strength and sheer presence to occupy defenders and wear them down. This allowed others around him to exploit both space and also tired minds and limbs.

The contest pitched and see-sawed through ninety minutes of regular time and then thirty minutes' extra-time. Coventry's man-of-the-match Bennett equalised Allen's strike. An own goal from Kilkline regained the lead for Spurs and Keith Houchen restored parity again on the hour with a diving header. In the fifth minute of the additional period, Spurs' Gary Mabbutt inadvertently turned a cross from McGrath into his own net. Spurs came storming back once more, but Coventry held on to the lead and the cup was theirs.

Their celebrations were gleeful, delirious. The team paraded around the pitch in triumph. Sillett danced a jig on the Wembley running track and in front of the TV cameras. All of them were sucking up the moment, and were also now seeming disbelieving of it. In the midst of it all, Regis stood tall. He wore the lid of the cup on his head and a big and untroubled smile on his face. For all the symbolic victories he'd won, this was his first tangible trophy, and also his last.

He spent four more seasons at Coventry. His and the team's form endured through two of them, Regis top scoring again in 1988 and Coventry finishing a best ever seventh in the First Division the next year. In October 1987, he was recalled to the England team to win his fifth and final cap as a substitute in an 8-0 romp over Turkey in a European Championship qualifier at Wembley. That return was fleeting for him and so also was Coventry's period in the sun. Relegation threatened the club once more in the 1989–90 season and Sillett was sacked.

By then, Regis had been left first devastated and then changed by a single, terrible event that occurred in Spain. He'd had a premonition of this the summer after Coventry's cup win and when he'd been visiting Laurie Cunningham in Madrid. In the early hours of one morning, Cunningham was driving them back to his house from a night out when he fell asleep at the wheel of his Renault 5 GTI. The car veered across the road and smashed into a barrier that ran alongside the city's main A6 highway.

'We'd been out drinking and partying and it was about 2 a.m.,' Regis says. 'The car rolled over three or four times. It ended up sliding on its roof. I can still see and hear it now, the sparks and the noise. I was waiting for the impact, but there wasn't one. It was a lucky escape, but we'd both had our seatbelts on.'

Both of them walked away from the scene of this crash with nothing more than cuts and bruises. The shock of it wasn't enough to curb Regis' drinking or save his marriage. He and Beverley were divorced, the wounds raw and painful. It would be another two years before he faced up to his demons and then only after receiving news that Cunningham had gone to his doom during the early hours of another Madrid morning on the same stretch of road. Today, he marks the loss of his friend as the turning point in his life.

'It got me to think about everything and ask what it was all about,' he says. 'Here's a guy whose life was very parallel to mine. He'd had a great career and all the riches – the houses, the cars and the whole thing. Yet he'd left it all behind. Within a year I'd reached out to a group called Christians in Sport and become a born again Christian.'

'Cyrille did everything that a young man in his twenties would do,' says Martin Swain. 'He lived the life and it cost him Beverley, who was lovely. And he knows that. But he came out the other side and this fantastic person emerged. He's a very rounded man and totally understated. One of my great pleasures in life is being able to sit with Cyrille and talk with him about everything from spirituality to the demon drink.'

In all, Regis played one more League game for Coventry than he did for West Brom and scored thirty-five fewer goals. Former Ipswich and England centre-half Terry Butcher took over as the club's new manager at the start of the 1990–91 season and deemed him surplus to requirements. He was given a free transfer and picked up by Ron Atkinson, who'd just then taken over at Aston Villa. He spent two seasons at Villa, at thirty-three the elder statesman in a strong side that finished runners-up to Manchester United in the inaugural season of the English Premier League in 1992–93. That Villa squad provided ample evidence of the legacy Regis had bequeathed to the game, since it included eight other black players: Earl Barrett, Ugo Ehiogu, Bryan Small, Paul McGrath, Tony Daley, Dalian Atkinson, Martin Carruthers and Dwight Yorke.

He was a bit-part player by the end of his time at Villa and after being released by them dropped down through the Leagues. He went first to Wolves and then to Wycombe Wanderers and finally to Chester City in the old Fourth Division, where he played out his final season before retiring in 1996 at the age of thirty-eight.

'I wanted to do twenty years as a pro, one more, but I'd had an injury to my ankle that we couldn't diagnose and it was causing me too much pain,' he says. 'It was hard going as well. You never had the luxury of staying anywhere overnight. You'd travel for three, four hours on the coach and then get off to play in front of a thousand people at Scunthorpe.'

In the final analysis, Regis's career tailed off and perhaps he was never again as magnificent as he was in those first three years at West Brom. However, the scope of his time in football was so much bigger and more significant than that – bigger than the fact of his having played over 700 games and scored more than 200 goals. To the likes of Dwight Yorke, Ian Wright, Paul Ince and the countless others for whom he kicked down the doors and showed the way, he remains a hero, an icon and a giant of the game.

He went back to West Brom in 1997 as reserve-team coach, when the club was still floundering, but left again three years later. He says he didn't grow to love coaching and that 'there was a bit of pride involved as well. I was in danger of becoming the guy who got wheeled out like an old bit of furniture, the Albion legend.' He moved on to his current role as a football agent, his first client being his nephew, Jason Roberts, also a striker. In 2006, he married his second wife, Julia, and two years later was awarded the MBE in recognition of his charity work for organisations like Water Aid. He is fifty-six now, a grandfather and at peace.

'I have no regrets,' he says. 'Some decisions I made were right, some were wrong, but that's the way life is. You're young, you make mistakes. And things look different through the eyes of a 50-year-old. At the time I was playing for West Brom, all I focused on was staying in the team. Now I'm able to appreciate the impact we had. That there was a generation of black kids out there who were thinking, "If he can do it, so can I."'

In 1984, Brendon Batson left the West Midlands after finally admitting defeat in his battle against injury. He says there was 'only so much pity and sympathy that I could take.' He moved his family to Cheshire and gradually found a route back into the game. He tried management, applying for the vacant post at his old club Cambridge but failed to even get an interview.

'I find it remarkable that Brendon didn't become the first black manager,' says Pat Murphy. 'Ron Atkinson had written him a glowing reference and felt he was an absolute shoo-in for the Cambridge job. I remember doing a piece for the radio and being furious about the fact he hadn't been interviewed, because we all got a little bit more vociferous about things in the eighties.'

As a player at both Cambridge and West Brom, Batson had been his team-mates' union representative and progressed to being the first black member of the PFA's management committee. In the spring of 1984, he accepted the offer of a full-time job from the union's Chief Executive, Gordon Taylor. He proved to be one of the game's most able and influential administrators, rising to the position of Taylor's deputy during his eighteen years at the PFA. He championed the conception of the Kick It Out initiative in 1993 and describes its subsequent evolution into a campaigning organisation as 'a watershed moment for football. It is without doubt the success story of the game in terms of dealing with a social issue.'

Batson left the PFA in 2002 to take up a position as West Bromwich Albion's new Managing Director. Like Regis, his return to the club was an unhappy one. West Brom had been promoted to the Premier League for the first time at the end of the previous season, but too soon for an inexperienced board and a labouring team to grapple with. Batson lasted a year in the job. During this time relations between the club's new chairman, Jeremy Peace, and its manager, Gary Megson, deteriorated to the point of open warfare and the team was relegated back to the First Division. Peace terminated his contract, claiming the club's demotion had forced him into a cost-cutting restructure.

'Brendon could only do so much in an environment that was like a madhouse,' says journalist Chris Lepkowski. 'The club wasn't ready for the Premier League. Megson was also a very political animal and someone who didn't seem at all easy to work with; he also fell out with Peace's predecessor, Paul Thompson, and with strikers Jason Roberts and Bob Taylor. You could ask him about a groin injury to a player and he'd turn it into an attack on the chairman.'

'The one regret I have is that I didn't make a success of that job,' says Batson. 'I was frightened when I left it. I hadn't been out of work since I was sixteen. My wife convinced me I'd be fine. Sure enough, we were going off to our house in Spain soon after when I got call to do some consultancy work for the FA.'

Today, Batson runs his own successful sports consultancy business and holds a number of directorships, among them the chairmanship of the Professional Players' Federation. He is widely acknowledged as one the most impressive and respected figures in the game and was awarded an MBE for his services to football in the New Year's Honours List of 2000. As a player, he survived the worst the sport could throw at him, and its occasionally treacherous political machinations as an administrator. The same strength and resolve got him through his grief at the shattering loss of his rock, Cecily, who was taken from him by cancer in September 2009.

'At the times when I needed it, my wife was always the one who gave me the right advice,' he says. 'She never doubted me or my abilities, even when I doubted them myself. Losing her changed my life and the life of my family forever. Things will never be the same. But I've got two children, five lovely grand-children and no complaints. I wouldn't change anything.'

During the years since he retired from the game, Batson has also felt the pangs of another significant loss in his life. In 2003, he co-founded the West Brom Former Players' Association with the club's 1968 FA Cup-winning captain, Graham Williams. The organisation has more than 100 members and meets at regular social functions and fund-raising events. These have brought back together the boys of 1978–79, reigniting their shared memories of the time when they were filled with hopes and dreams and came within touching distance of greatness. For Batson, they are also haunted by the ghost of the man who is no longer among them. The one of them who promised most of all, but fell furthest and hardest, and left them on a summer's morning in 1989.

Chapter Seventeen: Swansong

All things considered, 1982 was an awful year for Laurie Cunningham. His 1981–82 season at Real Madrid had been wiped out by injury, and as a result he was omitted from Ron Greenwood's England squad for the summer World Cup in Spain. His anticipated participation in the tournament had been one of the driving factors that took him to the country in the first place, but he was a mere spectator when it kicked off in his adopted homeland. Here was especially withering evidence of how wrong it had gone for him in Madrid, and he was dealt a series of other savage blows in the coming months.

The first of these was the loss of his most accommodating supporter at Real Madrid. Failure to win back La Liga or a European prize had cost Vujadin Boskov his job as head coach and he was replaced by Alfredo Di Stefano. One of Real's greats, the Argentinian was also a notoriously severe and unforgiving character. In particular, he was intolerant of footballers whom he viewed as shirkers or dilettantes and whom he saw as taking a relaxed attitude to their physical conditioning.

He brooked no challenge to his authority. The Brazilian playmaker Didi arrived at Real in 1959 as a World Cup winner and as the club's first black player. Didi was a terrifically gifted footballer, but his journalist wife wrote an article criticising his team-mate Di Stefano's influence at the club. In response, Di Stefano ostracised the Brazilian and he was forced out of Real at the end of his first season. There was no doubting that as a coach Di Stefano's kind of player was going to be Uli Stielike and not Cunningham.

If this was wounding to Cunningham, Nicky Brown's departure from Spain and the ending of their relationship was ruinous. Brown had been the one constant in his life since they were both teenagers, when he was starting out in the game. She had shared in his highs and lows, helped him to fight his battles and encouraged his dreaming. The two of them had agreed long ago on the terms that bound them. They had an understanding that if one of them ever decided to leave the other then there would doubtless be a good reason for it, given how tightly locked together they were. The abandoned party was to respect this and not attempt to change the other's mind or follow them.

'I didn't want to lead that kind of life anymore,' Brown says now. 'It was like living in a goldfish bowl. I also wanted Laurie to get out of football. He'd had too many injuries. We had enough money to go around and didn't need it. We'd realised how happy we were back at Orient and with our parents. Laurie's goal was always to help other people. We used to lie in bed at night discussing what we were going to do. He wanted to build villages that would offer a home life to the kind of kids we'd seen at children's homes in London.

'If I left, I thought he'd come with me. I didn't realise how tied up he was. It was a huge mistake on my part. We thought we'd betrayed each other, but we'd not. We'd just done what the other one wanted. I was waiting for my prince to come and get me, but he couldn't because of what we'd agreed. We couldn't talk to each other for the first three months after I left, it was too painful. But we never lost touch. Then things changed rapidly for him.'

Dave Harrison, who'd ghosted Cunningham's column for the *Evening Mail* when he was in his pomp as a player at West Brom, remembers running into him in a nightclub in Madrid during the World Cup. It was in the weeks immediately following Brown's leaving and Cunningham appeared to Harrison more animated than he'd ever seen him during the time the two of them were working together. He was talking a mile a minute and showing off his Michael Jackson moves on the dance floor. Yet there was also something lost and needy about him.

'He made such of fuss of me that night,' says Harrison. 'I think that might have been a reflection of the fact that he was lonely and looking for a bit of company. We chatted for quite a while and then he asked me if I wanted to come back to his place. I'd got an early start in the morning, so I declined. I've wondered ever since if we'd have driven down the road he was killed on.'

Soon after the World Cup, Cunningham's old sparring partner Bobby Fisher visited him in Madrid. Fisher was immediately confronted with a vision of all that his friend had been in Spain and also proof of the trajectory that he was now on. When Cunningham arrived at the airport to pick him up, Fisher looked on agog as he was clapped through the arrivals lounge by the waiting crowd. A more shocking sight met him when he got to Cunningham's once palatial home in Las Matas. It seemed to Fisher like a 'war zone'. The outdoor swimming pool was filled with rubbish and unusable. Inside, the first two floors of the three-storey house were near-derelict. Cunningham had confined himself to the kitchen and the master bedroom on the third floor.

'He told me he'd hired some Spanish builders to come and sort the place out for him, but that they'd never turned up,' says Fisher. 'It was desperate. That was my first point of thinking that there was something not quite right about the situation, and especially with Laurie. He'd split with Nicky and got this freaky Spanish girl living with him. She didn't speak a word of English and he didn't speak Spanish. She was just there for the sake of being there.

'I spent a week with him and we went out every night to different clubs, but I never once saw Laurie smile or laugh. He was like a dead soul. In many ways, I was glad to get away from him. He'd lost the one person that could ground him and I think he'd just bought into all that bullshit, living that kind of false life. The clubs we went to and the people we met were all false. None of it was real. He didn't find it easy to make friends and all these people wanted him for was football. Laurie never wanted to be the archetypal footballer. He'd talk about the game for five, ten minutes, but then want to get on to something else. The frustration he must have felt being out there would have been horrendous. He seemed to me a really lonely figure.'

Whatever torment Cunningham was going through, he continued to present a positive face to his brother. Keith Cunningham also came out to Madrid that summer and remembers his younger sibling seeming in good spirits. He was shocked at the news of Brown's going, but Laurie Cunningham otherwise avoided the subject. Normally, Keith would bunk up at Las Matas for weeks at a time. However, on this occasion his visit was brought to an abrupt and dreadful end.

In the depths of a Sunday night in July, Keith received a phone call at the house from police back in England. He was told that his partner, Norma Richards, and two of her three daughters from a previous relationship had been found murdered in the home the couple shared in Dalston, north-east London. Richards, twenty-seven, was raped and stabbed to death. Nine-year-old Samantha Richards had also been stabbed and seven-year-old Syretta Richards drowned in the bath. Their four-year-old sister, Rhodene, had spent the weekend with her grandmother and was spared. The two of them discovered Richards's naked body and those of her children when Rhodene was returned home. The interior of the house had also been daubed with National Front slogans.

'I told Laurie, he went straight to the football club and they got me a flight back home,' says Keith. 'It was a Monday morning when I got back to London. That's when I found out the full story of what had happened for the first time.'

Laurie Cunningham never got to see the case resolved. It remained open and its horrors ever present for twenty-eight long years. In December 2010, Wilbert 'Tony' Dyce, who'd been a casual acquaintance of Keith Cunningham's and Richards's, was convicted of the murders and sentenced to life in prison. Dyce had a history of sexual assault and had followed Richards home from a club. He was black, but had left the National Front graffiti in her house to cover his tracks. It had worked until advances in DNA technology finally linked him to the crime scene.

With events in his career and personal life lurching from crisis to catastrophe, Laurie Cunningham appears to have been desperate to bring about some form of normality. In short order, he entered into a relationship with a Spanish girl, Maria, and had a daughter with her, Georgina. He soon split from Georgina's mother, but just as quick met Sylvia Sendin-Soria, a petite brunette and a familiar face around the fringes of the football club. The couple were married within a year and subsequently had a son together, Sergio. Belatedly, Cunningham offered up to Real Madrid the image of a stable family life that the club preferred for its players.

'Me and my mom went out there for the wedding,' says Keith Cunningham. 'I asked him what he was getting married for, but he wouldn't discuss it. He hadn't been with her long. I think it was a little stunt. I think the club wanted him to get married, but he didn't. Cyrille had told him that he should come back to England and finish his career here. He didn't have to stay in Spain.'

'Laurie's old friends never got to know Sylvia too well,' says Fisher. 'It seemed to us like the ending of a big old chapter when he got married. We'd always seen it as being set in stone that Nicky and he would be together. The two of them parting was like the ravens leaving the Tower of London. Right away I felt that nothing good was going to come of it.

'I think Laurie also sensed that he wasn't going to be able to finish football with a great name and the power to get out all those other ideas that he had going on in his head. It's a horrible thing to say, but I felt he knew he couldn't get his old life back and so settled for second best. I may be completely wrong and he might have been very happy, but I really don't think so.'

However much Cunningham appeared to have conformed, it cut no ice with Di Stefano. UEFA's regulations at the time permitted clubs to have two overseas players in their squads and during the summer Real Madrid signed defender Johnny Metgod from the Dutch side AZ Alkmaar. Di Stefano paired the Dutchman with the German Stielike down the spine of his side and exiled Cunningham. He was left to brood until almost the end of the season and then sent out on loan to Manchester

United. This reunited him with Ron Atkinson and also with Bryan Robson and Remi Moses.

He featured in five games at the tail-end of a campaign that United finished third in the League. Now and then at Old Trafford he was able to flash and flare, though it was clear enough to his former colleagues how much he'd been curtailed by his catalogue of injuries. He could still enhance a game with a flick or a trick and use his experience to buy himself space and time on the ball. However, it was beyond him now to shape and change the course of a match.

'I hadn't stayed in touch with Laurie after he went to Spain, but we roomed together when he came to United,' says Robson. 'He'd changed. He wasn't as flamboyant on or off the pitch and was even quieter. There wasn't any sort of drama with him about what had happened in his career. He kept it to himself. But then, I never got the impression he was a deep thinker.'

United's last game of the season was the FA Cup final against relegated Brighton at Wembley. Atkinson still thought enough of Cunningham to pencil him in for a role in the game. Given the biggest stage he might even then have been lifted up and restored, but it wasn't it to be. His body again denied him. He pulled a muscle in training and failed to recover in time for the game. United went on to win the cup 4-0 after a replay. Cunningham went back to Spain to nurse his physical ailment and deeper, more painful psychological scars.

The pattern was set for the rest of his career. At twenty-seven, cameo roles were all that were left for him, quickening moments in the spotlight. He was like an old gunslinger riding from town to town, drifting from one club to the next. Never putting down roots and all the while knowing that a time was bound to come when he would get too slow, too broken and it'd all be over for him.

In the summer of 1983, Cunningham went to Sporting Gijon on Spain's north-west coast. Gijon is the largest city in the mountainous province of Asturias and the football club had been central to it since 1905. True glory hadn't been won at Sporting, but the club had been competing in the top division of La Liga since 1944 and finished runners-up in 1979. They played their football at El Molinon, the oldest surviving football stadium in the country. It was hundreds of miles and a world away from the Bernabeu.

Cunningham spent a season at Sporting. He was fit enough to manage thirty games for the club and scored three goals as they finished thirteenth in La Liga. The next season his contract with Real Madrid came to an end and he went to Marseilles in the south of France. Compared to Gijon, Marseilles was a teeming and cosmopolitan metropolis, but its football club had been under-achieving for years. Marseille had last won the French title in 1972 and wouldn't do so again until 1989. The club was in such a dysfunctional state that Cunningham played under three different managers during his one season with them. He got through another thirty games and then moved on once more.

He returned to England and went to Leicester City in the East Midlands. It was his most transparent step down to date. Leicester were traditionally one of English football's yo-yo clubs, too strong for the Second Division, not good enough for the First, and trapped in a purgatory of forever ping-ponging between the two. At the point of Cunningham joining, the club was embarking on a third consecutive season in the top flight, which counted as success. However, their most prolific player, striker Gary Lineker, had been sold to Everton and this left them toothless.

Leicester's 1985–86 campaign was a war of attrition. Battling against relegation, they won just two of their first fourteen League games and required a 2-0 victory over Newcastle in their last match of the season to keep them up. West Brom was one of the three teams that were worse off than them and went down instead. Attendances at their creaking Filbert Street ground averaged 11,000, and they also gave their supporters nothing to cheer in either of the two cup competitions, exiting both in the first round.

In this grim, grey environment, Cunningham's light was turned down low. The statistics show he had fifteen games for Leicester and no goals, but speak nothing of his torment. He was falling through the cracks and scrambling for something to hold onto. Much later, his wife Sylvia told the TV documentary *First Among Equals* that 'there were days when you saw him low. When a man has been so high and has to settle for less it shows.' Most often he kept his tumult buried deep and hidden from view. He put up, shut up and carried on.

'The injuries had fucked him up, but he didn't cry about it,' says Keith Cunningham. 'My brother wasn't a moaner or a weakling. He just got on. He was cool with it. It didn't make a difference to him which team it was for, so long as he was playing football, which he loved.'

'Guys don't talk about stuff like that with each other, not at that age anyway,' qualifies Cyrille Regis. 'You don't ask how someone's feeling and what's going on in their life. I didn't know what was going on inside with Laurie, because we didn't talk on that level. It was more about football, partying, birds and having a laugh. We were blagging it.'

Cunningham's next stopping off point was Rayo Vallecano, the third of Madrid's professional football clubs and in the shadow of Real and Atletico since its founding in 1924. Rayo was located in the working class Usera district to the south-east of the capital and wore its proletariat roots and left-wing leanings like badges of honour. It was an otherwise humble club with a small stadium and as fitful in Spain as Leicester was in England. Cunningham arrived during one of Rayo's frequent spells in the second tier of La Liga and left them fifth in the table at the end of the 1986–87 season.

From there his odyssey took him on to Belgium and Sporting Charleroi, in the industrialised south of the country. There was an odd echo given that Charleroi was historically a steel and mining city and known by locals as 'Pays Noir', the Black Country. It is likely Cunningham never found this out, since he was there just long enough to play a single game for Sporting and then gone again. Off to a club that was as far from the vision of balletic grace he had once been as was possible: Wimbledon.

Wimbledon Football Club was the ugly duckling of a leafy corner of south-west London best known for its spacious common and annual tennis tournament. Founded in 1889, the club wasn't elected to the Football League until 1977, but had since enjoyed a meteoric rise. Wimbledon had won promotion to the First Division in 1986 and finished sixth in their first season in the top tier, but the set-up and spirit of the club remained that of a lower-league underdog.

Their home ground was Plough Lane, a small and ramshackle arena that belonged to an earlier era of the game. Under impish manager Dave Bassett, the team had established a style of basic, bruising football that was as effective as it was simplistic. Wimbledon's approach to the game was two-fold: to hit the ball long and often, and to rough up the opposition whenever and wherever possible. Their sheer coarseness earned them the unofficial nickname of the 'Crazy Gang', which was ideally suited to some of their more combative players, most especially midfielders Vinnie Jones and Dennis Wise. Jones was a footballer of limited talent, but boundless aggression. With his close-cropped hair, tattoos and an expression that seemed to snarl even in repose, he was like a cartoon villain. The rodent-like Wise had more to his game, but a mean streak that suggested he would be able to start a fight in an empty room.

However, the Wimbledon side had a smattering of craftsmen as well as warriors. The young John Scales would evolve into an accomplished defender and Lawrie Sanchez added a degree of finesse to their midfield. Straddling both sides of this divide was John Fashanu, a centre-forward with a sometimes deft touch, but also so imposing he was known as 'Fash the Bash'. Fashanu was one of a handful of black players to have been brought up at the club. Among the others were three more regular first teamers: centre-halves Eric Young and Brian Gayle, and full-back Terry Phelan. Bassett resigned the summer before Cunningham's arrival and Bobby Gould had been handed the reins. Gould rescued his diminutive ex-Coventry striker Terry Gibson from an unfulfilling spell at Manchester United, but otherwise followed Bassett's blueprint.

The 1987–88 season was another good one for Wimbledon. They were comfortable in the top half of the table and on a run to the FA Cup final when Gould signed up Cunningham to complete the season with them. He featured in their last six League games and scored a couple of goals, but seemed a fish out of water – rather like a sleek sports car that had lost its top gear and was being forced to participate in a demolition derby. He nonetheless found a surrogate for Regis in the form of Fashanu and showed enough glimpses of his old self to win over most, if not all of his new team-mates.

'He was a gentleman,' says Phelan, who was then twenty-one. 'In terms of the way he presented himself, very elegant, smart and clean cut. To tell the truth, I was bowled over to be sat next to him in a dressing room. I suppose it would be like a kid today being sat next to Lionel Messi. He was struggling a little bit with his knee, but still in great shape. He often used to come in and say to me he wouldn't be training that day because he'd got gout.

'One morning, I asked him if he'd show me how he took those corners with the outside of his foot. He said, "No problem." All the lads just stood there and watched him curling in one ball after another, left and right side. It was absolutely brilliant. He gave me a smile and a little wink afterwards. He seemed a happy chap, but he was in a different league to the rest of us.'

'We had nothing in common,' says Sanchez. 'He was pally with John Fashanu and I wasn't. If you weren't in that camp then to an extent you didn't have anything to do with them. I don't even recall having a conversation with him. He seemed very humble and shy. He glided when he was on the ball. You could tell he had ability, but he certainly wasn't outstanding.'

Laurie Cunningham's swansong in English football was the FA Cup final at Wembley on 14 May 1988. The month before, he'd been a substitute for Wimbledon's semi-final victory over Luton Town at Spurs' White Hart Lane stadium and made it onto the pitch at the end of the game. Gould again selected him on the bench for the final against Liverpool, who were chasing the second part of a League and Cup double.

On a sweltering day and across the wide expanse of Wembley's pitch, it was thought that Liverpool would retain the ball, exhaust Wimbledon and beat them at a canter. However, their expected procession never got going before the watching Diana, Princess of Wales. Wimbledon stopped them in their tracks, scratching and scrapping, no lambs to the slaughter. They took the lead as half-time approached through a Sanchez header. Liverpool came at them in the second period, but Wimbledon soaked up the pressure and held firm. The result was assured when goalkeeper Dave Beasant saved a penalty from Liverpool's most reliable poacher of goals, John Aldridge.

Cunningham made his entry in the fifty-sixth minute. He had such a minimal impact on the game that both Sanchez and Phelan now wrongly believe that he didn't make it onto the pitch until its last seconds. His involvement added up to filling the space down which Liverpool sub Craig Johnston might have gone raiding, and a teasing moment when he slipped his marker and ran with the intent and poise of old, but into a dead-end.

At the final whistle the Wimbledon team were united in their exaltation at a famous triumph. However, one has to look hard at the surviving TV footage of the contest's aftermath to pick out Cunningham among them. He's there in the line of players waiting to receive the trophy from Princess Diana and as they group together on the pitch for a gaggle of press photographers, but like a silhouette or a ghost in the machine.

'Laurie had taken Brian Gayle's place in the squad for the final,' says Sanchez. 'Gayley was gutted. I remember seeing him in tears before the game. It was a bit naughty of the manager to have left him out. He'd been an integral part of the club since we'd got up into the top division. The whole team was being paid a pittance, but he got a pittance of a pittance. Laurie had been at the club for two minutes. He only touched the ball once or twice in the final. But there you go, he got a cup winners' medal.'

Wimbledon's victory party was held in a marquee that was erected on the furrowed pitch at Plough Lane. The BBC's *Match of the Day* programme was broadcast from it that night and the cup was given pride of place on a plinth sited in the middle of the makeshift room.

'I remember Laurie being there and throwing some shapes when we were all dancing,' says Phelan. 'He was joking with me, telling me he was going back to his castle in Spain. I never saw him again.'

Cunningham could have taken a different path. Don Howe, Wimbledon's assistant manager at the time, said later that he had impressed during his short spell at the club. The management were considering offering him a contract for the next season, but he left abruptly after the cup final and without a word. He was doubtless compelled by the fact that Sylvia had not long given birth to their son and wanted to go back to Spain.

Yet even then he might have been persuaded to stay on had Wimbledon been able to offer him the carrot of European football. Ordinarily, the club would then have gained entry into the European Cup Winners' Cup. However, English clubs were still under an ongoing ban from continental competition imposed by UEFA following the Heysel Stadium disaster of 1985. This held Liverpool fans responsible for the sickening crowd trouble that broke out inside the venue before that season's European Cup final with Juventus resulting in the deaths of thirty-nine Italian supporters.

Instead, Cunningham accepted an offer to return to Rayo Vallecano for another season in La Liga's second tier. It was a successful one for the club and they won promotion at the end of it. Niggling injuries kept him out of the side for half the campaign, but he managed nineteen games and the goal that sealed promotion. The team also included Argentinian midfielder Hugo Hernan Maradona, the younger and less blessed brother of the more heralded Diego. During the last weeks of Cunningham's life, he was negotiating with the club over the terms of a possible new contract. The process dragged on and Cunningham grew frustrated. He contacted Brendon Batson at the PFA and asked his old team-mate to help find him an English club.

'I spoke to him not long before his accident,' says Batson. 'There was almost like a kind of sadness in his voice. I think he was looking to find his way back home. At the PFA, we had a service for disengaged players and I put Laurie's name on it. I said I'd have a look round for him, but I could never pin him down on what he wanted to do.'

The acute sense of dislocation and of being unfulfilled that were felt by Cunningham sharpened when he went back to Spain. Slowly, irrevocably, he sank into despair and came undone. His family and closest friends aren't, or can't be specific about where and what this led him into, but what is clear is that at the end of his life he was profoundly conflicted. Bobby Fisher recalls Mavis, Cunningham's mother, voicing her concerns to him. She expressed a fear that her son had got involved in something that was potentially perilous to him, and that he had also run into financial troubles. The 'dead soul' Fisher saw in Madrid seven years earlier had slipped further into the shadows.

'We were worried about Laurie,' he says. 'Had he got into something that was deeper and quite dark down there? Was he mixing with some really villainous people? There is that idea. I don't think anyone knew exactly, but there was this darkness about him. A mutual friend told me Laurie had rung and said he needed to borrow some money. They said that the sum was £350 and that Laurie had told them it was to get some curtains fixed. There was something weird about the whole situation.

'Sometime before that, I know he'd been approached in a bar

and told to get out of the place. A guy had opened up his jacket and shown him a gun. I spoke to him on the phone two or three weeks before he died. It was a quick, very superficial conversation. "How're you doing? What's happening?" Again, it was like speaking to someone who wasn't there.'

'Yes, he was a troubled man and also deeply hurt,' says Nicky Brown. 'You have to know someone intimately for a long time to understand how they're affected and whether they're faking it or not. Laurie and I could never put a face on for each other. I got from him a terrible sense of sadness.

'Somehow, somewhere, I think he felt betrayed along the way by the money, the fame, by being for sale. He was no angel and he could be a bugger too, but he was too nice to be that clued up. It was so tragic, because he was beginning to develop as a man who recognised himself and was ready to stop playing games. He was ready to go on to something other than football.'

Brown had entered into another relationship and had given birth to a daughter since leaving Spain. However, she and Cunningham had stayed in touch and remained close. She'd spoken with him a week before he died. She was on holiday in Cornwall when the phone rang on the morning of 15 July 1989.

'I heard about Laurie's death four or five minutes before it was televised,' she says. 'My family had been desperately trying to get hold of me. In Spain, they bury their dead the next day. Mavis and her sister-in-law had to take off straight away to go and get his body because they'd already started that process. There was a big battle over the body.

'As soon as Mavis landed back in England, I was in attendance. I had to be with him, and I didn't leave his side till the funeral.'

Bobby Fisher heard the news from Mavis Cunningham, who called him at 8 a.m. 'She was crying and just said, "Laurie's dead,"' he says. 'I turned the radio on and there was no more Laurie. It was a really odd, empty feeling.'

Ron Atkinson was the first person from Cunningham's West Brom days to get the call. He had the difficult job of breaking the news to Cyrille Regis and Brendon Batson. Regis had spoken to Cunningham just two days before and was silent, crushed. Even now Batson says he 'can't remember the whole of that day. I was just numb.'

Speaking to the *Birmingham Post* two days later, Atkinson described Cunningham as 'the best player since George Best'. The new West Brom chairman, John Silk, added he was 'a tragic loss to football. Laurie was in a class of his own during his time at the Hawthorns. Albion supporters saw the best of him and will always treasure memories of his partnership with Cyrille Regis.'

Cunningham was buried near his family home in Tottenham, north London. The occasion was a public spectacle conducted before hundreds of mourners and in the glare of television cameras. Writing later in his autobiography, Atkinson claimed it was 'very evident that certain influences had been at work involving what can only be described as a black brotherhood of people connected to the sporting world.' Cunningham had latterly taken on an agent, Ambrose Mendy. A colourful self-publicist, Mendy's other clients included Cyrille Regis and John Fashanu, and he would go on to represent the boxer Nigel Benn. Among the many black footballers who attended the service were Carlton Palmer, who'd just then left West Bromwich Albion for Sheffield Wednesday, and his new team-mate, Dalian Atkinson.

'It was almost as if a bandwagon had taken over,' affirms Bobby Fisher. 'Quite a few people were there that day who wanted to use Laurie's passing to nurture their own profile. It felt almost as if we'd lost Laurie again. I wanted to remember him with a little bit of joy and not the dark periods that he seemed to have later in his life. How he used to move and some of the things we'd done together growing up. Going out dancing till 3 a.m. and coming in late for training and getting fined.

'After the service, a long train of cars and people followed on to the cemetery. Nicky and I didn't go along with that. We went on later to say our farewells and when no one else was there.'

'A year later, Laurie's family held a memorial service for him,' says Regis. 'On that occasion, it was just the family and his close friends that turned up. It showed you how very quickly people move on. Even within a year, he'd gone.'

The people who loved Cunningham and knew him best were left to pick up the pieces and to try to make sense of his death at thirty-three. His wife Sylvia returned to Spain after the funeral and later remarried. Their son Sergio has no recollection of his father other than through flickering TV footage and photographs. Keith Cunningham says that he and his mother still speak with Sylvia, but that their contact isn't close or regular. It is a fact that Nicky Brown's ties to the Cunningham family have remained firmer, more binding. Ultimately, among the aspects of Laurie Cunningham's end days that remain hidden and out of reach, the tragic accident of his death might be the clearest thing of all.

As Cyrille Regis says: 'My best mate was gone and I heard a smattering of things [about his accident]. But from all I can gather what happened was that he had been out at a nightclub, was on his way home and smashed up his car. He banged his head being thrown from it and died on the roadside.'

In more recent years, Laurie Cunningham has been named among the greatest players to have represented Real Madrid and West Bromwich Albion in surveys of supporters conducted by both clubs. However, outside the bosom of his family he has been best remembered at his first club, Orient. A bar at Orient's Brisbane Road ground and a block of flats adjoining it has each been named after him.

On 12 October 2013, Keith Cunningham, Brown, Fisher, Cyrille Regis and Brendon Batson were all present at Brisbane Road for the unveiling of a blue plaque commemorating Cunningham's flowering at the club. It is displayed on the outer wall of the main stand and the testimonial contained within it reads: 'Laurie Cunningham – 1956-1989 – Football legend; pioneering England international; player for Leyton Orient FC 1974-1977.' Simple words, but conveyed within them is the extent of a remarkable and all too brief life.

'We had fun together, man,' says Keith Cunningham. 'My brother had a lot of qualities. He was truthful, outspoken and very friendly. He was a nice guy, an all-rounder, but also a star and one in a million. There wasn't another player who could dance with the ball like him. It was a lovely thing to watch. I loved him. I loved him very much.'

The last time Ron Atkinson saw Laurie Cunningham was in May 1989. Atkinson had returned to the Spanish capital to agree the terms of his departure from Atletico Madrid, having been sacked as their manager after just one eventful season in charge of the club. He got in touch with Cunningham and the two of them arranged to meet up.

'He was going to see Real Madrid in a European game with his president at Rayo Vallecano and invited me along,' says Atkinson. 'He'd just won promotion with Vallecano and as he was sat there at the Bernabeu he said to me: "I can't wait to get back here next year. I'll show them what they've been missing."'

Epilogue: Legacy

It is the simplest of images. An unadorned portrait of Laurie Cunningham, Cyrille Regis and Brendon Batson lined up in their West Brom shirts. Cunningham and Regis balance a ball between their heads and each of them is smiling. The mood is relaxed and carefree. Without the benefit of context, it would be nothing more than a snapshot. However, a deeper understanding of its backdrop transforms the photograph into an intimate, captured moment from the beginnings of a revolution. Its chief instigators framed together for the first time not as novelties or curiosities, but as men. Contained within it there is a powerful truth. When it was taken thirty-five years ago it conveyed something that was extraordinary, exotic even, and also to some a vision that was both alien and unacceptable. Now, it is the norm – an image of three black sportsmen representing one British team.

When Cunningham, Batson and Regis were first united at West Brom there were just fifty or so black footballers playing in the four divisions of the Football League in England. Today, more than a quarter of the professionals in the English game are black or from ethnic minorities. In the years since Cunningham made his pioneering debut for the England U21 team in 1977, close to 200 black and mixed-race players have gone on to be capped by the country at both U21 and senior level. The three men in the photograph were the lightning conductors for one of the most profound developments in the sport, and perhaps its greatest and most abiding achievement.

In the journey from then to now, there have been other notable turning points and victories. None of these was navigated without difficulty or won without a battle. John Barnes's £900,000 transfer from Watford to Liverpool in the summer of 1987 marked another crossing of the Rubicon for the game in Britain. Barnes was the first black player to be bought by one of the proudest but most insular institutions in British sport. Magnifying the significance of Barnes's arrival at Liverpool was the fact that the city was home to the longest established black community in the UK. Three months later, when he made his first appearance in a Merseyside derby at Anfield, the visiting fans chanted, 'Everton are white.' Not out of shame, but as a boast.

The dreadful deaths of ninety-six Liverpool fans before an FA Cup semi-final at Sheffield Wednesday's Hillsborough stadium on 15 April 1989 gave rise to another major development. In his subsequent report into the tragedy and on the wider issue of ground safety, Lord Justice Taylor recognised a correlation between racist attitudes and the football hooligan mindset. Taylor's recommendations on this were a catalyst for the introduction of the Football Offences Act of 1991, which belatedly criminalised racist chanting within stadia and during matches.

In June 1993, Paul Ince became the first black man to captain the full England team on a post-season tour of the USA. That same year, the Professional Footballers' Association launched the Kick It Out campaign, aimed at combatting racism in the sport. By 1997 Kick It Out had evolved into an operating organisation and continues to be funded by the PFA, Premier League and the FA. It has had its critics. In October 2012, Manchester United's Rio Ferdinand and Jason Roberts of Blackburn Rovers were the most outspoken of several black footballers to boycott its annual week of action. Their protest was at Kick It Out's perceived lack of influence, and also at an apparent failure of strength and will from within the game to advance football's fight against racism. However, Kick It Out's sheer existence continues to represent another landmark for the sport. Its chairman, Lord Herman Ouseley, recalls how ignorance of racist abuse and intransigence towards tackling it were so long pervasive in the game.

'Right back in the 1980s I'd tried to pick up the issue in London with people like Ken Bates, the Chelsea chairman,' he says. 'I was basically told that there was nothing to be worried about and to go away. I later became chairman of the Commission for Racial Equality and at least had some basis from which to challenge people, but there was still a great deal of resistance. Senior figures at the FA and Football League told me there wasn't a problem. There was a whole lot of crap that I had to put up with.'

Eventually, walls came down. In the summer of 2001, the FA made a formal apology to black footballers and supporters alike for its failure to address racism and racist chanting throughout the seventies and eighties. The giant leap made within the game was further emphasised in February 2005. That month, Arsenal manager Arsene Wenger selected a sixteen-man squad comprised entirely of overseas players for a League match against Crystal Palace. Arsenal's 5-1 winning team was made up of six Frenchmen, three Spaniards, two Dutchmen, a German, a Swiss, a Brazilian and a player each from Cameroon and the Ivory Coast. It included five black players: Lauren, Kolo Toure, Gael Clichy, Patrick Vieira and Thierry Henry.

There were also five black players in the West Bromwich Albion side that won 2-1 at Manchester United in a Premier League fixture on 28 September 2013. One of them, striker Saido Berahino, recalled Cyrille Regis's explosive entry into the game, when making his first-team debut weeks earlier in a League Cup tie and scoring a hat-trick. West Brom's victory at Old Trafford was the club's first at that ground since Ron Atkinson's men recorded their 5-3 triumph in the freezing winter of 1979, when Regis and Cunningham ran riot. It is that team that stands out as the jumping off point for all of these momentous events and the attendant changes that have since swept through the national game in Britain, making it so much the better.

'There was a whole unsung generation of black guys who came up in the early seventies and who never made it into the game,' says Regis. 'Why? It was because of racism and the idea that they lacked bottle or couldn't stand the cold. We broke that stereotype. Young black boys watching television in the late-seventies saw Laurie shining for West Brom in the snow, or myself knocking heads with big, no-nonsense defenders, and what that did for their spirits.

'The next generation, guys like Ian Wright, John Barnes and David James, it's only when they tell you their story that you're able to see the influence we had. At the same time, there was a sea-change in the mentality of football managers. Guys like Big Ron, Brian Clough, Johnny Giles, David Pleat at Luton, Alan

Durban at Stoke and Sammy Cheung at Wolves were crucial to what happened. It was a double-edged thing.'

Ron Atkinson for ever compromised his role in the story on the evening of 21 April 2004. By then he had carved out a successful second career as a television broadcaster, providing expert analysis on matches for ITV Sport. On that night he was commentating on the first leg of Chelsea's European Champions League semi-final with Monaco in France. The English side slumped to a 3-1 defeat. In its aftermath, and believing that he was now off-air, Atkinson vented his thoughts at the lacklustre contribution of Chelsea's veteran midfielder Marcel Desailly, a Ghanian-born Frenchman coming to the end of a fine career. During the course of his rant, Atkinson described Desailly as 'a lazy fucking nigger'.

Unbeknown to him, ITV was still transmitting to the Middle East at the time and his comments were aired in Egypt and Dubai among other countries. The erupting firestorm consumed Atkinson and torched his reputation. He lost his job at ITV the next day and has been banished from the mainstream media ever since, lurking like a pariah on the fringes of local radio and newspapers in the West Midlands. In the immediate fall-out, Ian Wright branded his remark 'disgusting'. Brendon Batson was more measured in his response, but withering too, expressing shock and disappointment.

Writing later in his autobiography, Cyrille Regis said: 'I was staggered. In all the years I'd known Ron, I knew he would fly close to the wind when it came to jokes but I'd never heard him use that particular word. Do I think the words were racist? Yes. Do I think Ron's a racist? No. I can say without hesitation that Ron was brilliant with us black players.'

This is the view that continues to prevail among Regis's former West Brom team-mates and is also shared by Atkinson's erstwhile TV colleague, Gerald Sindstadt, who asserts there is 'no one less racist than Ron'. Regis fast forgave Atkinson his aberration. 'I still see him,' he says. 'He's great company, tells great stories and we have a great crack.' Batson was slower to thaw, less accommodating of the notion that Atkinson was guilty of nothing more than belonging to an older and less enlightened generation.

'I was hugely hurt by his words,' he says. 'I said at the time that I didn't think he was a racist, but a lot of people didn't believe me. I think Ron had just got carried away with his own self-importance. There was a vast amount of bravado about what he said. He thought that everybody should have a laugh at everything and anything goes. And I know he felt that he had to pay a heavy price for it. Well, that's the consequence.

'Yet I think this is the measure of the man: when my wife fell ill, the first call I got from outside of my immediate family circle was from Ron. When I think of what my wife and family went through, what Ron said in that broadcast is of no significance to me now. I said some harsh things about it back then, but I've got over it. We've got over it. There's no way I'd ever accuse him of being anything other than a bloody idiot for using those words.'

For his part, Atkinson is wary of revisiting this dark corner of his past. At the time, he confessed to having made 'a stupid mistake for which I am very sorry'. Reluctantly, he allows now that 'what I should have done back then is made a bigger stand. What I was doing was quoting somebody that I knew.'

'Sorry, I haven't heard that one before,' responds Batson when this is relayed to him. 'Even if that were true, you wouldn't repeat it verbatim, would you?'

Of course, football hasn't rid itself entirely of racism any more than it's been driven out of society as a whole. However, to hear racist abuse at a British football ground is now as rare as it is shocking. Batson contends that 'naked racism' is under control within the confines of the professional game, but cautions that there are still 'big issues' to confront at grassroots level in that regard. He believes it imperative that football also now addresses the paucity of both black managers and administrators working in the sport.

'We've come a long way, but we need to move quicker now,' he concludes. 'People in the upper echelons of the game tend to appoint in their own image and there's a lot of talent out there screaming for a chance. The structures of the game need to become more equitable.

'I love football. When people are brought together at the major international tournaments and you rid it of all that parochialism and xenophobia, it's great. The game has been good to me. My brother trained as an electrician and I know I've been lucky from hearing the things he told me about the way black kids were treated on the production line at places like Ford.'

'We're hoping football can be an example to the wider society of how you can conquer prejudice and hatred,' says Lord Ouseley. 'There is a new morality emerging in the game and a very impressive generation of players coming through who want to take the mantle on and move things to the next level.

'But people at the top of the game also want to tell you that we've dealt with racism now and move on. That's the bigger danger, believing that it's been solved. Part of the problem is that there isn't a history of people telling stories of what went on in the game to get that across to the next generation. It's like Andy Cole once said when he was playing for Newcastle: "When I'm on the pitch I'm a king and when I'm on the street I'm just another black cunt.'"

Ouseley's fears were flamed by the manner in which both the FA and the parent clubs dealt with two notorious and more recent high profile incidents of racism in the game, and these also sparked the Kick It Out player boycott. They involved the Chelsea and then England captain John Terry and Liverpool's Uruguayan striker Luis Suarez. Both occurred during Premier League matches in October 2011. Terry was accused of racially abusing QPR's Anton Ferdinand, younger brother of Rio. Suarez of the same offence against the elder Ferdinand's Manchester United team-mate, Patrice Evra.

Terry was stripped of the England captaincy and months later found guilty of the offence by an FA panel. His punishment amounted to a £220,000 fine, around a week of his wages, and a four-game ban. Chelsea took no further action against their player. Liverpool's handling of the Suarez case was if anything more shameful. On 20 December 2011, the FA found Suarez guilty of calling Evra 'negro' on at least ten occasions and with racist intent. He was fined £40,000 and banned for eight games. The following evening Liverpool's players took to the field for a match at Wigan wearing white T-shirts emblazoned with Suarez's smiling face as an expression of 'total support' for their team-mate. He was also given the unequivocal backing of his manager, Kenny Dalglish, who sought to portray his star player as the victim. A more general view was that the game's governing body had been far too lenient in dealing with both Suarez and Terry.

'People in the game have got to recognise that football is never going to get better if the clubs automatically defend a player no matter what he's done,' says Lord Ouseley. 'At Kick It Out, we want football to get to a position where the clubs themselves take action if a player is found guilty of racial, sexual or homophobic abuse, just as any other employer would do.'

The FA established a fresh set of anti-discrimination rules in the wake of the Terry and Suarez furore. Ironically, the first substantive test case of these involved a West Bromwich Albion player, the French striker Nicolas Anelka. In December 2013, Anelka celebrated scoring a goal against West Ham by performing the 'quenelle' – a hand gesture popularised on the continent by the controversial French comedian Dieudonne M'bala M'bala, and described by Jewish groups as a form of inverted Nazi salute. The game was being televised live in France and Anelka's actions were condemned by the French Sports Minister, Valerie Fourneyron, as 'disgusting'.

Hit with an FA charge, Anelka was subsequently found guilty of using an offensive gesture, but not out of anti-Semitic intent. In his defence, Anelka claimed M'bala was a friend of his and he had made the sign in support of him. Effectively, he asked the FA's adjudicating panel to accept that he had no prior knowledge that the 'quenelle' was more often used outside synagogues and Holocaust sites, or of M'bala's numerous criminal convictions in France for promoting anti-Semitism. He was fined £80,000, ordered to attend an education programme and banned for five games. This was the minimum penalty available to the FA under its new guidelines and prompted another outburst of protest. However, the club did act on this occasion. West Brom initially suspended Anelka on full pay pending an internal inquiry and soon after cancelled his contract. In a statement the club said it could not 'ignore the offence his actions caused, particularly to the Jewish community, nor the potential to damage the club's reputation.'

Racism also continues to infect the world game. In such

Eastern European countries as Russia, Ukraine and Poland, black players are still routinely subjected to the sort of hate-filled barracking that largely disappeared from British stadia in the 1980s. The response to this from football's global governing body, FIFA, and its European counterpart, UEFA, has most often been abject.

FIFA's president Sepp Blatter once suggested that incidents of racism between players could be resolved with a handshake. In 2013, Blatter also criticised AC Milan's Kevin-Prince Boeteng for walking off the pitch during a supposed 'friendly' match in Italy when he was made the target of racist chanting. UEFA issued the Serbian FA with a relatively paltry £65,000 fine in October 2012 after supporters of its U21 side subjected several England players to sustained racist abuse during a European U21 Championship match in the country. Earlier that summer, at the senior Euros tournament in Ukraine and Poland, Danish striker Niklas Bendtner got an £80,000 fine from UEFA for flashing underpants with a bookmaker's name branded on them after scoring a goal.

Yet for all the barriers still to be broken and the resolves still to stiffen, British football's acceptance of and tolerance towards racial differences has improved dramatically in the time since Cunningham, Regis and Batson came into the game. On 13 August 2013, the FA and Kick It Out hosted an Under-21 international match between England and Scotland at Sheffield United's Bramall Lane ground. It was held in honour of Cunningham and replicated the fixture in which he made his international debut. Regis and Garth Crooks were invited to address the England squad beforehand, and spoke about their formative experiences in football.

'The guys had no concept of what we went through,' Regis says. 'They're purely judged now on being a player and being black doesn't come into it. It's phenomenal that we've come that distance. Laurie, Brendon and I were the spearhead for that, the focal point. The three of us in one team, it was iconic, it was radical. We changed the face of football.'

On the twenty-fifth anniversary of Laurie Cunningham's death, 15 July 2014, a statue depicting him, Regis and Batson will be unveiled in West Bromwich town centre. Two miles down the road from where an election campaign was once made infamous by the slogan, 'If you want a nigger for a neighbour – vote Labour.' And from where a pub wall had been painted with graffiti that read, 'Cunningham is a black cunt.'

The work of Yorkshire sculptor Graham Ibbeson, the statue stands ten-foot high, is cast in bronze and portrays the three players celebrating a goal in their heyday together at West Brom. It is a proper and lasting monument to how much and how far they moved along their sport and their country.

'As a young man you don't dream that one day there's going to be a statue erected to you or to us,' says Regis. 'You dream of winning the FA Cup or playing at Wembley for England. It's very humbling. But also, and Brendon will tell you the same thing, it really isn't about us, it's about what we represent. We were the crest of the wave.'

According to Bobby Fisher, the thought of there being a statue dedicated to him would have left Cunningham 'pissing himself with laughter. He'd have said, "What are you guys doing?" But then, he'd have wanted it to be of him with a Fedora, a cane and a double-breasted suit, not as a footballer.'

'Laurie's dying changed all of our lives,' says Nicky Brown, 'and none of us who knew him is able to properly describe what we feel about it. I still get a warm feeling inside when I think of him. He was a beautiful man. I loved him and admired him too, because when he touched things they turned to gold. I know that sounds sickening, but it's true.

'He had great strength of character and stood up for what counted in the face of so much adversity. He was a huge loss. I do believe he'd have kept on changing things. It might have been in the most normal of ways – a children's home or a donkey sanctuary. But it would have made a difference.'

Brendon Batson treasures another photograph of him, Cyrille Regis and Laurie Cunningham together. It is the only one he has of them all and was taken one Christmas in West Bromwich. In it they are each wearing Santa Claus hoods. He got Cunningham to sign it for him before he left for Real Madrid.

'I had it framed and it hangs in my home in Birmingham,' he says. 'Cyrille lives just a couple of miles from me now and we're getting older together. But Laurie's never aged. He will always be to me what he is in that picture. We were blessed to have him.'

Acknowledgements

This book could not have been written without the selfless help, influence and support tendered to me by a great number of good and kind souls. I am especially indebted to Cyrille Regis, Brendon Batson, Keith Cunningham and Nicky Brown for allowing me to share their time and memories and to tell their story. I would as well particularly like to thank Cyrille for making introductions along the way and for his encouragement throughout. As more than one person described him to me, he is 'The Man'.

I hope that Laurie Cunningham walks tall through these pages. The indelible impression that he left on me during his all too brief but glorious pomp at West Bromwich Albion started the ball rolling for this book. It will remain with me and anyone else who ever saw him grace the Hawthorns.

I would also have been lost without the invaluable assistance of Geoff Snape at West Bromwich Albion Former Players' Association. The Association was founded in May 2003 by Brendon Batson MBE, then Chief Executive of West Bromwich

Albion, Graham Williams, captain of Albion's 1968 FA Cup-winning team, and two of the club's supporters, Norman Westbury and Snape. It has grown in strength over the past eleven years and membership now stands at just short of the 150 mark. It does a fine and laudable job and I would have been lost without it.

There are other 'man of the match' performances to which I am indebted and very much grateful: to the great Laurie Rampling for the photographs and the keys to his remarkable library; to John 'Simmo' Simpson and Dave Bowler at West Bromwich Albion, Martin Swain at the *Express & Star*, Chris Lepkowski at the *Evening Mail*, Paul Campbell at the *Guardian*, Graham Hunter, Matt Allen and Neil Storey for counsel and contacts; Steve Jenkins at the Leyton Orient Supporters' Club; Danny Lynch at Kick It Out; Andy Lyons at the peerless *When Saturday Comes*; David Goldlatt; Phil Ball; Sid Lowe; Rachel Clare at Birmingham Central Library; Alf Russell at Wolverhampton Archives & Local Studies; Gavin Schaffer and David Metcalfe-Carr at Birmingham University School of History and Cultures; Nick Bell at Hayes & Yeading FC; Jim Cadman at Celebration Statue 1979; and to Peter Law for time and generosity that extended above and beyond the call of duty.

In the course of writing this book, I was also fortunate enough to meet and interview many other people. All of them were generous with their time and often as much with their hospitality. For throwing open the doors to me, thank you to: Ron Atkinson, Bobby Fisher, Tony Brown, Tony Godden, Ally Robertson, John Wile, Bryan Robson, Willie Johnson, Len Cantello, Derek Statham, Ally Brown, John Trewick, Peter Barnes, Gary Owen, Viv Anderson, Terry Phelan, Lawrie Sanchez, John Homer, Bob Downing, Dave Harrison, Pat Murphy, Bobby Ross, Helen Scott,

Valerie Holiday, Derrick Campbell, Gerald Sinstadt, Eustace 'Huggy' Isaie, David Hinds, Roger Huddle, David May, Ali Campbell, Brian Travers and Lord Herman Ouseley.

The good stuff in this book belongs to all of the above. Any mistakes or inaccuracies in the text are entirely my own responsibility.

On the front line, I retain a deep well of gratitude for Matthew Hamilton, my agent, consigliere and friend, who planted the seed and then tended it with his usual care, expertise and attention to detail. Hats off also to ace editor Andreas Campomar for faith, direction and encouragement – no man deserves to enjoy his 'boat rock' more – and to all the good folks at Constable. At Andreas's urging I read *People Who Eat Darkness: the Fate of Lucie Blackman* by Richard Lloyd Parry, which helped to inform the structure of this book. It is a remarkable and profound work and I can't recommend it highly enough.

Love and thanks to Mick Rees for taking care of business and to all the members of the Rees and Jeffrey clans. And above all, my boundless love and appreciation to Denise, Tom and Charlie, who encouraged and indulged me in the months of writing this book, and who make it all worthwhile.

Sources
Foremost among the many invaluable sources of reference for this book were the following:

Books
Samba in the Smethwick End by Dave Bowler and Jas Bains [Mainstream Publishing]
Cyrille Regis: My Story [Andre Deutsch]
Big Ron: A Different Ball Game [Andre Deutsch]

Attack Attack: The Story of West Bromwich Albion 1978-79 by Dave
  Bowler [Britespot]

100 Greats: West Bromwich Albion Football Club by Tony
  Matthews [Tempus]

West Bromwich Albion: The Complete Record by Tony Matthews
  [Breedon Books]

West Bromwich Albion: 100 Great Matches by Glenn Wilmore
  [Breedon Books]

Black Lions: a History of Black Players in English Football by
  Rodney Hinds [Sports Books]

Stoke City: 101 Golden Greats by Simon Lowe [Desert Island
  Books]

Out of His Skin: The John Barnes Phenomenon by Dave Hill
  [WSC]

White Storm: 101 Years of Real Madrid by Phil Ball [Mainstream]

Crisis? What Crisis?: Britain In the 1970s by Alwyn W. Turner
  [Aurum]

Estates: an Intimate History by Lynsey Hanley [Granta]

The National Front by Martin Walker [Fontana]

*The Divisive Decade: a History of Caribbean Immigration to
  Birmingham in the 1950s* by Peter L. Edmead [Birmingham
  City Council]

A Question of Colour? by Peter Griffiths [Leslie Frewin]

Race Community and Conflict: a Study of Sparkbrook by John Rex
  and Robert Moore [Oxford University Press]

Whitewashing Britain: Race and Citizenship in the Post War Era by
  Kathleen Paul [Cornell]

The Empire Strikes Back: Race and Racism in '70s Britain by the
  Centre for Contemporary Studies [Hutchinson]

Wheels Out of Gear: 2-Tone, the Specials and a World in Flame by
  Dave Thompson [Helter Skelter]

A History of Popular Music by Piero Scaruffi [Amazon Media Kindle edition]

Murder at the Farm: Who Killed Carl Bridgewater? by Paul Foot [Headline Review]

Jeremy Thorpe: a Secret Life by Lewis Chester, Magnus Linklater and David May [Fontana]

Articles

Till Death Us Do Part and the BBC: Racial Politics and the British Working Classes 1965-1975 by Gavin Schaffer, *Journal of Contemporary History*, 2010

The *Express & Star* newspaper archives at the Wolverhampton Archives

The *Birmingham Post* and *Evening Mail* Archives at Birmingham Central Library

All Blacks article by John Edwards, *Daily Mail*, 23 August 2012

Guardian article on Tony Dyce's conviction, 17 December 2010

The Forgotten Story of Willie Johnston, the *Guardian*, 23 December 2008

Laurie Cunningham article by Ed Aarons, the *Independent*, 4 March 2013

Brendon Batson interview by Martin Swain, *Express & Star*, 17 September 2010

Brendon Batson interview by Chris Lepkowski, *Evening Mail*, 7 December 2012

Interview with Carl Bridgewater's parents, by Anuji Varma, *Evening Mail*, 7 September 2008

From Jail . . . to What?, by Seth Linder, the *New Statesman*, 28 February 1997

Television

Laurie Cunningham: First Among Equals, ITV documentary

Enoch Powell: Rivers of Blood, BBC TV documentary

Section 1

Laurie Boys Brigade team, copyright unknown, c/o Laurie Rampling, p 1

Brendon playing for Arsenal 1972, copyright unknown, c/o Laurie Rampling, p 1

Laurie in his gangster suit at Brisbane Road, copyright *Daily Mail*, p 1

Laurie and Cyrille soul mates, copyright *Daily Mail*, p 2

Big Ron signs Brendon, by Laurie Rampling, p 2

Regis goal vs. Forest, Laurie Rampling, p 2

Players in bath after Forest game, by Laurie Rampling, p 3

Laurie and MG car, copyright unknown, c/o Laurie Rampling, p 3

Laurie shirt-pulled at Derby, by Laurie Rampling, p 3

Regis goal vs. Man City, copyright *County Press*, p 4

1978 team squad, copyright *Express & Star*, p 4

Laurie and parents, by Bob Thomas, p 5

Laurie and Cyrille in dressing room after Valencia game, copyright *Birmingham Mail*, p 5

Laurie in action against Valencia at the Hawthorns, copyright *Birmingham Mail*, p 5

Laurie vs. Bristol City in the snow, by Laurie Rampling, p 6

Regis goal vs. Norwich, by Laurie Rampling, p 6

Laurie, Cyrille and Three Degrees night out, copyright unknown, c/o Laurie Rampling, p 7

Brendon with wife Cecily, by Laurie Rampling, p 7

Cyrille Young Player of the Year, copyright Sport & General, p 7

Cyrille headed goal vs. Manchester United, Laurie Rampling, p 8

Cyrille's All Blacks team line-up, by Laurie Rampling, p 8

Section 2

Laurie playing for England, copyright unknown, c/o Laurie Rampling, p 1

Colour Cyrille vs. Manchester United in 5-3 game, copyright unknown, c/o Laurie Rampling, pg 1

Big Ron on Great Wall of China, Laurie Rampling private collection, p 2

Brendon, Laurie and others in China, Laurie Rampling private collection, p 2

Laurie with John Gordon, copyright unknown, c/o Laurie Rampling, p 3

Laurie colour Real Madrid strip, copyright Coloursport, p 3

Laurie and Nicky Brown at the Bernabeu, copyright *Daily Mail*, p 4

Laurie with Bryan Robson, copyright *Daily Mail*, p 4

Cyrille in Wolves strip, copyright ASP, p 5

Brendon outside the PFA, copyright PFA, p 6

Three Degrees statue night with Frank Skinner, by Laurie Rampling, p 6

Cyrille colour in his WBA pomp, by Laurie Rampling, p 7

Laurie pace and grace colour at WBA, copyright unknown, c/o Laurie Rampling, p 8